About the Author

James Wallman is a journalist, trend forecaster, and speaker.

He has commented on trends happening now, and predicted what will happen next, for publications like GQ, the New York Times, and the Financial Times, and for clients such as Absolut, BMW, Burberry, and Nike. He wrote the futurology column in T3 magazine from 2008-2012, and was editor of a trend consultancy called The Future Laboratory's forecasting publication, LS:N Global, from 2009-2013.

He has an MA in Classics from Oxford University and an MA in Journalism from the University of the Arts London. He has lived in France, Greece, and Palo Alto in California. He currently lives in London, with his wife and daughter.

Follow him on Twitter @jameswallman

STUFFOCATION

*How We've Had Enough of Stuff and
Why You Need Experience More than Ever*

JAMES WALLMAN

First published in the United Kingdom in 2013
by Crux Publishing

ISBN-13: 978-1-909979-00-0

Also available as an ebook:
eISBN: 978-0-9575245-2-1

www.cruxpublishing.co.uk

For Thiru and Indy-May

And for Jack, Pam, Guy, and Elsie

CONTENTS

A Note from the Author

The case studies in the book are not compound characters. They are real people. Their stories are true. All scenes and events actually happened.

James Wallman, London, October 2013

INTRODUCTION

How We've Had Enough of Stuff

A few years back, on a Monday morning in September 2010, a man by the name of Ryan Nicodemus woke up in a room that was bare except for a bed. Outside, the sky was blue. There was a light breeze. People were starting the week, sipping coffee, starting their cars, driving north for Dayton, south for Cincinnati. It was a day like any other.

Nicodemus, a square-jawed Irish-American who could pass for the movie star Ben Affleck, sat up and squinted. There was no bedside lamp or table, no pictures, no nothing, except for the bed he'd slept on and the sheets he'd slept under.

He pulled the sheets back and padded across the carpeted floor, past the empty closets, into the hallway. It was all the same – stripped bare. The only thing there was, was an eerie sound. "It was really strange," Nicodemus recalls. "Like silence, but very echoey."

If you had been there, waking up alone in that house, you would have thought you'd woken up in some sort of surreal dream, in a strange house the day after the owners had moved out – and left all their things in boxes and bin bags at the foot of the stairs.

Nicodemus went down and picked up a box. He read the label – "Miscellaneous no. 7" – and put it to one side. He picked up another – "Kitchen junk no. 2" – and did the same. He kept going till he found "Bathroom no. 1". He rummaged inside. He pulled out shower gel, toothpaste, toothbrush. He started on the bags, till he found, and took out, one towel. He tied the bags closed, he shut the boxes, and he went upstairs to shower.

As water washed over him, Nicodemus wondered. How did it feel? Odd? Better? Was a home with no stuff better or worse? He hadn't woken up in a dream, you see. He'd woken up in an experiment.

At the time, Nicodemus was 28, and doing well. He had a girlfriend, a house, a job. He was making over $100,000 a year, working for a telecoms company called Cincinnati Bell. He liked what he did. He liked the people he worked with. He got a kick out of seeing his employees develop and helping them sell one or two more things, so they could make their bonus or win that incentive trip to Hawaii. He wore Brooks Brothers suits, $300 shoes, and $100 ties. He had a hundred $100 ties. At the weekend, he went off-roading on a $8,000 four-wheeler with his buddies. He played Xbox and watched movies on his top-of-the-line, 53" Samsung TV. He drove a brand new, metallic blue Toyota Tacoma, one of those big boy's toys that looks like a life-size Tonka Truck.

"If you'd told my 18-year-old self what I was going to have at 28," Nicodemus says now. "I would've been the most excited 18-year-old there ever was. I would've been, 'like, are you kidding me? This is gonna be the best life ever!'"

But ten years later, it did not feel like the best life ever. Nicodemus was not happy. Instead, he was confused. "I almost felt," he says, "ungrateful – 'cause I had everything I'd always wanted."

At first, he kept plugging away, working, spending, hoping the feeling would go. But no matter how much he earned and how many things he bought, he could not shake it. Then a thought occurred to him. Maybe there had been a mistake. Maybe the happiness equation was wrong.

The Happiness Equation

Nicodemus grew up poor, in a place called Lebanon – population 20,000, average income $20,000 – in Ohio in the north-eastern United States. When his parents split he stayed in a run-down apartment with his mother. She was too busy with drink and drugs to notice the cleaning, the cockroaches, Ryan. Aged 12, he moved in with his father. Eric ran a small business called Nicodemus Fine Paint and Wallcovering. He was a devout Jehovah's Witness. He kept a clean house. Was it inevitable that Ryan ricocheted like a pinball between his father's god and his mother's demons? He took drugs. He went to church. He ate a lot.

During school holidays, he worked for his father. He saw how the other half decorated their homes and how they seemed to have the sort of happiness he longed for.

One day, father and son were in their overalls at a job. The house was nothing fancy. Everything was modern and new, apart from a grandfather clock in the hallway. As Ryan was setting things up, taking the family pictures off the walls, he noticed that the people in the pictures looked real happy. That morning, the owners had seemed pretty happy, too. Maybe they were. Looking around, he wondered: maybe this nice, middle-class house was the kind of home happy people lived in.

"Dad," he said. "How much would I have to make to own a house like this?"

"Son," Eric replied in his gruff, American-Dad voice. "About $50,000 a year."

It was that simple. Happiness had a look: the inside of that house. And it had a price tag: $50,000. Nicodemus shared this golden secret – "happiness = $50,000 a year" – with his best friend, Joshua Fields Millburn.

Today, Fields Millburn is slim and good-looking. He looks like a younger version of the actor Christopher Walken. He has a wave of blond hair that rises straight up like Walken's. His smile is halfway between pleased-with-himself and please-listen-to-me. Back then, though, he was just like Nicodemus: a fat teenager from a broken home.

After they left school, Fields Millburn and Nicodemus worked their tails off to fulfil their side of the happiness equation. A few years later, they reached the magic number. That meant they should be happy, right? If only life was that simple. Fields Millburn soon worked out the problem.

"The equation is wrong," he told Nicodemus one day. "We didn't adjust for inflation. Maybe it's not $50,000, maybe it's $80,000." Now that made sense. After all, inflation meant things cost more, especially the things you wanted, the good stuff. And if the cost of the good stuff rose, that meant the cost of the good life would go up too.

So they kept on, working, spending, competing. Nicodemus bought a 1700-square-foot house. Fields Millburn got one that was 2,000 square foot. Nicodemus drove a Toyota. Fields Millburn had a Lexus. Nicodemus owned a hundred ties. Fields Millburn couldn't keep up with that, but he did have seventy shirts by Brooks Brothers, and fifteen of their suits – three more than Nicodemus's twelve.

But it did not matter how much they earned or what they bought, whether they had more than before or more than each other. Every time they hit the new inflation-adjusted target, the happiness equation did not work. It was like chasing the pot of gold at the end of the rainbow. Eventually, another thought occurred to Fields Millburn: what if they didn't only need to adjust for inflation? What if the happiness equation was just plain wrong? There seemed to be something in that.

"All the things around me that were supposed to bring happiness weren't bringing me happiness at all," Fields Millburn says now. "In fact, it was the opposite. Instead of happiness, I got debt, stress, discontent. I was overwhelmed. Eventually, I got depressed."

Around that time, Fields Millburn came across some people online who had a radically different idea of happiness. They were called "minimalists", and they thought that the best route to happiness was not by getting *more*, but by having *less*. If it worked for them, could it work for him and Nicodemus too? It had to be worth a shot, they decided.

But what if it didn't work, and they only found that out after they had got rid of all their stuff? So they hatched a plan. To find out if they would be happier living with less stuff, they decided to run an experiment. They would put all Nicodemus's things in his house into bags and boxes, just like he was moving. Each time he wanted something, he would take it back out. The experiment would last twenty-one days. They had read it took that long for a new habit to stick. By the end of that time, Nicodemus would find out how much stuff he really needed and if living with less made him happier.

It did. He never got round to unpacking all the things he had stuffed into bags and boxes. He took some things out, of course, a few things as he needed them each day – toothbrush, toothpaste, shower gel, clothes for work, a glass to drink out of.

After day ten, Nicodemus did not take anything else out. By then, he realized he had everything he needed. It wasn't the sound of the house that felt odd now. It was the waste. "It really opened my eyes to how little I used all the stuff I owned," he recalls. "Thinking about all the money I'd wasted on all that stuff – now that was a really surreal feeling."

He had worried what his girlfriend would think, but she thought the whole thing was funny. "She'd come into the living room grinning," recalls Nicodemus, "and say 'honey, have you seen *the spoon?*'"

Satisfied that he had enough and that less really was better, Nicodemus got rid of all the stuff still packed away. He sold some things on eBay and Craigslist. He gave others away. He filled a truck with stuff for his father to take to church. And then he started a new life with far fewer material possessions.

Many of us, at some point, have questioned whether we are really happy with our lives and our jobs, whether we're just working to pay the payments on the things we own, and if we really need all that junk cluttering up our homes and our lives. So, every now and then, to keep that wondering voice quiet, we do a quick clear-out, spend less time working, and more time at home – and we stop there. Nicodemus didn't.

When he did a clear-out, he packed everything away, and most of it stayed boxed and bagged up till he gave it away. He stopped wanting and buying new things. He stopped working so many hours to pay for all those things he didn't really need. He started living with much less stuff. Instead of trying to reach materialistic targets, he started striving for other goals, like being healthy and having good relationships. And it worked.

Nicodemus is now, as he has told me many times, much happier. Why? Why did he find that living with fewer things meant more happiness? And is this new happiness equation good only for him, Fields Millburn and a handful like them, or will it work for the rest of us?

Are you stuffocating?

Stuffocation is the story of one of today's most acute, till now unnamed, afflictions. It is about how you, me, and society in general, instead of feeling enriched by the things we own, are feeling stifled by them.

Instead of thinking of more in positive terms, as we once did, we now think more means more hassle, more to manage, and more to think about. In our busy, cluttered lives, more is no longer better. It is worse. Overwhelmed and suffocating from stuff, we are feeling *Stuffocation*.

Nicodemus, you see, is not the only one. There are millions, right now, all around the world, feeling like they have too much stuff. There are the two million, to begin with, who read the blog and books Nicodemus and Fields Millburn write about living with less stuff each year. There are more.

Twelve million – as many as live in Greater London, or in New York and Los Angeles combined – have seen a film online called *The Story of Stuff*, about the disastrous ecological impact of materialism. Most of them probably feel, especially after watching the film, they would like less stuff in their lives. There are many more.

A political scientist by the name of Ronald Inglehart has been following people's attitudes toward material things – stuff – since 1970. When he began his research, he found, in the six countries he surveyed – the UK, France, West Germany, Italy, the Netherlands, and Belgium – that four out of five people held materialist values. Political scientists have been conducting similar surveys, at regular intervals, ever since in more than 50 countries. The message from the research is clear: we are becoming far less materialistic, as only around one in two now hold materialist values. "Almost half the people are now post-materialists," says Inglehart. It may even be more than that.

When one of the world's largest advertising agencies conducted a survey recently in countries like the UK, France, and the United States, they found that "people in mature markets have had enough of excess", that they are "tired of the push to accumulate more", and that one in two have thrown out or thought about throwing out stuff in recent years. They also discovered that two in every three think they would be better off if they lived more simply – with less stuff, in other words. If that is right, that means there could be around 40 million in the UK and 240 million in the US who would prefer a simpler life with fewer material things.

Maybe you feel it too. Have you had enough of excess? Are you tired of the push to accumulate more? Would you, truth be told, be happier if you had fewer things than you have right now? Take a trip through the cupboards, drawers, and shelves of your homes in the quiz on pages 24 and 25 to find out if you – like Nicodemus and millions of others around the world – are also feeling *Stuffocation*.

Why have we had enough of stuff?

So why have so many of us had enough of stuff? Why are we turning away from materialism? As with anything as seismic as *Stuffocation*, there are many explanations.

A political scientist, like Inglehart, for instance, would say that because more of us have grown up in stable situations where we haven't had to worry about where our next meal was coming from, we have become less concerned about materialistic needs like food and shelter, and more interested in "post-materialist" needs such as having the freedom to say what we want to say and do what we want to do.

A psychologist, like Oliver James, or a philosopher, such as Alain de Botton, will tell you we've had enough of stuff because our possessions, and the lifestyle that comes with them, are causing us more stress than happiness. James calls this problem "affluenza". De Botton says keeping up with the Joneses is giving us "status anxiety".

An environmentalist will tell you we've had enough because of global warming, landfill, our carbon footprint. We are worried that we are using up more resources than the planet can sustain.

A demographer might say that they can see that the stress of stuff, our stable upbringing and the environment may all be valid, but there are four other, much more important, reasons for *Stuffocation*: the ageing population, the growing population, the rise of the global middle class, and the move to cities.

As people get older they are less interested in having more things. As there are more people on our finite planet and more of them are becoming middle class, there is ever more pressure on resources. And as more of us move to cities, we are buying fewer cars, and our homes are getting smaller, meaning less room to put things.

Social scientists would say that all these reasons – the stress of stuff, the stable upbringing, the environment, the ageing population, the growing population, the rise of the global middle class, and the move to cities – they are all relevant, but that we are also increasingly fed up with materialism because we simply don't believe in the system anymore. One social scientist, such as Ruth Milkman, for instance, might point out that we are disillusioned with its inherent inequalities, that the protesters in the Occupy movement reflected the anger the rest of us felt. Another might highlight the fact that, till recently, we thought that if we earned more and bought more things, it would make us happier. But researchers like Tom Gilovich have shown that this is not the case, and as this truth reaches the mainstream it is changing the importance people place on possessions.

An economist might smile at all these explanations. Sure, she might say, the environment, the stress of stuff, the stable upbringing, the ageing population, the growing population, the rise of the global middle class, the move to cities and the lack of belief in the system – all of these are important. But the real reason for *Stuffocation* is obvious: it is economics, stupid. In a world of rising costs and stagnating incomes, most people simply do not have enough money to keep on buying things right now. So rather than "had enough", it may be more accurate to say that we cannot afford so much anymore.

A technologist might agree with all this, and then tell you the real reason why we are turning away from material goods is, actually, because we can. After all, what's the point in owning physical books and CDs when you can access them from the cloud?

And, finally, what do I, a trend forecaster, think?

The Perfect Storm

Stuffocation is the outcome of more than 10,000 hours of analysing trends and forecasting the future. In the past, I have commented on trends happening now and predicted what will happen next for publications like *GQ*, the *New York Times* and the *Financial Times*. But most of the time, I have been doing this for clients like Absolut, BMW, and Nike, at a consultancy called The Future Laboratory. The company is based in London, but during that time I was flown to places like Amsterdam, Beijing, and New York, and always with the same aim: to help people prepare for what's next.

Why did they listen to me? How do I know what the future holds? I don't read tea leaves or breathe in vapours or gaze into a crystal ball. The method I use is far less esoteric, and, I like to think, a fair bit more robust. It is inspired by something a futurist called William Gibson once said: "The future is already here — it's just not very evenly distributed". More importantly, it is informed by a way of reading cultural change that, since it was first described in 1962, has been applied more than 5,000 times. I will tell the story of how that method was discovered, and how I use it to tell the future, in the next chapter.

Of all the social, cultural, economic, technological and political shifts I have observed and reported during my years of analysis and forecasting, there is one that has stood out, and it is this: that people in rich countries are becoming less impressed by, and less interested in, material goods. Instead, they increasingly prefer intangible, experiential goods – in other words, experiences. Instead of stuff to have and hold, they want stories they can tell others, and tales that tell them something about who they are as well.

That insight led me to spend countless more hours of research and investigation. I discussed the idea with psychologists, economists, historians. I heard the stories of people experimenting with new ways of living from Adelaide to Barcelona, from California to Germany. I interrogated their motives, and the outcomes of their decisions. I ran up many blind alleys. And the aim of all this was to understand the Zeitgeist, to work out what is happening, analyse why it is happening, and forecast where it will lead. The insights from that work are in this book.

When I write down the list of factors causing *Stuffocation*, a number of thoughts strike me. One is that they are more like waves than building blocks.

Each has its own starting point, in other words, but does not rely on any of the others. So even if you disagree with the environmentalist, for instance, and you do not think people care enough about the environment to consume less stuff, that does not affect whether you agree or disagree with, say, the technologist or demographer. It is also perfectly possible to believe that each of the explanations is relevant and partly responsible for *Stuffocation* – and I do.

Even more importantly, I think that the changes taking place are not minor blips that will be here one year, gone the next. The one exception is the economy and the fall in incomes. But as the economic situation improves and our incomes rise, and people have and feel like they have more money to buy stuff again, that will only exacerbate other factors, such as the environment. It may also encourage more people to switch to digital sooner.

All of the other factors causing *Stuffocation* – the stable upbringing, the stress of stuff, the environment, the lack of belief in the system, the ageing population, the growing population, the rise of the middle class, the move to cities, the rise in costs, and the switch to digital – are the result of observable, observed, unavoidable long-term trends. Taken singly, each of these would have an effect on the world like a wave as it swells and crashes against a sea wall. Since all are arriving at the same time, becoming more urgent, less avoidable and more obvious, they are creating a perfect storm for our mixed-up materialist culture. That is why, right now and for the foreseeable future, so many of us are disillusioned with material goods and materialism, and feeling *Stuffocation*.

Sherlock Holmes and the Mystery of the Krispy Kremes

When I look down the list, though, I can't help but think there is something missing. All these factors make it plain why *Stuffocation* is happening now, but they do not make sense of how we got here. They do not explain why we have kept on buying more and more and more things, even though we already have more than we need and more than we can cope with. The best way to throw light on that is through a story I think of as the "mystery of the Krispy Kremes".

On Thursday, 14 February 2013, the Lothian and Borders police received what sounded, on the face of it, like a routine call. There was a jam out on the ring road, by a retail park called Hermiston Gait. Most other places wouldn't have mattered so much, but Hermiston Gait is by the start of the M8, one of the busiest motorways in the UK and the main artery connecting Scotland's two biggest cities, Edinburgh and Glasgow. Commanders at HQ soon decided to do what any police force anywhere round the world would have done, given the circumstances. They warned drivers to avoid the area, and sent a couple of squad cars over to check out the reason for the problem – the new Krispy Kreme doughnut store.

When it had opened for the first time at 7am, an hour before sunrise, the previous day, three hundred people were lined up outside. Staff served coffee and the brand's doughnuts as quickly as they could. They served 400 customers in the first hour of opening, setting a new Krispy Kreme record. But even that was not fast enough.

No matter how hard they tried, the queue of people would not budge. The line of cars for the store's drive-thru kept building up, too. First it jammed the retail park. Then it slowed down the cars and trucks on the roundabout. By the next day, it was clogging up the traffic for the M8. That was when the police came over to check on the queue, and the doughnuts.

Not everyone was as excited about the new store as all those people lining up. "If Edinburgh is overweight today," grumbled a man from Britain's National Obesity Forum called Tam Fry, "it will be obese tomorrow."

Krispy Kreme's Original Glazed contains two hundred and seventeen kilocalories, including three grams of protein, twenty-two grams of carbohydrates and thirteen grams of fat. The calorie counts go up from there. Krispy Kreme doughnuts are, it's fair to say, not the world's healthiest snack.

The people standing outside knew this. The people sitting in their cars knew this. So why did they wait – for up to two hours – to get served, when they knew the thing they were queuing for was not even good for them?

Before you decide the answer is obvious – this is Scotland, home of the deep-fried Mars Bar, and therefore "case closed" – consider your own behaviour for a moment. You know that Krispy Kremes, and all sorts of things, are not very good for you. Yet, every now and then, you eat them. Sometimes, you even queue up for them. Why? Why do you, and me, and all of us crave foods we know aren't good for us?

There is no one better to solve this riddle than Brian Wansink, a food scientist sometimes introduced as the "Sherlock Holmes of food". Wansink has been working out why we eat what we eat for more than two decades. The answer to the Krispy Kreme question is in his book *Mindless Eating*. "We are hardwired to love the taste of fat, salt, and sugar," he wrote. "Fatty foods gave our ancestors the calorie reserves to weather food shortages. Salt helped them retain water and avoid dehydration. Sugar helped them distinguish sweet edible berries from sour poisonous ones. Through our taste for fat, salt, and sugar, we learned to prefer the foods that were most likely to keep us alive."

Wansink's explanation as to why we like certain foods draws on a branch of the social sciences called evolutionary psychology. This not only makes sense of the sort of foods we are attracted to but also how much we eat. "We have millions of years of evolution and instinct telling us," Wansink wrote, "to eat as often as we can and as much as we can."

That wisdom made sense when food was scarce. But it made a lot less sense when, in the 20th century, combine harvesters and synthetic fertilizers and higher-yielding seeds produced not only enough, but much more than enough.

This gave us an entirely new problem. Because, although the automatic, hardwired impulse to eat as often and as much as possible was no longer relevant, we were not able to simply switch it off like a light switch. Trained to cope with scarcity, we have struggled with abundance.

Having evolved over thousands of years to eat as often and as much as we could, many millions have become fat. This has happened on such a massive scale that we have a new name for it: the obesity epidemic.

The idea that we are making decisions in an age of abundance using mental tools honed in an age of scarcity might seem obvious. But it is worth repeating at a time when many millions of us not only have enough stuff, but way too much. Evolutionary psychology, I think, is key to understanding why we keep wanting and buying more, even when we already have far more than enough.

We are now living in an age of material abundance. Before, material goods were expensive and scarce. Clothes, for instance, were so hard to come by they were handed down from generation to generation. A shirt, before the Industrial Revolution, cost around £3,000 in today's money. But now, things – shirts, shoes, cups, cars, glasses, books, toys and a zillion other things

– are ubiquitous and cheap. Once again, though, our inbuilt impulses have yet to catch up. As a result, many millions of us are filling our homes and lives with stuff.

Overwhelmed and suffocated by stuff, we, as individuals, are feeling *Stuffocation*. As a society, we are feeling *Stuffocation*. *Stuffocation* is the material equivalent of the obesity epidemic.

A New Happiness Equation

There is a radical idea at the heart of *Stuffocation*, and it is one that is going to fundamentally alter our lives and upset a lot of apple carts – a lot of very big, very institutionalized apple carts, a lot of medium-size apple carts and a lot of small, personal apple carts. Perhaps even yours.

Because an individual feeling *Stuffocation* will make very different choices from the ones she or he made before, and a society responding to *Stuffocation* will look radically different from the one we have grown up in. How?

Till recently, the capitalist system we have been living in was largely based on a consumer who was materialistic. In that system, as in Nicodemus's original happiness equation, possessions and the pursuit of those possessions gave us status, meaning, and happiness. In that world, greed was good, more was better, and material goods were the best way to keep up with the Joneses. They aren't anymore.

I don't want to belittle all the things we've bought, though. I don't want to bash materialism either. Or, rather, not *just* bash it, at any rate. (I want, of course, to replace it.) Materialism, and the consumer culture and capitalist system it underpinned, was the right idea for the right time. It meant that the masses, for the first time in human history, lived in abundance rather than scarcity. It gave us washing machines, TVs, and indoor toilets. It delivered clean water, the welfare state, and health care that has improved the length and quality of our lives. It has lifted living standards for us, and it is now doing the same for billions of others, from Beijing to Bangalore and Sao Paolo.

But materialism's success has caught up with us. All that abundance has, paradoxically, brought scarcity once again. Now, for all the reasons causing *Stuffocation*, materialism is no longer such a great idea.

This book is about what I think should happen next. It is a call to arms. But it is much more than that. As well as a prescription of what needs to change, it is also a description of what is going to happen in the future, and the changes happening right now.

As more people, like Nicodemus, question the system and decide that more is not better and that they will not find happiness in possessions, we will see nothing less than a cultural revolution.

We will buy less, fewer and different material goods. What marketers call our buying motivators or consumption triggers will change, and they will change their business models. We will choose our jobs based on what we want to do, rather than what we have to do to pay for possessions we don't really need. We will judge status differently. Instead of focusing on how much money someone earns or how many things they own, we will calculate them in more experiential terms. Government policy will shift as well, with less concern for gross domestic product and the economy, and more interest in new measures of progress.

I am not suggesting that this will all happen suddenly, that we will all wake up on the morning of, say, the New Year sales in 2014 or 2015, and our interest in material things will have vanished overnight. This cultural change, after all, is as significant as the shift our ancestors made when they gave up thrifty ways to become wasteful consumers in the 20th century – and that took a good half century or so to really take hold. From the perspective of later historians, this will be seen as revolution, but from ours, living it every day, it will feel much more like evolution.

And I am not claiming, even then, that we will get rid of all our things and become a bunch of possession-free ascetics. I do not think we will head for the hills and live naked in caves. We will still need and use shoes, bags, clothes, cars, and mobile phones. But as we increasingly respond to *Stuffocation*, we will consume far less. And so, if our focus is gradually shifting away from material goods, where will we increasingly get our status, meaning, and happiness from?

To answer that question and understand what the world after materialism will look like, we will cross continents and eras in the search for clues, from the damp, candle-lit workshops of 18th-century England to Barbra Streisand's sunny, bluff-top California home in the 21st century.

We will smell Tahiti's technicolour flowers at dawn. We will hunt elk on a foggy day in Montana, carrying nothing but a stone-age bow and arrow. We will be voyeurs in Los Angeles, watching people through the windows of their homes. We will get stuck in a snowstorm in Peru, wearing only flip-flops on our feet. We will see the Sangre de Cristo mountains turn scarlet red as the sun sets. And along the way, we will meet the trailblazers who made materialist culture happen and the trendsetters solving *Stuffocation* today: the economists and the psychologists, the Mad Men and the innovators whose revolutionary, counterintuitive ideas changed, and are changing, the world we live in.

The point of all this is not only to have a sharper view of the Zeitgeist and a more informed opinion on the defining problem of our generation. It is to ask and answer the essential questions that we, as parents, policymakers, marketers, entrepreneurs and individuals, should be, and are, asking right now: how can we solve *Stuffocation*? Would we be happier if we lived with less stuff? If we are becoming less materialistic, where do we go from here? How, in other words, should you and I and the rest of society live today in order to be happy?

HAVE YOU HAD ENOUGH OF STUFF?

1. In your home generally, do you ever worry about the mess and that things aren't in the right place?

2. Is there a part of you that wishes there was a "clutter fairy" who would clean it all away, work out what you really need, and get rid of the rest?

3. When someone you live with brings something home is your typical response "but where are we going to keep it"?

4. In your bedroom now, if you wanted to hang a new dress or shirt in your wardrobe, would you have to heave the stuff that's already there left and right to make a gap, and jump in with the new thing, because if you weren't quick enough that gap would close up?

5. Do you have clothes you haven't worn for more than a year or, even, never worn?

6. When you open a drawer, do clothes pop out like they're trying to get some air?

7. In your kitchen, when you put something away in the cupboards, do you have to push and pull and poke, to fit the thing in your hand around all the other stuff that's already there?

8. Even when the kitchen looks clean and tidy, like a picture in an interiors magazine, are all those cupboard doors camouflage for the bedlam behind?

9. If you have a garage, is it packed so full with junk there's not enough room to house the number of cars it was designed for?

10. Think back to a time someone gave you something in the last year. Perhaps it was at Christmas, when Auntie Doreen and Uncle Peter held out a gift-wrapped box. Maybe it was your birthday, when your mother really shouldn't have, but did, and handed over something, she said, was just the perfect thing for you. Was your gut reaction ever to think "not more stuff"?

If you answered "yes" to any of these questions, you, like millions of others, are feeling *Stuffocation*.

ONE

The Farm Boy Who Discovered
the Secret to Forecasting

In late 1984, the economics editor of *The Economist*, a man by the name of Rupert Pennant-Rea, set out to make a point. Formerly an economist at the Bank of England, Pennant-Rea was rather fed up with predictions. "Was I frustrated?" he asks now. "Anybody who's ever been close to economic forecasting always is. At the Bank of England we'd spent a huge amount of time and money producing forecasts – and they were invariably unsatisfactory. Every now and then we got close to being right. But most of the time, we didn't."

So Pennant-Rea decided to poke some fun at forecasting. He asked four groups of people to predict what inflation, growth, and the pound's exchange rate would be like in ten years' time. The four groups were ex-finance ministers, company chairmen, economics students at Oxford University, and London dustmen. Contacting the chairmen, the students, and the former finance ministers was simple: he wrote to them. He did not know the addresses of any dustmen, though.

So early one morning, as he heard the dustcart coming down his street in Wandsworth, south London, Pennant-Rea threw on a coat and went out for a word with the foreman. What time did he and the boys finish the round? Would they mind helping with a short survey?

"He looked at me suspiciously," Pennant-Rea remembers, "as if to say – who *is* this nutter?"

The foreman agreed, though, and later that morning, with a notebook and some cans of beer in hand, Pennant-Rea made his way over to the depot. He picked his way past the dustcarts and a few windblown bits of rubbish, and poked his head through the door of a shed. "It wasn't exactly my milieu," he says now. "But as a journalist you have to be brazen."

The dustmen, as you can imagine, were not used to well-spoken economist-types asking them their thoughts about inflation. "They started slow," says Pennant-Rea. "But they soon got the hang of it, and even started egging each other on. One would say, 'How about 20%?' and another would cut in, 'Nah, mate, that can't be right, that's unthinkable,' until they decided on a figure they could all agree on."

Soon, Pennant-Rea had all he needed, handed over the beers, heartily shook hands, and left to write up his notes. The article became one of the lead features in that year's Christmas edition. It was called "Guessing the Future".

Ten years later, *The Economist* checked the results to see who had been more accurate. Who would you have bet on? The economics students and ex-finance ministers came third and fourth. And the dustmen were equal first with the company chairmen.

How was that possible? How could the dustmen do so well compared with people who have been trained to know and who had far more information, the so-called experts? And, which is more worrying, what is the point in trying to forecast the future if an expert's forecasts are no more accurate than a prediction from the proverbial man on the street, no better, you might say, than rubbish?

Forecasts Are Not Facts, They Are Maps

The author Nassim Nicholas Taleb painted a similarly gloomy picture in his book *The Black Swan*, especially in a story about a turkey farmer and a turkey. See the world, for a moment, through a turkey's eyes. Each day, the farmer comes to feed you. For a thousand days or so, he turns up, red bucket in hand, pulling out oats and corn and carrot peelings, sprinkling them on the ground. Every one of those thousand days, you go gobble-gobbling over, pecking at the food.

Assume for a moment that, although you're a turkey, you have a good memory, you can talk and like to draw graphs. Now, if you were asked what was going to happen tomorrow, you would have a thousand separate pieces of data on which to make a prediction. You might draw those thousand data points on a graph and extrapolate them to predict that, yes, in fact, your nice, predictable, breakfast-bringing farmer will come out to feed you tomorrow, same as always.

But what if the farmer's long-lost cousins are coming for dinner tomorrow? What if instead of scattering food, he is going to wring your neck? What use would all your data points from the past be then?

Life, Taleb says, is like that. No matter how much data we have, the world is unknowable. We can never know what is going to happen in the future. No matter how sure and safe and good things feel, fate might have other plans. It might even wring your neck.

What all this tells us is that someone with no special knowledge, dustmen, for instance, can be just as good as people with insider knowledge at predicting the future. It also shows that wild, unexpected unforeseen events can happen, and suggests that any attempt to tell the future will therefore be pointless.

But we need not conclude, as Taleb does, that all forecasting is futile and that we should simply give up on forecasts altogether. After all, every one of us, and every business, and every government, uses predictions every day to work out what might happen and what we should do to plan for that. If we did not, how could we plan how many products to produce, how many homes to build, or what time to turn up at the airport? A departure time, if you think about it, is nothing more than a prediction of when your plane will take off.

Besides, we should not, in truth, expect forecasts to be perfectly accurate. We should not even think of them as facts. Instead, we should see them the same way we view models or maps. A good forecast, like an accurate roadmap or a well-constructed model, should provide us with enough information about the future so that we are able to plan. It may not mention every detail – every bump in the road or sight or unexpected traffic jam – but it will tell us when to turn left or right, it will give us ideas on how to get to our destination, and it will sketch out what it will look like when we get there.

It is easy to see why men like Pennant-Rea and Taleb get all gloomy and frustrated about forecasts. But there really is no need, if you remember that a forecast is not a fact. It is a map.

Using the Past to Tell the Future

The best way to draw a map of the future is through detailed knowledge of two things that are far easier to know: the present and the past. There are two instances, in particular, when knowing the past can help. The more obvious is when there is a long-running trend, which started many years ago and which looks likely, given certain circumstances, to continue in the future.

Consider, for instance, the rise of the Chinese economy, or the growing tolerance of our societies towards gay people. These changes are not smooth. They do not always fit convenient graphs – like the ones turkeys draw. There is often plenty of noise around the signal. Sometimes they blip, make unexpected leaps, up, down, back, forward. Sometimes the Chinese economy surges. Sometimes it stalls. Every now and then, local laws make significant steps towards tolerance or intolerance, swiftly altering homosexual rights. But it is clear that these are both long-terms trends from the past that are likely to continue in the future.

The second way the past can help is by showing how the world works. This is how weather and electricity and population forecasters do their jobs, for instance: they observe and analyse a set of circumstances from the past, and see what outcomes they led to. Using those insights, they create models that describe how the world works, and how change happens. Then, by viewing the information they have about the present through those models, they forecast how many people there will be, how much electricity will be needed, and whether it is going to be sunny tomorrow.

None of these are perfect – as you will know if you have ever been caught out without an umbrella and blamed the weatherman – but they do work. Take weather forecasting, for instance, and, in particular, high temperature and hurricane forecasts. In the 1970s, the high temperature forecasts were wrong, on average, by about six degrees. Today they are only wrong by half that amount, three degrees. When hurricane forecasters predicted where a hurricane would hit land in the 1980s, they were usually out by 350 miles. Today, their predictions are only wrong by 100 miles. These improvements in forecasting save a lot of money, many lives, and millions of us from suffering that uncomfortable feeling of wearing too much or too little.

Proving that forecasts based on knowledge of the past and the present are useful by showing that they are less wrong today than they were yesterday, it must be said, may seem a little odd as a way to show that we can forecast. But an error rate of three degrees is really quite accurate. It is accurate enough to be of use to energy companies planning demand for electricity, and to help us work out what sort of shirt or coat to put on.

And it is also worth making this point because this is one of the key ways cultural forecasters like me work. With a reasonable understanding of how things changed in the past, and reasonable knowledge of what is happening in the present, in other words, we can make sensible forecasts about what will happen in the future.

There is one model that is better than any other for understanding how culture changes, a way of tracing the spread of ideas that has been applied more than 5,000 times. It is the method most cultural forecasters use to work out the future today. It is the principal model I will be using in this book. Called the *Diffusion of Innovations*, it was discovered by a farm boy from Iowa by the name of Everett Rogers.

The Farm Where the Corn Did Not Grow Tall

When the pioneers ventured west to settle Iowa in the 1830s, it looked like a sea of grass. The prairie grass grew taller than a man back then, seven, eight, even twelve feet high.

For those who could see it, that tall grass told its own story – of the fertility of the soil beneath and how that would one day be the making of the state, putting it at the heart of America's Corn Belt. To this day, the chorus of Iowa's unofficial anthem, which is called the Corn Song, ends with the proudest boast an Iowan farmer could make:

"We are from Ioway, Ioway,
That's where the tall corn grows."

The corn was not growing tall on the farm where five-year-old Everett Rogers lived in 1936, even while the corn grew just fine in all their neighbours' fields. Ev knew that this was a tough year and that there was a drought on. But still, why had his father's crop failed when others hadn't? He only found out why years later, when he was a young man studying at the local university.

The answer, it seemed, lay in a paper by two researchers called Bruce Ryan and Neal Gross. In the early 1940s, they had studied how an agriculture innovation had spread through two small farm communities in Greene County, Iowa, about 30 miles from where Rogers had grown up. It must have been like reading about home.

The innovation was hybrid corn seed. It delivered 20% more yield. Even better, it was drought resistant. It was much better than the seed the Iowan farmers had been using before. And it had also been available since 1928.

Yet most farmers – like Rogers's father – did not instantly start planting the new, better seed. By 1933, only a handful were planting it. Then, the rate of adoption sped up. In 1934, 16 started planting it. In 1935, 21 followed, then 36 in 1936 – the year of the drought. The next year, 61 took up the new seed, and then 46, 36, 14, and 3.

When they plotted those numbers on a graph, where the x-axis is time and the y-axis is the cumulative number of farmers, they discovered it made a smooth S-shape.

By the time of the study in 1941 – thirteen years after the better seed became available – two were still not using the better, more efficient, more profitable seed. Why? Why had some farmers adopted it earlier and others been so slow to catch on, even though it was far more likely to produce tall-growing corn?

To find out, in summer 1941, Ryan knocked on the doors of all the farmers in the area. He would arrive for his first call of the day before dawn, and keep going all day, asking each farmer a long set of questions: what was their level of education? How old were they? How many acres was their farm? What was their income? How often did they go to the state capital Des Moines? Did they read farm magazines? And when had they first started planting the hybrid corn?

Ryan and Gross now cross-referenced the information they had gathered with the data on the graph. The first pioneer farmers to plant the hybrid corn, they found, tended to have larger farms, higher incomes, more years of education, and were more cosmopolitan – as calculated by how often they went to the state capital, Des Moines. Ryan and Gross labelled these "innovators".

The later a farmer took on the new innovation, they found, the smaller his farm, the lower his income, the less education he had, and the less interested he was in the world outside his immediate surroundings.

The next group who adopted the innovation, after the innovators, they called "early adopters". Next were the "early majority", then the "late majority", and finally the "laggards". They had the smallest farms, the lowest incomes and the least education, and they did not get out very much. This group included the two farmers, out of the 259 farmers in the study, who had still not adopted the hybrid corn when Gross went knocking in summer 1941.

Rogers was captivated by the revelations in the paper. The time lag between a farmer finding out about the innovative seed and planting it was, on average, nine years. There were many barriers that stopped farmers trying the new corn out: it meant, for instance, that they had to change their method of planting. The innovators and early adopters were far more likely to experiment, and to listen to salesmen and advertisements. Later adopters – the early and late majority – preferred to hear what their neighbours thought.

And if you read the numbers carefully and looked at the S-curve, there was clearly a moment when the idea really took hold, like the moment in dry prairie grass in high summer when a small fire catches the wind and spreads like wildfire. Looking at the curve, Ryan and Gross called that the moment the innovation "took off". Rogers later thought of it, with reference to the importance of the neighbours in terms of spreading an idea, as a "social snowball". Many years later, Malcolm Gladwell would call it the "tipping point".

Reading the paper must have been a lightbulb moment for Rogers. Finally, he could make sense of the time, all those years before, when his father's crop had failed as everyone else's corn had grown tall. His family's plot was relatively small. They were not rich farmers. His father had not spent time reading farm magazines. He was more interested in tinkering in his shed than farming. His father, it was plain to see, was not an innovator. But he was.

Ev Rogers reviewed hundreds of other studies of the diffusion process, from other disciplines like medicine, marketing, and anthropology, and he made a fascinating discovery: that Ryan and Gross's S-curve held for them too. Rogers published this discovery, in 1962, as the *Diffusion of Innovations*. Now, more than fifty years and thousands of diffusion studies later,

Ryan and Gross's research method has become the one that all innovation researchers use, and Rogers's *Diffusion of Innovations* curve has become the de facto method of studying how ideas spread.

Rogers spent the rest of his career, until his death from cancer in 2004, travelling the world, to countries like Mexico, Colombia, and India, using the model to diffuse good ideas – such as the use of condoms to prevent the spread of AIDS. He would use the *Diffusion of Innovations* model to analyse the situation and work out the best way to engage with the local people, and the best way to speed them along the curve so that they would get the benefits from the innovation sooner rather than later.

Perhaps, there was always a little of that confused five-year-old boy inside of Rogers. But now, as an adult, he didn't have to worry any longer. Now, he could do something about it. By helping people around the world get to the innovation that bit sooner, maybe he was making sure that, when everyone else's corn grew tall all around, theirs did too.

Using the Present to Forecast the Future

As well as providing social scientists with a definitive method for tracking change, Everett Rogers also created, for those who could see it, a powerful forecasting tool. Because if you read the S-curve from left to right, along the timeline of the x-axis, you are essentially watching a graphical movie of an idea spreading through time. If you can work out what is happening at a certain point, and you know which point you are at, you can use the curve to not only analyse the past, but also forecast the future.

If, in other words, you look around the present and notice an innovation – which could be a new type of computer that has no need for a keyboard, a new brand of more comfortable flip-flops, or a new way of living – and then notice that certain people are adopting it, and then that more people are also adopting it, you can, with caution, make reasonable predictions of the future.

This is what cultural forecasters do. They believe, as William Gibson did, that "The future is already here — it's just not very evenly distributed." Their job is to observe and interrogate the noise of the present to identify signs of that unevenly distributed future. Then, using the S-curve, they make forecasts about when and how those ideas will become more widely distributed, and what the world will look like as a result. This is the method I use. This is what I am doing in *Stuffocation*.

To use the curve, according to Rogers, there are five key factors that will determine whether an innovation will be adopted or not. To begin with, there is the question of the innovation itself. Is it better? Is it easy to understand? Is it easy to try out? Is it easily available? And if one person tries it, and assuming it works, will other people notice? If the answer to each of these is a resounding "yes", it is more likely to spread.

You also need to understand the decision-making process, and whether it takes people a long time to decide to adopt the innovation or not. If it takes nine years from knowing about something that is 20% better to using it, it is little wonder that it takes a long time for everyone to adopt an innovation. Compare that, though, to the uptake of smartphones or a superfood like blueberries. Since people tend to change their handset every year or so, and they tend to buy fruit every week, the change is likely to be quicker.

Third, what are the communication channels within the system, and how do ideas, information, and inspiration pass through the community? This is an especially important consideration for us today, as in our hyper-connected world of the mobile internet and social media, ideas spread, and change happens, very quickly. Till recently, for instance, new fashion ideas were disseminated by the select few at monthly glossy magazines. Today, they can be blogged, texted, tweeted and Instagram-ed in an instant by almost anyone.

Fourth, you also need to know how innovative the culture is. Compare London and Kabul in Afghanistan, for instance. In one of those markets, people are fairly open to change. They change their clothes, the foods and places they eat, and even the people they spend time with almost with the season. You are likely to come into contact with people from different cultures with different ideas every day. In the other, far more conservative system, people tend to eat the same food, and spend time with the same people, who hold the same views that they do.

If you were launching an innovation – say a new exercise, toy or TV show – in which of these two cities would you launch yours? The more innovative and connected a system is, the more quickly an innovation will spread.

Fifth, are there any "change agents" involved? That is, are there any powerful people or organizations which might actively try to diffuse the innovation? Examples might be Krispy Kreme's marketers trying to get people to make more occasions for doughnuts, or the government trying to make people shop more, or stop smoking, or eat more fruit.

By considering these factors and answering these questions, it is possible to make an accurate forecast about whether an innovation that is happening today will spread in the future. In this book I will, as I mentioned, use the *Diffusion of Innovations* model to consider the most exciting, innovative new ways of living that are happening now, and forecast the one that will replace materialism, and solve the problem of *Stuffocation*. I will, in other words, examine the present to forecast the future.

Before we come to the present, though, we need to be sure that major cultural change is the sort of thing that happens.

To do that, we need to look for precedents in the past. And to do that, we will investigate the last time the world faced a problem as significant as

Stuffocation. The trouble then was not overconsumption. It was overproduction.

TWO

The Original Mad Men
and the Job of Creating Desire

On Monday, 11 May 1925, just after 10am, as sun streamed through the windows of a hall in Houston, Texas, a hush settled among a group of men and women from the advertising industry, as a tall, distinguished-looking gentleman walked in and took the stage. A man in his 50s, his brown hair, now greying at the sides, was slicked back and parted left of centre. He was wearing a dark three-piece suit and a white shirt with a rounded collar.

"Advertising was not always looked upon as a vital part of our economic system," said the future president of the United States, Herbert Hoover. It was now, though. "You have taken over," he told the assembled audience of Mad Men and women, "the job of creating desire."

Advertising, Hoover believed, was one of the best ways of solving the most pressing problem the

US economy faced at the time – overproduction. Since the Civil War had ended in 1865, peace and farming and factories had transformed the country. Millions of acres of prairie grass had been turned over and made productive, for raising pigs, growing wheat, and producing countless other things. Entire industries had sprung up.

The nation was now littered with foundries producing iron, mills spinning textiles, and workshops making cars, tractors, trains. Railroads criss-crossed the continent, bringing radios and razors and toasters, as well as magazines and influence from the skyscrapers in New York and Chicago to the north, south, east, and west. Even World War I had helped, as it had destroyed crops and closed factories in Europe, and meant more work for America's industries.

In the sixty years since the Civil War's end, the population had increased by a factor of three, from 35 to 114 million. Over the same period, output had risen between twelve and fourteen times.

The United States industries had grown, in other words, four times faster than the population. Now, in the 1920s, America's manufacturing and agricultural industries were producing far more than they could sell. The Europeans were producing more of their own food and goods once again.

And the American people had reached, so the US secretary of labor James J Davis told *The New York Times*, the point of "need saturation".

By 1927, the country's textile mills could produce enough cloth for the whole year by operating only six months of the year. Less than a fifth of America's shoe factories could produce a year's supply of footwear.

As the 1920s progressed, the problem of overproduction loomed larger. Soon it threatened to blow the country and its folk off their happy, bumpy road to prosperity. As supply outstripped demand, the United States was coming to a fork in the road. The dilemma was simple: either the farmers and factories needed to produce less, or its people had to consume more. If you had been in a position to choose the path the country took, which way would you have picked: produce less or consume more?

The obvious answer would have been to get the farmers and the factories to produce less. This was what men like the economist Arthur Dahlberg and the cornflake capitalist W K Kellogg proposed. This solution would be simple to achieve. Its outcome was more predictable. The people would work less. They would have more time off. They could use their spare time to indulge in what John Maynard Keynes called the "Age of Leisure". They could play in the park, sing in the choir, contribute to the community, take up a hobby, contemplate God, spend more time with their family and friends, even listen to the radio. Would you have chosen this option?

There were many others, though, who thought the other solution, to consume more, was better. These people – politicians like Hoover and industrialists like the General Motors CEO Alfred Sloan – did not even think of the problem in the same way. To them, the trouble was not overproduction. It was underconsumption. The solution, therefore, was to get people to consume more. The logic of the argument was really quite compelling.

It had first been made, in fact, hundreds of years before, by an Englishman called Bernard Mandeville, in a satire published in 1715 called the *Fable of the Bees: or, Private Vices, Public Benefits*. The satire was about a group of prosperous bees who lived, so the story went, a life of luxury and ease. But after grumblings that their way of living lacked virtue, they turned away from their fraud and greed and extravagance, to a new life of simplicity and honesty and temperance. You might think that would be a good idea. But, as the fable showed, if the bees gave up their vices, especially their greedy, high-spending ways, that would be the end of their easy, luxurious life as well.

This was a revolutionary, counterintuitive idea. The conventional wisdom, hardwired over thousands of years till then, had been that the best way to increase prosperity was by saving, not by spending. But Mandeville showed that things that were sins in the eyes of the church, like being greedy and buying more than strictly necessary, or showing off by throwing extravagant parties, produced work, jobs, and wealth – in other words, the private vices of the rich led to public benefits for all.

The same logic which had worked for Mandeville's bees, and the noblemen and merchants they represented in the fable, also made perfect sense for society in the 20th century. If people bought more, they would create a virtuous circle where everyone benefited. They would create more jobs and more wages. The industrialists' profits would go up. The government would receive more tax revenue. Everyone would enjoy a higher standard of living. If more people spent more, in other words, and paradoxical though it might at first seem, they would have more. It all hinged, as you can see, on consumers acting like hard-working and, even more importantly, high-spending bees.

But before the leaders of industry and government, who New York academic Stuart Ewen has named the "captains of consciousness", could hurry everyone along into this sweet new future, there was one problem. The decision to produce less was clearly theirs to make. They could make it happen simply by reducing work hours. But getting people to consume more was far more complex. It was far *less* certain – that the outcome would be as they hoped – and far *from* certain – that they could make it happen in the first place.

For that future to happen, the captains of consciousness would have to get the good men and women of America to buy more things, more often – even though, at the point of "need saturation", they already had enough. To make the people buy more, they would have to change behaviours and attitudes that had evolved since the dawn of time, the sort that said: prize the possessions you have, then, be careful with them and look after them, because they cost a lot of time and effort and energy to get. How could they get the people of America to change the habits and customs, not only of their lifetimes, but of all the lifetimes that had ever come before them?

The New and Improved Throwaway Culture

Earnest Elmo Calkins's first break in advertising came in 1891. He won a competition, out of 1,433 other entries, to write the best advertisement for a household cleaner. His advert claimed the new cleaner "stays newer longer, and sweeps cleaner than a broom". He had, you could say, the gift of the ad. He wrote the kind of words that made people go out and buy things. He continued to use this method, which became known as "reason-why" advertising throughout his career.

As his career progressed, though, his adverts became more sophisticated. To add dramatic appeal, he started using art. He created one of the first art departments in an advertising agency. In the first decades of the 20th century that had worked well enough, especially since many people were still buying their first of any product category, and manufacturers often had some genuinely new and improved breakthrough to announce. But in the later

1920s, when the problem of overproduction was looming, Calkins wondered if even that was enough.

As an adman, of course, Calkins's role was to sell whatever his clients made as well as possible. But he realized that, as the culture was changing, so his role needed to change too. So he set to thinking, and eventually came up with a new idea. The best way to make people consume more products was not to change the products. It was, he realized, to change the people. The key to stimulating consumption was to take the happy, thrifty people of America and turn them into dissatisfied, wasteful, conspicuous consumers. Instead of manufacturing products, industry should engineer consumers. How could they do that?

Calkins had two answers. The first way to make consumers was by giving people enough money to buy products. This could be achieved either by the industrialists paying them the right wages, or by companies helping people purchase by giving them the financial means to buy now. In other words, companies should offer credit. "It is [as] necessary to provide consumers as goods," two employees of Calkins, Egmont Arens and Roy Sheldon, would later write in their 1932 book *Consumer Engineering*, "and as necessary to provide the consumers with money as with goods."

The second idea was even more revolutionary, and colourful too. This new way to sell more products was inspired by the art Calkins had brought into the world of advertising. Just as advertising had evolved from those early, functional messages into works of art, so he felt that was what products also needed. This, so it seemed to him, was the natural progress of any industry.

First, a person would be amazed by the fact of something's existence and the added value it would bring to their lives, and the industrialist only needed to create a functional product. After that, the consumer will want to see that product beautified, through colour, style, beauty. This is the stage, he believed, industry had come to.

"The appeal of efficiency alone is nearly ended," he wrote in an article for *The Atlantic Monthly* in August 1927. "Beauty is the next logical step."

If you think about this idea for a moment, it is clear that it is the statement of both an aesthete and a businessman. Because the beauty, if you will, of this idea is that the concept of what is beautiful can also be engineered, and manipulated according to a manufacturing cycle, to keep people buying. In other words, Calkins's idea was to take the idea that underpinned the success of the fashion industry and use it in all other industries.

"People buy a new car," Calkins wrote, "not because the old one is worn out, but because it is no longer modern. It does not satisfy their pride. They refurnish the house, not because the old furniture is unable to perform its duties as furniture, but because it is out of date, out of style, no longer the thing."

The topic of how to create the new regular-buying consumer was one of the most important areas of debate for the Mad Men and women of the 1920s and 1930s. It would be discussed at meetings of the New York Sales Managers' Club and the New York Advertising Club, and in the pages of leading trade publications like *Printer's Ink* and *Advertising and Selling*. Many agreed with Calkins that the solution was to create a new consumer with a new attitude.

"We must induce people," wrote another adman, J George Frederick, in a lead article in *Advertising and Selling* in 1928, "to buy a greater variety of goods on the same principle that they now buy automobiles, radios and clothes, namely: buying goods not to wear out, but to trade in or discard after a short time." Frederick even gave this new and improved throwaway culture a name. He called it "progressive obsolescence".

The Birth of Death Dating

The idea of obsolescence, this culture of "use and discard", it must be said, did not suddenly appear in the 1920s. Americans had been throwing some things away since the 19th century – like disposable razors, and even, in an era where getting whites very white was difficult, shirt collars and cuffs. American men bought 150 million throwaway collars and cuffs in 1872.

To trace the idea of progressive obsolescence, as J George Frederick called it, back to its origins, though, you really have to go back to the 1830s, when a three-masted sailing boat called *The Beagle* rounded the world carrying a gentleman naturalist by the name of Charles Darwin.

Till that time, the scientific establishment had been closely aligned with the church. Any theory – and there were a few around at the time – that humans were not divinely created and had evolved instead was considered heresy. But now, for the first time, this was not just a theory. There was now scientific proof. Darwin found it on that trip and published it, in November 1859, in *On the Origin of Species by Means of Natural Selection, or the Preservation of Favoured Races in the Struggle for Life*. In it, Darwin proved that all animals had evolved through a process of natural selection, where only the fittest survived, and those that did not adapt did not.

If you were a man of letters or industry in the 19th century, Darwin's theory was both interesting and inspiring. If you thought about this idea for a moment, it sounded an awful lot like the industrial revolutions of recent years.

When James Hargreaves had invented the spinning jenny in Lancashire in the 1760s, for instance, the spinner could now spin yarn twenty times more efficiently than if she had been using her old spinning wheel. That new spinning jenny not only revolutionized how quickly a spinner could produce yarn. It also meant the spinning wheel would now only be useful for burning. It had become, in a word, obsolete. And as Hargreaves's jenny had replaced the wheel and made it useful only as firewood, so, a few years later, the spinning jenny became obsolete – as the new spinning frame made much stronger yarn.

Once you had noticed this happening with the process of producing yarn, you would also see that it was a natural part of the progress of other industries. Once someone discovered that making railroads with steel was better than iron, for instance, the iron tracks were obsolete. Actually, while you were about it, this theory did not just sound like a number of industries, it sounded a lot like capitalism.

The Austrian American economist Joseph Schumpeter noticed this. "The same process of industrial mutation – if I may use that biological term," Schumpeter wrote, "incessantly revolutionises the economic structure from within, incessantly destroys the old, incessantly creating a new one. This process of Creative Destruction is the essential fact about Capitalism."

Seen this way, it is little wonder that obsolescence and the waste that came with the throwaway culture resonated so strongly with the captains of consciousness. To them, obsolescence and waste were more than simply ways to increase profits. They were not just by-products of the industrial equivalent of evolution. They were proof that industry, and society, was evolving.

In the 1920s and '30s, these ideas gained ground with business people. "America's triumphs and rapidity of progress are based on progressive obsolescence," wrote Frederick's wife, Christine, who had become one of the leading consumer experts of the day. "We have more because we spend more – this is our American paradox."

Keeping people spending – solving the problem of underconsumption – became a key business focus.

"Are the consumers consuming fast enough?" wondered Arens and Sheldon, in *Consumer Engineering*. "Goods fall into two classes, those we use, such as motor-cars or safety razors, and those we use *up*, such as toothpaste or soda biscuit. Consumer engineering must see to it that we use up the kind of goods we now merely use. Would any change in the goods or the habits of people speed up their consumption? Can they be displaced by newer models? Can artificial obsolescence be created? Consumer engineering does not end until we can consume all we can make."

In the same year, a real estate agent in New York called Bernard London, in a pamphlet called *Ending the Depression Through Planned Obsolescence*, suggested that the government stimulate demand by defining the time any product was allowed to be used. It would work like the use-by date that comes with food. After a time, in London's vision, the product you had bought would be "legally dead". You would have to trade it in or get rid of it – and buy a new one.

Not everyone, it must be said, got on board straight away. Henry Ford, for instance, resisted calls to obsolescence. "We want the man who buys one of our cars never to have to buy another," he had stated in 1922. "We never make an improvement that renders any previous model obsolete." That was a noble sentiment, and Ford no doubt meant it. But in 1933, in the face of flagging sales, Ford gave in and, like his great competitor Alfred Sloan at Chevrolet, started changing the styling of his cars each year.

If there was a watershed moment in the history of obsolescence, this was it. Now that the leader of America's flagship industry was using beauty to make last year's model less attractive and thereby encourage people to spend more often, other businesses in all industries soon adopted the idea, if they had not already, and obsolescence became standard business practice.

To begin with, this new culture separated America from the rest of the developed world. "The progressive obsolescence is the very knife-blade which is carving this cleavage," Christine Frederick observed in 1929. "In Europe people buy shoes, clothes, motor cars, etc., to last just as long as possible. That is their idea of buying wisely. You buy once and of very substantial, everlasting materials and you never buy again if you can help it. It is not uncommon for English women of certain circles to wear on all formal occasions, the same evening gown for five or ten years. To us this is unheard of and preposterous."

Frederick was right. The ideals and practice of materialistic consumerism had spread quickest in America. It was there that production capacity had most quickly outpaced consumption, and where overproduction had created the possibility, as well as necessity, for manufacturers and government and the people to uproot the old ways. But the success of progressive obsolescence was soon obvious in the soaring American living standards – and soon everyone wanted to emulate America's success.

As the profits of US businesses soared, so companies elsewhere copied their methods. As the US national income increased, raising more taxes and creating more wealth, governments around the world sought to copy the mass production, mass consumption model of the capitalist-consumerist-materialist system that the United States' captains of consciousness had created. As the material wellbeing of ordinary American households improved, so ordinary people wanted to hear more about how America's women did it.

Frederick, for instance, despite her harsh words, was invited on lecture tours of Europe. In early 1927, she spent three months lecturing in the UK, taking her message of consumerism to chambers of commerce and women's groups in Birmingham, Liverpool, Glasgow, and London – where she stayed, and shivered, in the Berners Hotel. Her room's wall-heater and wood-burning fireplace were not, apparently, enough to keep the room warm.

"No wonder my women sponsors wanted me to present the advantages of central heating," she would write later in her unpublished autobiography.

That year, she also spread the gospel of consumerism to other European countries, including Italy, where she met Mussolini – who reminded her of "a head-waiter in an Italian restaurant on 45th Street in New York City".

Where once, people all around the world had been careful with their money, they, gradually, as the 20th century progressed, emulated the American model and became wasteful, conspicuous consumers. As the century wore on, especially after World War II, it became clearer that the world's fastest growing economies were those based on that model. They were all hinged, in other words, on consumers eagerly using up what they previously only used, buying new things a little sooner than was strictly necessary. The American paradox – to have more by spending more – became a universal paradox or, at least, a paradox for those of us in the wealthy West.

Richard Nixon in the Kitchen and the Best Idea of the 20th Century

In 1959, Richard Nixon visited Nikita Khrushchev in Moscow, and had one of the oddest, and possibly funniest, superpower summits of the 20th century – a rough-and-tumble, boyish debate in a kitchen. It was a time of some tension between the US and USSR. In the hope that a little more understanding would stop either country using the nuclear weapons each was then stockpiling, the two countries had agreed to a few cultural exchanges.

The centrepiece of the Russian exhibit which landed in New York in June 1959 was the world's first successful satellite, Sputnik I. The intended message, which came through loud and clear to everyone in the American administration, would not have been clearer, even if a Russian politician had stood there thumbing his nose blurting "ner-ner-ner-ner-ner". The message was this: our communist system is better than your capitalist one, as proved by the fact that we Russians have superior space technology.

When the doors opened to their exhibition in Moscow a few months later, the Americans wanted to deliver an equally powerful, and perfectly opposite, message. How could they do that? What would show those pesky Russians that capitalism was in fact better than communism?

They decided to do so by creating a real-life suburban home, the sort of house Richie Cunningham lived in, in the television series *Happy Days*. It was in this home's kitchen that Nixon met Khrushchev.

If you look up the CIA transcript it reads like a comedy sketch where the director has asked one to be reasonable, and the other to act the defensive, blustering ruddy-cheeked oaf. Can you tell who was given which directions?

The Kitchen Debate - transcript
24 July 1959

[Both men enter kitchen in the American exhibit.]

Nixon: I want to show you this kitchen. It is like those of our houses in California.

[Nixon points to dishwasher.]

Khrushchev: We have such things.

Nixon: This is our newest model. This is the kind which is built in thousands of units for direct installations in the houses. In America, we like to make life easier for women...

Khrushchev: Your capitalistic attitude toward women does not occur under Communism.

Nixon: I think that this attitude towards women is universal. What we want to do, is make life more easy for our housewives...

Nixon: This house can be bought for $14,000, and most Americans can buy a home in the bracket of $10,000 to $15,000...

Khrushchev: We have steel workers and peasants who can afford to spend $14,000 for a house. Your American houses are built to last only 20 years so builders could sell new houses at the end. We build firmly. We build for our children and grandchildren.

Nixon: American houses last for more than 20 years, but, even so, after twenty years, many Americans want a new house or a new kitchen. Their kitchen is obsolete by that time... The American system is designed to take advantage of new inventions and new techniques.

Khrushchev: This theory does not hold water. Some things never get out of date – houses, for instance, and furniture. Furnishings – perhaps – but not houses. I have read much about America and American houses, and I do not think that this exhibit and what you say is strictly accurate... You think the Russian people will be dumbfounded to see these things, but the fact is that newly built Russian houses have all this equipment right now.

But Russian houses had nothing like all that equipment.

"There is no more truth in showing this as the typical home of the American worker," fumed the Soviet state news agency Tass, "than, say, in showing the Taj Mahal as the typical home of a Bombay textile worker."

Rather than expose the US delegation as lying, though, this comment showed that the exhibit had done its job. It also highlighted the gulf that was opening up between the standards of living in a capitalist system and those under communism.

Moreover, what the entire episode – the exhibits, meeting, conversation, and reporting – demonstrates is that "keeping up with the Joneses" is not merely a petty concern for suburban housewives, city bankers, and those people who live next door. While it is easy to laugh at people who try too obviously to keep up, it is an essential human trait. And, as Khrushchev and

Nixon's conversation makes plain, it is as fundamental for nations as it is for individuals.

That realization, I think, is fundamental to understanding the history of the 20th century, and the importance of capitalism as an idea. Because, as the century progressed and capitalism hauled millions out of poverty in the United States, the West, and Japan, it made the stagnating standards of living elsewhere, and the systems their leaders had chosen, look ever worse. It became progressively harder for official news agencies to deny that their countries were falling behind. And it became more obvious that the capitalist system, driven by consumerism and underpinned by materialistic values, was not just different. It was better.

Eventually, especially after the fall of the Berlin Wall and the Iron Curtain, many communist, and other, countries started adopting elements of this system too, especially materialistic values, conspicuous consumption and the throwaway culture. Just as it did over here, so it is now giving hundreds of millions over there better lives as well.

Again, the way is not entirely clear, but international trade, with materialistic consumerism at its heart, is pulling more out of poverty now than ever before. By 2030, so many believe, we may even have eradicated poverty. For this reason, materialism was unquestionably the best idea of the 20th century. How ironic, then, that it has also given us the most pressing problem of the 21st century.

THREE

Barbra Streisand and the Law of Unintended Consequences

In February 2003, the entertainer Barbra Streisand was, as she'd say, pissed – meaning angry, not drunk. A man had gone up in a helicopter. He had flown over her 8-bedroom, 11-bathroom bluff-top home in Malibu, California. He had pointed the telephoto lens of his camera through a rear door, which had been deliberately removed, and he had taken a photograph of Streisand's 10,485-square-foot home.

Then, he had put the picture on the internet for anyone to see. If you really liked the shot, he was selling prints too.

The picture showed Streisand's home, including her garden, the swimming pool, and how she had arranged the tables and chairs on her patio. Streisand was not in the picture. Nor was her husband. But that was hardly the point. She was one of the world's biggest stars. She was followed everywhere by paparazzi. Couldn't she at least have some privacy at home?

Streisand's lawyers contacted the man. They asked him in what they would later describe as amicable terms to take the photo down and stop selling it. When he refused, they served a cease-and-desist notice on him, which is a legal way of amicably asking someone to stop doing something. In the notice, they invoked California Civil Code Sections 3344 and 1708.8 – better known as the Anti-Paparazzi Laws. They also wrote the following: "Please be advised that no part of this letter may be published or disseminated without our prior written consent."

The man, who also lived in California and went by the name of Ken Adelman, did what any good, law-abiding citizen would have done. He scanned the letter and put it on his website.

The website was CaliforniaCoastline.org, the place of record for the California Coastal Records Project. Adelman was not a paparazzo, you see. He was not aiming to sell his photos to the *National Enquirer* or *The Sun*.

He was an environmentalist who had been trying to protect the California coast, by documenting its state from the air, since 1997. The aim of the California Coastal Records Project was to shoot all 12,000 kilometres of the state's coastline – and it just so happened that Streisand happened to live on that coastline.

Streisand's team of anti-paparazzi lawyers sued for $10 million. By doing so, they must have realized that filing the papers would not only bring the case to court. But they must also have known that this would bring their client to the public's attention. And they are unlikely to have foreseen, in all fairness to them, the full consequences of what they had done.

Reaction, at first, was mixed. A few felt Streisand was right, that Adelman had crossed the line. Most thought Adelman was well within his rights, though, and when the news became public they expressed their feelings by clicking onto Adelman's website, and then downloading the image.

If Streisand's anti-paparazzi attorney's plan was to stop people looking at Streisand's home – and it seems reasonable that that was the aim – it backfired in the most public and spectacular fashion. Before the lawsuit, the image had been downloaded six times, including twice by her lawyers. After the case became public, the image was downloaded 420,000 times.

Then it became even bigger news. The story went down the coast to the *San Jose Mercury News*. It crossed the Pacific Ocean to the *Japan Times* and the *Sydney Morning Herald*. It was reported in *Le Monde* in France and by the BBC in the UK.

Whenever someone tries to stop people seeing something online – like when the French secret service wants Wikipedia to delete an article about a spy listening station, or Celine Dion does not want people looking at a site called Ridiculous Pictures of Celine Dion – but merely draws more attention to it, that is now called, in honour of the great entertainer, the Streisand effect.

The Prince and the Rabbit-Proof Fence

In October 1859, Thomas Austin was excited. Like the rest of the family in the village of Baltonsborough in Somerset, England, he had been poor. But in the tough times of the 1840s, like three dozen other Austins, he had emigrated to Australia.

Things had turned out well for him down here. He had grabbed the opportunities that Australia offered. He had occupied large sections of as yet unclaimed land, and raised lots of sheep there. He was the first to bring over the Lincoln Longwool, which grew the longest and most lustrous fleece of any sheep in the world. He had thrived in this green and pleasant land down under.

Now, twenty years later, he was the Australian equivalent to Britain's landed gentry, a bona fide member of Australia's "squattocracy". Back in Britain, the gentry would have manor houses. Here, he had bought Barwon Park, and was in the process of having it re-done in fashionable bluestone. In Britain, the landed gentry would hunt rabbits.

This was why he was so excited that October, because twelve rabbits had just arrived from England and he was about to release them into the wild. They would be ideal for shooting and eating, and making him look and feel not only a member of the squattocracy but, in some way, a member of the aristocracy.

The plan worked. When Prince Alfred made the first visit of any British royal to Australia, some years later, in 1867, he came rabbit shooting at Barwon Park. Alfred enjoyed the shoot so much he delayed an official engagement to spend a second day shooting there. No doubt at some point during those two days, Austin let on that he had been founding other rabbit colonies, by passing breeding pairs to his friends – much like the prince's ancestor, Henry III, had done in England in the 13th century.

The prince came to shoot a second time, a few years later, but by then the rabbits had turned from a source of pride to a cause of complaint. The year before, his neighbours had moaned about how his rabbits had crossed over from his estate and were destroying their land. Austin put up a wire-cage fence to keep his rabbits in. But it was too late.

This part of Australia, it turned out, was ideal for this particular type of rabbit. Back in Britain, there were other animals that would chase and eat the rabbits, and they would spend winter in their burrows, sleeping a lot and not reproducing. But here the rabbits had no natural predators and the winters were mild, so the rabbits bred all year round.

Like a biblical plague of locusts, there were soon so many they were eating and destroying everything in their path. They killed young trees before they could grow. They ate all the native plants. As they did so, they left the topsoil exposed, causing widespread and wholesale erosion, and ruining what had been great farmland. The price of an acre halved.

By 1869, there were so many bunnies running wild in Australia that even a cull of two million made almost no difference. In the 1880s, the New South Wales government offered a bounty for every rabbit killed, but when locals claimed the bounty on more than 25 million rabbit scalps, it withdrew the offer, fearing it would bankrupt the state.

In 1901, the federal government began construction of a rabbit-proof fence. It was to run from the south to the north coast. At 3,256 kilometres long – about as far as from London to Marrakech, or from San Diego, California to Jacksonville, Florida – it would be the longest fence in the world. It took seven years to complete. When it was done, the government appointed a Chief Inspector of Rabbits.

His job, and that of his team, was to make sure the fence was secure against the furry, long-eared pests. His brave men drove cars along that fence. They rode bicycles by it. They travelled by horseback. When the horses could go no further in the desert, they went ahead on camels. All the while, they were on the lookout, trying to spot holes in the fence where the rabbits might have chewed through.

But, like the fence around Barwon Park, it was too late. By 1950, Austin's original twenty-four had criss-crossed the country, intermingled with other rabbits, and multiplied to create a total rabbit population of six hundred million.

The Law of Unintended Consequences

Although they are oceans apart, these two stories, about a man in Australia and a woman in California, have a certain something in common. They are both archetypal examples of the law of unintended consequences. This law, which was codified by a sociologist called Robert Merton in 1936, states that for any action there will be results that were unintended.

Streisand's aim had been to stop people peeping at her home, not to get hundreds of thousands to take a look. All Austin had wanted to do was have a few hundred rabbits to shoot on his estate, a few to give out to friends, and to establish his social status. The last thing he wanted was to ruin the land that had treated him so well, slash land prices, and create a plague that would waste millions of man-hours and cost millions of dollars.

The law of unintended consequences is a helpful model for understanding how people cause cultural shifts to happen. "Change," so the British historian Ian Morris believes, "is caused by lazy, greedy, frightened people looking for easier, more profitable and safer ways of doing things. And they rarely know what they are doing." In other words, as per the law of unintended consequences, they rarely know what the outcome of their actions will be.

This law, I think, holds whoever the people are who are making the changes – whether they are "change agents" deliberately trying to engineer change, or innovators trying out new ideas. No matter what they intend, there are likely to be consequences they did not intend.

Consider the creators of the Industrial Revolution. Did they know, or even imagine, where their actions would lead? Did each of those men, working out easier, more profitable and safer ways to weave, make metal, and move from one place to another, realize how their inventions would, collectively, change the world? Of course not.

It is unlikely that they were trying to create a revolution of any kind, except in their own area of expertise and fortunes. It is also unlikely that they would have anticipated the consequences of their actions and inventions, especially the widespread overproduction of the 1920s.

They had been born and raised in a time when scarcity was the natural condition of society, when the greatest concern for the greatest number was that they did not have enough. It would have been very hard for them to imagine that their inventions, collectively, would create such abundance that the greatest concern for the greatest number was that there was too much.

By the same token, it is unlikely that the captains of consciousness, those men and women who decided waste was good and then created a culture of materialistic consumption, would have realized that their throwaway system would lead to all the problems of *Stuffocation* today – especially what it has done to wellbeing and the environment.

Mad Men, Silent Spring

In one, infamous, scene in episode seven, series two of the television series *Mad Men*, Don Draper takes a picnic with his wife Betty, and their children, Bobby and Sally. The grass is green. The sun is shining. The birds are singing. Don lies on a red-and-white checked picnic blanket in the shade of a tree. Betty leans on him, her head on his chest.

"We should do this more often," she says.

"We should only do this," he replies.

And they lie there, enjoying the simple joy of nature. Soon, though, the world creeps in. They should get going, Don says, to avoid the traffic. Hauling himself up, he drains the rest of his beer and, like a baseball pitcher pitching a ball, tosses the can into the parkland.

The camera pulls back to a wider shot. We can see the car in the background at the top of the frame. Betty now gets up, dusts herself down. She carefully takes one corner of the picnic rug in each hand and flicks it, tossing the remains of their picnic onto the grass. She folds the rug, and walks to the car as Don watches her.

The camera shot stays wide. We watch them get in the car, hear the first revs of the engine. And the car drives off. But no one in the audience is watching the car. We are still staring, open-mouthed, at the bottom of the frame where Betty left all that rubbish without a second thought.

This scene sums up the attitude that earlier Mad Men and women had bequeathed to people like Don and Betty Draper: a casual disregard for the environment.

Yet even in the resounding economic boom of the post-war years, the environmental movement raised its hand and asked if there was another, not so idyllic, side to materialism. The movement began in 1961 when a woman named Rachel Carson published a book called *Silent Spring* about a dystopian future where industrial practices had destroyed nature.

"The birds, for example – where had they gone?" she wrote. "Many people spoke of them, puzzled and disturbed. The feeding stations in the backyards were deserted. The few birds seen anywhere were moribund; they trembled violently and could not fly. It was a spring without voices. On the mornings that had once throbbed with the dawn chorus of robins, catbirds, doves, jays, wrens, and scores of other bird voices there was now no sound; only silence lay over the fields and woods and marsh."

Carson had first noticed silences like this just after the war. She had tried many times to publish articles about the problem. Magazines refused to print them, even though Carson was a celebrated author, in case they upset their advertisers. Eventually, she gave up and wrote the book.

When it was published, the chemical companies causing the problems did all they could to suppress her message. For all their efforts, though, all they did was create much needed media noise for *Silent Spring*. By doing so, they not only created a Streisand effect, decades before it would be called this. They also helped shine a light on what has turned out to be one of materialism's darkest sides: the senseless trashing of the planet we live on.

Despite occasional victories, like the banning of the CFCs that harmed the ozone layer, environmental damage has really only got worse through the years. The runaway success of consumerism is now not only causing what may be irreversible climate change, for instance, but also, which is perhaps worse, the greatest extinction of plant and animal species since the dinosaurs died out.

Materialism, in other words, might mean that whole swathes of our planet could one day wake up, as Rachel Carson foretold, to spring mornings that are entirely silent. What would a picnic in that kind of countryside be like?

The Dark Side of Materialism

There is another side of materialism that is just as dark as the many blots on the environment: its effect on our happiness. Now that it has provided so many millions of us with the basics of material wellbeing, materialism seems unable to also improve our overall wellbeing. Instead, it increasingly looks like it is doing the opposite. Rather than making us feel good, materialism is making millions of us feel joyless, anxious and, even worse, depressed.

The first person to offer scientific proof of this was a researcher called Richard Easterlin. Easterlin wanted to find out: did having more make people any happier? (Easterlin, to be clear, was asking about economic growth rather than only material goods. But since the economy was driven by consumerism, and consumerism is largely driven by materialism, I think it is an acceptable proxy in this case.) To find out, Easterlin compared data on economic growth and happiness since the end of the World War II from nineteen countries, including developed countries like the US and the UK and less developed countries like India and Brazil.

The results were startling. Once people had enough to meet their basic needs, happiness did not vary much with national income, he found. He also found that although people were earning ever more in the US after the war, they were not becoming happier. In fact, they had become less happy since 1960. Why?

Perhaps the best way to answer that is over a hot drink and a biscuit with a friendly philosopher.

Each morning, the British philosopher Jeremy Bentham liked nothing more than munching some hot, spiced, ginger nut biscuits, and sipping a cup of strong coffee. But, as Bentham once observed, while he liked the first cup of coffee very much, the second was far less enjoyable. Economists and sociologists have names for this: the law of diminishing marginal utility and hedonic contrast. But we do not need a technical term to understand Bentham's point.

In that simple observation, I think he has summed up the problem of *Stuffocation* and the paradox of materialism: that a little is good, but that you can have too much of a good thing.

A Hungarian-American economist called Tibor Scitovsky had another suggestion to explain why increasing prosperity was not leading to more happiness. In his 1976 book *The Joyless Economy*, he wrote that it could be because of materialism's "dark side": all the unintended consequences of material progress such as the harm it does to our health, the environment, and future generations because of "our reckless brandishing of weapons, extermination of pests, squandering of resources, popping of pills, ingesting of food additives, and use or overuse of every mechanical aid to our comfort and safety".

"Could it not be," Scitovsky asked, "that we seek our satisfaction in the wrong things, or in the wrong way, and are then dissatisfied with the outcome?" The answer, I think, is "yes" – if those things are material goods.

Material goods, it must be said, can be useful for self-expression and signifying status – the type of shoes or shirt you wear says a lot about you, for instance. But in our materialistic consumer culture, we have come to rely on material goods too much, and they are letting us down.

In today's materialistic culture, many people believe material things can solve emotional problems.

But this, as the psychologist Oliver James wrote, is a "false promise". Retail therapy, in other words, does not work. Instead, it is more likely to make your problems worse – by putting you in debt, for instance.

In today's culture, material goods have become substitutes for deep and genuinely meaningful human desires and questions. Consumer culture has become a sort of pseudo-religion. Once we sought answers to meaningful questions, like: why am I here? What happens after death? How should I live? Now we ask questions that are far easier: the blue one or the red one? Will that go with the top I bought last week? What will she think if I buy that?

Instead of trying to understand who we really are, we reach for the "Real Thing". And when the goods we buy fail to match up to those deep desires, instead of giving up on material goods, we just keep banging our heads against the wall and buying more.

Mass-produced goods, which are the natural product of the system, are the worst of all. They are so stripped of meaning and novelty that they have little chance of genuinely exciting or inspiring us. "The monotony of mass production is fully matched," Scitovsky wrote, "by the monotony of its product." So we become quickly bored with the goods we have – sociologists call this hedonic adaptation – and in the search for novelty, move on to the next thing, and begin the process again.

Even where material goods are helpful, by helping us signify status, they create more problems than they solve. Because in today's meritocratic society, having goods signifies success and, equally, not having goods says failure. As a result, we are not only smugly or painfully aware of who is above or below us in the pecking order, we also know we can clamber up or slip down the rankings at any moment.

It is like living in an immense, stomach-churning session of Snakes and Ladders, where the game never stops and where everybody is a competitor. To play this paranoia-inducing game – and it is a game we all play – millions of us spend our days and nights worrying about our place in the pecking order, and scheming to get up the ladders and avoid the snakes. The end result is millions suffering from material-focused status anxiety.

Even worse than anxious, materialism is making people feel depressed, in record numbers and to a record extent. From the 1970s to the turn of the century, mental illness in children and adults in developed countries doubled. A quarter of Britons now suffer emotional distress. Americans are three times more likely to be depressed today than in the 1950s. The level of emotional illness, it turns out, increases with income inequality, which also tends to be higher in English-speaking nations.

The more a society becomes like the most wasteful, status-obsessed and materialistic country on Earth – the United States – the higher the rate of emotional distress. The unavoidable conclusion is one of the darkest sides of materialism: that mass production and mass consumption, ultimately, cause mass depression. That, surely, is not what anyone would call progress.

From the Pyramid to the Pancake

We have come, once more, to a crossroads. Once more, the choice we make is critical. It will change the course of history just as much as materialism did. But do we, the people, even have a choice? Is the path of history simply a matter of what the captains of consciousness decide, as it was in the 1920s?

The last time we faced a great crossroads, the debate was framed and discussed and decided by the elite, by the captains of consciousness of the day. (I say "we" because I believe a significant part of Western culture, the practice of the materialistic consumer culture we live in today, is descended from the decisions made to solve overproduction in the USA in the early part of the 20th century.) The industrialists and the government and the Mad Men and women were, if you like, the puppet masters deciding what would happen. The people, in that era, were more like puppets.

Back then, just as the industrialists had learned to mass produce products by taking advantage of the new machines and systems of the Industrial Revolution, so the Mad Men and women learned to mass engineer consumers by leveraging the new tools of mass media that appeared in the 19th and

20th centuries: magazines, newspapers, cinema, radio and television.

But then came the internet, and everything changed. Suddenly the puppets had a chance to speak as well. In this new internet-enabled era, it is much easier for everyone and anyone to become successful, and influential. The effects of this flatter world are everywhere.

The internet has revolutionized publishing, for instance. *Fifty Shades of Grey* was rejected by professional agents. Its author published herself via an online e-book and print-on-demand publisher, and was then picked up by a mainstream publisher. It then became the fastest selling paperback ever.

The internet has recast fame. When Jenna Mourey posted a video of herself getting ready to go to work as a dancer called "How to Trick People Into Thinking You're Good Looking", five million watched it in a weekend. Now she is Jenna Marbles, her video channel has nine million subscribers, and her videos have been watched more than a billion times.

The internet has also transformed fashion. Once the front of catwalks was strictly Hollywood A-listers and VIPs. It still is – only the VIPs now include bloggers like twelve-year-old Tavi Gevinson. And it has revolutionized politics: consider the impact of Facebook and Twitter on Egypt, Iran, and the Occupy movement.

Because of the internet, the direction of influence and the structure of power have changed. Instead of the old, top-down system, where information and influence flowed from the top, now they also flow in other ways, from the bottom upwards, and also sideways. And before, the few at the top held sway over the many at the bottom. If you wanted to visualize it, you could describe this system as a pyramid.

Now, though, because of the infinite connections enabled by the web, many talk to many, those at the bottom are more powerful. The system is far flatter. If you wanted to draw it now, the structure of power and influence would look much more like a pancake.

The world is not, it must be said, perfectly flat. There are still peaks of influence. The government is still far more influential than most people. And the world's big media and advertising companies, like Disney, Google, News Corp and WPP are certainly more likely to influence what you and I think and do, and especially when we spend and what we buy.

As we come to this crossroads this time, though, it is clear that the world is not the same as before. This time around, it is not simply a matter of what the incumbent captains of consciousness, the government and big business, decide. They are not the only ones pulling the strings anymore. They no longer have the same control of what we read and watch and think and want. Now, more than ever before, we, the people, do have a choice about what happens next.

One message that most governments and businesses do not want us to hear about is minimalism. Why would they, when their economic and financial models are based on materialism, on us wanting and buying more? If the incumbent captains of consciousness – government and industrialists and advertisers who rely on materialism – had it their way, there would be no mention of minimalism.

But, partly because of the internet, and blogging especially, the minimalist movement is a growing and powerful sub-culture. There is nothing the government or business can do to stop them. After all, if they tried to interfere with the *Minimalist Woman*, the *Minimalist Mom*, the *Minimalist Journey*, the *Minimalist Freak*, *The Minimalists*, or any of the hundreds of other anti-materialist websites, they would most likely end up creating their own Streisand effect.

FOUR

I Love to Count:
the 33, 47, 69 and 100
Things of Minimalism

A few years ago in Sacramento, California, a slim, tanned, immaculately dressed young woman called Cheryl walked in to her walk-in closet. She was followed by another woman, also smartly turned out, by the name of Tammy Strobel.

Strobel had a cropped brown bob and a pixie nose. She had a sing-song lilt to her voice: "Hi, I'm Tammy". Her eyes were green like a cat's. In those days, she would accent them with blue eye shadow, and lashes curled so hard the tips stood straight up.

Strobel inhaled the sweet smell of new closet and clean clothes. As she looked round, her eyes widened, her pupils dilated. You could *shop* in here. Everything – the dresses, the sweaters, the pants, the shoes, and all of it colour coded and neatly folded – everything looked beautiful. No wonder Cheryl always looked like she had just stepped off the pages of a magazine.

It was a lunch break, Strobel recalls, like any other. The two friends from university had just been to the mall, their way, most days, of getting off the campus of the financial company they worked for, so they could talk about more important stuff, like clothes, fiancés, and engagement rings.

Strobel spent ages finding hers. Truth be told, she had got a little obsessed. She had devoured catalogues. She had made secret trips to the mall. "When she talked about that ring, her eyes sparkled," her sister-in-law, Tina Smith, remembers. "It was like, all of a sudden, she had purpose."

When Strobel's boyfriend, Logan Smith, proposed and put the ring she had chosen on her finger, life felt perfect – till she saw Cheryl's. Because while Strobel's had a single diamond, Cheryl's had three, and no matter how hard she tried, she could not get that thought out of her head. But how could she get a ring as good as Cheryl's, especially when, as she knew, that ring was all Smith could afford? Well, she soon figured, she could at least make a start by offering her ring as down payment.

Smith is one of those men who looks like a boy they just stretched to make taller. He grew up, the elder of two brothers, on a ranch in northern California. He has curly blond hair. He wears rimless glasses. He put a cartoon, black handlebar moustache on his picture on Google+.

How did Smith feel when Strobel told him what she wanted to do?

"I guess it hurt my feelings a little," he recalls now, "to know that all the ring I could afford still wasn't enough for her." But if a new ring was what Tammy wanted, so be it. He borrowed some more money from his younger brother and he bought it. Yet even that, after the initial, wide-eyed rush, did not keep Strobel happy for long. Nor, it seemed, did anything else.

That was odd, because she should have been, at the very least, content. She was doing well at work. Her firm had picked her for its management-training programme. She was with a great guy, and they lived in a pretty town near Sacramento called Davis, in a luxury apartment surrounded by manicured lawns and McMansions.

"I felt like I had it made," Strobel recalls. "Like I had everything I could possibly want." From the outside looking in, to anyone who caught sight of her new three-diamond ring, or saw her and Smith out partying in town, or came over to their fancy home and saw the rooms full of stuff and closets full of clothes, she did.

Life was not so great on the inside, though. The two-hour drive to work and back was getting to her. So were the hours crunching numbers in her cubicle, and she began to wonder if she really believed in what she was doing. She started drinking more, and her weight ballooned. She was getting back pain, and it was getting worse. She was worrying about their bank loans, and they always seemed to be growing. She began picking fights with Smith, even in public.

"She'd say things, even in front of him, like 'If he was making better money I wouldn't have to go get money'," Tina Smith recalls.

Somehow, in the midst of all that debt and stress and unhappiness, the sing-song, happy-go-lucky Tammy had gone. Something had to give.

Smith had the idea first. It came to him in, of all places, the shower. He was in there when Strobel arrived home one night. He had had an idea, he called out, that could solve all their problems. "Oh, yeah?" was her muttered reply (which he did not hear). She could give up her job, he said. They would live on his income. To make that work, they would get rid of some of their stuff and move to a smaller apartment.

"Are you insane?" Strobel shot back. "Where the hell are my Mom and Dad going to stay? Where are we going to put all our things?"

"But your Mom and Dad hardly ever stay–" Smith began.

"We're not doing it," was Strobel's firm reply.

Smith heard that. He tried another tack.

"What if I get rid of my crap first?" he offered. "I'll get rid of that table you hate."

Now that was an idea Strobel could agree with. So Smith got rid of the table. Then he sold his car and started cycling instead.

"That's when Tammy got it," Logan says. "That's when she saw that getting rid of stuff wasn't wrong, that there was no shame in it. And without all the car payments, it meant we had a lot more money. That was when the lightbulb went on in her head."

After that, they devised a safe, reversible way to find out if the reality of fewer possessions and less space would work for them. They would move everything out of their second bedroom. They would pretend they lived in a smaller apartment that had just one bedroom. That way, if they did not like it, they could go back to their old life. Then, with their plan in place, they emptied the second bedroom and got rid of things they barely used or that just took up too much room, like Smith's guitars, a bookshelf Strobel's Dad had made, and even their television.

Instead of being tough, as Strobel had worried, it was a revelation. After six months, they realized they were paying for a room they did not use anymore, and that having less did not feel worse, it felt better. They were spending less time managing, moving and cleaning their things – and feeling guilty about not using them. They had more time, they were eating more healthily, they were feeling less stressed and getting on better.

Now they had seen the upside of shedding their stuff, they got serious about it, giving some things away and selling the rest on Craigslist. They sold their other car. Strobel sold her wedding dress. They moved in to a one-bedroom flat.

Now they were paying less rent, Strobel gave up her commute and her job, to do something that meant more to her – helping abused women. Even though she had taken a salary cut, from $40,000 to $24,000, their bills were much lower, so instead of building up more debts, they were able to start paying them off.

"All I wanted to do then," Strobel recalls, "was have fewer and fewer things and move into smaller and smaller apartments."

Then she came across a woman online called Dee Williams. Williams had moved out of her three-bedroom house and into a tiny home, which she had built for herself on a flatbed trailer. Along the way, she had reduced the number of things she owned to less than 300, and got herself out of debt.

Strobel was transfixed.

If she and Smith moved into a tiny home, she figured, that would mean even less room, less stuff, less debt and, maybe, even more happiness. Now they had a goal, she and Smith kept downsizing their belongings. Strobel eventually slimmed her stuff down to only 69 possessions. That list included a camera, a toothbrush, a computer, three pairs of shoes, and four rings – including her wedding ring, though she was trying to sell it.

They kept moving into smaller and smaller apartments, paying off their debts and saving up, so they could buy a tiny home. Eventually, in September 2011, they moved into one. Designed by Williams, it includes a bedroom, a bathroom, a kitchen with the kind of cooker you use on a yacht, a pull-out desk, and even a porch – and it measures one hundred and fifty square feet. It could have fitted inside Cheryl's walk-in closet.

The 39 Socks

By pinpointing the things he owned as the root cause of his problems, Ryan Nicodemus exemplified the minimalist response to *Stuffocation*. With Strobel's 69 things, she highlights another: the minimalists' obsession with numbers. Because this chapter is not only brought to you today by the number 69, but also by the numbers 33, 43, 47, 50, 51, 100, and 288. You know how your more materialistic friends like to brag about how many, how much, and how good their possessions are? Minimalists do the same – but with how few things they have.

A Finnish man by the name of Henri Junttila and an American called Leo Babauta, whose blog has more than a million readers, lived for some time with only 43 things. A woman called Nicole Yau got by with 47 things. Colin Wright managed with 51. The counting all began in earnest, in case that counts at all, when a blogger called Dave Bruno ran something called the 100 Thing Challenge, in which he asked his readers if they could reduce the number of their possessions to, you guessed it, 100.

This slightly absurd obsession with numbers is funny. It is as if the minimalists are playing a sort of reverse I-Spy game, where the one who counts the fewest, rather than the most, things, wins. It is as if, instead of getting meaning and happiness from having things, they are getting meaning and happiness from not having things.

Instead of showing off how many possessions they have, they are showing off how few they have. This is how they get status in their peer group. They have given up conspicuous consumption, if you like, for conspicuous anti-consumption.

"It's a bit like a Buddhist running into a monastery," Colin Wright once admitted to me, "and shouting as loud as he can: 'I'm the humblest guy ever!'"

It is easy to laugh at the minimalists and their obsession with numbers. But think about those numbers for a moment, because there is something in them. How many things do you have? Stop reading for a moment. Count the things in your handbag, your wallet, or your wardrobe. Wait a moment, though, are you counting properly? How are you counting socks – does each sock count, does a pair count as one, or are socks one collective thing?

And here we have come across one of the thornier issues in the minimalist movement. Not everyone agrees on how you should count, and what counts when you are counting. Different people play by different counting rules.

There is the Rule of Permanence, of course, so perishable items are out. There is the Rule of Dependence, so the power cable to your MacBook does not count. And, crucially, there is the Rule of Ownership: if something is shared, like furniture everyone sits on, you do not count it. Or do you? Some do. Some don't. Dave Bruno's list of 100 things, for instance, does not include the dining room table, the family piano, and the plates everyone eats off.

Some start out saying they will count everything but soon realize how long that will take and give up. Some sound like they are going to count everything, but tail off when the count mounts up. Here is Joshua Fields Millburn on his 288 possessions:

"So, unlike many other people who count their stuff, I literally counted everything I own, including things like the clock on the wall, my toothbrush, photo frames, my solo oven mitt, the trash can under the sink, salt & pepper shakers, cooking utensils, and even that metal thing in the shower that holds shampoo. I even counted the items that other people leave off their lists—my couch, chairs, dining table, and other furniture—because they are considered 'shared items'; I live by myself so these things needed to be counted. I did group some things into groups (e.g., my underwear, clothes hangers, food, etc.), but I only grouped things when necessary (N.B. the only thing I struggled with grouping were my books. I don't own a ton of books/novels—I got rid of most of them this year—but I grouped the ones I still have because they all fit on my little coffee table, and I'm a fiction writer, so I use them as references quite often)."

So whose numbers can you trust, and how many things do you really own? This counting thing has become faintly ridiculous. But there is a serious point to be made here. Once you start your own counting, whichever rules you use, those 47, 69 or 100 things soon sound a lot more impressive. So, are you ready to count again? If that sounds like too much effort right now, take a trip to my sock drawer instead.

As I was writing this chapter, hoping you would play along and go count your stuff before reading any further, I realized two things. The first is that I would not bother. I would keep on reading, just like you have. The second is that, actually, if I am going to ask you to do it, I ought to share how my counting went.

Since the importance of *Stuffocation* dawned on me and I started researching this book, I have read about and talked to some of the world's most compelling downsizers, cross-shifters, minimalists and post-materialists. As I have found out more about how they are finding greater happiness and meaning in their lives, I have been influenced by them. I have cleared up and thrown out. I have stopped buying so much. I have started using what I already have. It turns out when I counted, though – and this shocked me as much as it may surprise you – that I am still quite the Sock Guy.

I am far from a minimalist – as you are about to find out – so I knew counting everything would take forever. Socks, I thought, would be a good place to start. And unlikely to cause me too much embarrassment if I ever had to share it. But before we delve into mine, picture your sock drawer for a moment. Is it tidy? Colour coded? Split between week day and weekend? Bursting out? Are all your pairs in there?

Okay, no more delays. Here is my sock confession: I have 29 pairs of everyday socks, plus the bright blue pair I am wearing now. Plus I have two pairs of sport socks, for the one time each year I play squash or go running. I have a pair of cycling socks. Who knew they existed? They were a gift from my stepdad. He loves cycling. I have three pairs of football socks, including a pair with so many holes I do not wear them anymore. They were my Dad's. They are sentimental socks. Who knew that was possible? I also have three pairs of socks that are not in the drawer: ski socks, kept in a bag at the far end of the loft. So I have 39 pairs of socks. I could go more than a month without washing any.

And there was me thinking I had – excuse the pun – pared back. A month or so ago, I threw out all the pairs I did not like. That was the end of the Bart Simpson Christmas-present socks, the England football team birthday-present socks, the Monday, Tuesday, Wednesday, Thursday, Friday leaving-present-from-a-job socks, and the long Italian, mustard yellow cashmere present-from-the-wife socks. They always made my calves sticky and ankles itchy.

And this count of 39, I must admit, does not include the six stragglers. When their other halves turn up from somewhere else around the house, that would mean I have 45 pairs – enough for a month and a half. I could, theoretically, only do eight sock washes each year. Weird though it sounds, there is no getting away from it. I am, I confess, quite a Sock Guy.

So where does that confessional count leave me? Easy. I would choose the counting rules that suit me. Socks? One item. (I should have done shirts. It would have made me look less avaricious. I have ten: one blue, two grey, six white and one denim.)

It is easy to laugh at how the minimalists count, and at me for having so many socks. You can see why some people might look down their noses at the minimalists and say all they have done is swap one status game for another.

There are two responses to that. Firstly, expressing status is an essential trait of all animals, including humans. So why should minimalists not have a way to express their status? Besides, ultimately, they tend to use the numbers as a target and a benchmark. They often only count at the beginning of their journey to having less.

This is how counting helped a woman in Colorado by the name of Courtney Carver, for instance. Carver had been a keen skier, a regular cyclist, a successful businesswoman and a dedicated shopper. Whenever she went out of state, for example, she would buy a new pair of sunglasses.

But when, a few years back, she woke up to find all her energy had gone and she was diagnosed with multiple sclerosis, she blamed it on her materialistic way of life. "It was my body's way of rejecting my lifestyle of more," she says.

To prove to herself she could live with less, she began by reducing her wardrobe to 33 items. That count included her purse, one handbag, and a single pair of sunglasses. Then, to bring minimalism into all areas of her life, she and her husband, Mark Tuttle, invented a game where they would hide things from the other. "If you didn't notice it, that meant you didn't need it," Tuttle says. "And that meant we could get rid of it."

By making minimalism more fun – by conducting Nicodemus's bin-bag experiment or Strobel and Smith's pretend-we-don't-have-that-room experiment, or by playing the reverse I-Spy counting game or Carver and Tuttle's "did you miss it?" game – it makes trying it out far easier and more engaging. That is useful, particularly when you bear in mind that it is not easy to get off the hamster wheel of materialism.

It may even be essential, especially when you remember that minimalists are, after all, fighting impulses about acquiring and accumulating that have been ingrained over millennia.

And although it is easy to laugh at the counting, the results are far from laughable. The way Smith and Strobel's life has improved is compelling proof of that.

By getting rid of their possessions, they reduced their outgoings. By reducing their outgoings, on rent and car insurance, for instance, they were able to reduce their debts and Strobel was able to leave her job. That meant no more long commute, no more back pain, more time to make healthy food and more time to exercise. As a result, her weight returned to normal, she felt healthier and happier, and she stopped fighting with Smith. That one decision – to have fewer things – set in motion a whole domino-line of good things.

It worked for them. It has worked for many others I have spoken with, like Nicodemus and Fields Millburn, Nicole Yau, and Colin Wright. Minimalism clearly works for many people – though it is still easy, at first glance, to dismiss it as a lifestyle choice for singletons in their twenties and thirties with minimal responsibilities.

But minimalism is also achievable for families: it has worked for father-of-two Chris Wray in Cambridgeshire, mother-of-two Rachel Jonat on the Isle of Man, and father-of-six Leo Babauta in San Francisco. And it has worked for Courtney Carver, who has a teenage daughter. Carver's sickness is now, as her doctors told her recently, "like it's in suspension".

So minimalism works for a lot of people. Does that mean if you want to be happier you should get rid of most of your stuff? Is it just these people, or does that mean there is a general rule that applies to everyone?

Will Less Stuff Make You More Happy?

Suppose, for a moment, that you are a sceptic. You are not the sort who is persuaded by one or two or even a dozen cases. There are, after all, millions of people out there. These so-called minimalists could be anomalous drops in the ocean of humanity. Even though less stuff has clearly helped them be happier, it is too early to conclude that there is a new equation for happiness, a new rule that says "less stuff equals more happiness". It might not work for everyone. It might not work for you.

As a sceptic, you would want to hear more convincing proof before you questioned the materialist creed of "more is better" and tried out minimalism's "less is more". You would certainly need to see something more concrete before you entertained the thought of shoving all your stuff in bin bags, emptying one of your rooms, or hiding things from the people you live with.

The problem is that, no matter how hard you look in the literature, or how many psychologists you ask, that proof does not seem to exist.

"There's a lot of anecdotal evidence regarding minimalism, there's a lot of people out there saying they feel like a burden's been taken off their backs," the psychologist Barry Schwartz told me. "But, no, there are no scientific studies that I've come across. And for all I know it could be true for ten minutes – and then these people go back to accumulating."

Constructing an experiment to test the hypothesis would be very difficult, because people have either reached the point of *Stuffocation* and want to get rid of things, or they have not. The people who came to take part in any experiment would most likely be self-selecting. That, of course, would skew the results and render them useless.

Could there be an alternative way to test the hypothesis and either corroborate or disprove it? Another psychologist, Oliver James, thinks there may be.

"Just as there is an electro-chemistry of buying, there could be a similar effect for getting rid of things," he says. "It wouldn't be the same neurotransmitters. It wouldn't be serotonin. It would more likely be oxytocin or cortisol, since they are key indicators of either stress or relief. If somebody measured changes in cortisol levels that could show relief."

A breakthrough, perhaps. If researchers tested the levels of cortisol in people with reference to their possessions, they could show whether stuff and stress go together. That could provide, for the first time, scientific evidence that getting rid of stuff is good for you. If that sort of evidence existed, would it help sceptical people – like you, perhaps – believe that less really is more? Would you consider getting rid of some of your stuff? Would you, at the least, take a look in your sock drawer?

FIVE

The Anthropologist
and the Clutter Crisis

Sometime in the summer of 2000, there was a knock on the door of Jeanne Arnold's office. It was most likely one of her doctoral or grad students, come to ask her about methodology or whether an inference they were making about some evidence they had brought back from a dig sounded reasonable. In those days, Arnold's salt-and-pepper hair swept up and back in a bouffant style that ended somewhere around her shoulders. The glasses she wore had oversized, '80s-style metal frames. She looked up from her research, and smiled when she saw Elinor Ochs, one of her colleagues at the University of California, Los Angeles.

"Got a minute, Jeanne?" Ochs asked – when what she really meant was, "Have you got ten years?"

Ochs was putting together a bid for a project, she explained. Would Arnold be interested in working with her on it? She was gathering a team, she said, to document life in the 21st century. They would use the same methods as anthropologists studying tribes in Africa, or archaeologists analysing a dead civilization's remains, like Inca ruins in South America – except they would be doing the work right there in Los Angeles, with case studies who were very much still alive.

The study would be the first of its kind. Well, there had been one or two studies a bit like it before, like one in New York that looked at the art people bought. But there had never been a study as ambitious as this. Instead of trying to understand people through one aspect of their lives, the plan was to record as much of their lives as possible, to create the definitive record of how people were living in the early part of the 21st century.

The project, Ochs said, could really use a material culture expert like Jeanne. Arnold was not sure, though. It sounded exciting, like it might be groundbreaking. But this wasn't really her field.

Arnold's speciality was the past, not the present. That had been her passion ever since she had got the bug as a little girl. Back then, she had spent her long summer holidays in the woods by her home near the Great Lakes, digging up crinoids and leaf fossils and arrowheads. "They were only little," Arnold recalls. "Nothing a real palaeontologist or archaeologist would be interested in."

They were a start, though. And as Arnold grew, so did her interest in the ancient past, especially archaeology, and its sister discipline, anthropology. She studied them at summer camp, at the local university, and then at the University of California. That is where, in 1980, she stumbled across her life's work – a native tribe called the Chumash and their old home on Santa Cruz, one of the Channel Islands off the coast of California.

When Arnold talks about the Chumash sites now, you can almost see her arriving on Santa Cruz those thirty-odd years ago. She would have just stepped off the navy supply boat. It was the only way to reach the island back then. It went once a week.

The wind would have been blowing her brown hair around as she hiked up the green hill to the site. There, she would have walked round wearing dark sunglasses, reading the landscape the way only an archaeologist could. Where you or I would have only seen dips in the ground, she saw the footprints of real people, and hints of where the Chumash had sited their pole-and-thatched huts. If you or I had ferreted around in the ground, we might have found some old fish bones.

"A Chumash toss zone," Arnold would say. "They weren't bothered about mess. After they'd eaten, they just threw them on the ground."

If we had kept looking we might have found, even up here, far from the sea, shell remains and the beginnings of beads. That is when Arnold would have asked us to stop. Those remains were for the professionals. With those, and many more like them, she could understand how the Chumash lived, what mattered to them, and how their society was structured.

After more than a decade of gathering and analysing Chumash artefacts, Arnold realized she was not only excavating a site, she was building a case. Until the late 20th century, the conventional wisdom had been that complex societies, in which there is an established hierarchy of a ruling elite and bureaucrats, had emerged only from agricultural communities – like Egypt under the pharaohs, for instance. That meant, so scholars believed, that complex societies *could* only have developed in communities based on agriculture.

Yet an archaeologist and anthropologist by the name of Michael Moseley had challenged the idea, after excavating a coastal site in Peru which, he believed, not only contained indications of fishing and gathering – and no agriculture – but also of a complex society. As the years went by and the evidence stacked up, Arnold became convinced that the Chumash – who hunted, gathered and fished but did not farm – had also lived in a complex society called a chiefdom.

"That meant," Arnold will tell you now, "that a society didn't have to be agricultural for complex systems to emerge."

In other words, as Arnold's work helped prove, the conventional wisdom was wrong, and it had to be replaced with a new theory that reflected the new evidence. "There are a few grumpy old men out there who still say they're not persuaded," Arnold admits. "But they're slowly disappearing."

The sort of person who was not afraid of confronting the conventional wisdom when it no longer accurately reflected the evidence – no wonder Ochs wanted Arnold, and people like her, on the team.

After a few days, Arnold said she was in. Then she and the rest of Ochs's team at the Center on Everyday Lives of Families (CELF) – of anthropologists, archaeologists, ethnographers, photographers and psychologists – worked out a methodology, got approval and the funds they needed. In 2000, the team set to work, and soon found themselves in the middle of a clutter crisis of epidemic proportions.

The Middle-Class Clutter Crisis

With funding and methodology established, the CELF team began the next task: finding some families – average, middle-class ones who were typical of households everywhere, and 32 of them – who were willing to open their lives to scientific enquiry. Once they had found them, explained what the commitment would mean to their lives, and what it would mean for social scientists who wanted to understand life at the turn of the 21st century, they began.

They noted the make-up of their households, the size of their homes, what jobs they did. Each family had at least one child aged between seven and twelve. Their homes ranged from 980 to 3,000 square feet. The professions of the parents included teachers and lawyers, dentists and business people, an airline pilot and a firefighter.

Ochs's team drew up plans of their homes. They photographed them – their bedrooms, bathrooms, kitchens, living rooms, playrooms, second bathrooms, garages, gardens. They came early. They stayed late. They asked questions. They stayed silent. But they never stopped taking notes – of where their case studies went, what they did, when they ate, what they ate. They were like flies on the wall or spy drones in the air, always there. They were the ultimate voyeurs, granted special permission to access all areas of their case studies' homes.

And even when the scientists were not there, they found another way in. They gave the families video cameras to record their own home video diaries.

Sometimes it got too much – for the scientists at least. Once, when one family was having a heated argument, the researcher who was following them round could not cope and had to go outside. Rather than stop recording what was happening, though, he carried on watching through the window of the family's bungalow. When the people inside – still arguing – moved to another room, he moved too. He stepped round the house and stood outside that room's window, still watching, still making notes.

Like the minimalists, Ochs's team counted. But they were not counting up to 33, 43, 69 or 100. The aim of their lists was not to show off how few things they had. They had no use for the Rule of Permanence, the Rule of Dependence or the Rule of Ownership. They were counting hundreds, thousands of items.

They wanted to produce tallies that were scientifically valid. So they used a different – and new – set of counting rules, devised specially for the project by someone who had gathered and counted and analysed hundreds of thousands of artefacts for more than two decades – Jeanne Arnold.

The aim of Arnold's rules was to help the counters all count the same way, and create verifiable results. The first rule was that they would not look in cupboards or closets. They would only count what was visible. Arnold's second rule was to count not in the case studies' homes but only from photographs – in case someone asked a question and put the counter off, in case the counter just forgot what number she or he had reached, and so they could double-check the counting later.

They would paste the photos together carefully to avoid double counting. Then they would begin: how many paintings? How many computers? How many chairs? And then they would tally all the different categories up.

CELF's researchers gathered a vast amount of data. They spent four years collecting it, and seven analysing it.

"It took that long to describe and digitize everything," Arnold will tell you, "and to work out what on Earth was going on."

In all, there were four terabytes of data, which is 4,000,000,000,000 pieces of information. The families made 47 hours of their own home video tours. Ochs's team shot 1,540 hours of videotape – mostly from inside the house. They took 19,987 photos. And they counted a tonne of stuff.

As the years went by and the mountains of evidence grew, some of the numbers and the observations, to tell the truth, shocked the researchers. They were amazed at how little time adults were spending outside in their gardens – less than 15 minutes per week on average, even though they had often spent a lot of money on fancy barbecues and outdoor dining sets. They were surprised at how child-centric the houses were. Thirty-one of the thirty-two homes had things on display in the living room – like plaques, ribbons, trophies, certificates, and beauty contest tiaras – that showed off how well the kids were doing.

They were, to be brutally honest, gobsmacked at what they saw some of the kids getting away with. One time, for instance, a mother told her little girl and little boy she had to make a conference call. It wouldn't take long, she said, but it was an important call with some important people at work. Could they keep it down for a few minutes? Then, moments after she had taken the call, as if that was their cue, her son started banging his drums and her daughter started playing her trumpet – both as loud as they could.

Above all, though, the researchers were astounded by how much stuff people had. The smallest home in the study, for instance, a house of 980 square feet, contained, in the two bedrooms and living room alone, 2,260 items. That count, remember, was only of the things that were visible. That did not include any of the stuff that was tucked into drawers or squeezed into closets.

The other homes were similarly packed. On average, each of the families had 39 pairs of shoes, 90 DVDs or videos, 139 toys, 212 CDs and 438 books and magazines. Nine out of ten of them had so many things that they kept household stuff in the garage. Three-quarters of them had so much stuff in there, there was no room left for the things that their garages were originally designed for – cars.

These families, these typical middle-class families, no doubt, have a lot of stuff. But, when you think about it, a lot does not necessarily mean clutter. A lot of things could be a collection, like a set of books, records, CDs, clothes, or even toys that are tidily arranged, perhaps colour coded or neatly folded, or in height or alphabetical order.

As well as being a large number of things, there are two further requirements, Arnold says, before you can call a group of objects clutter. Those are that the things should be messy, and they should be in the wrong place, like toys strewn all across the house, from the living room to the bathroom, and down the hallways and in the garage.

This – lots of stuff, in a mess, out of place – is what the CELF researchers found time and again in the homes of their case studies, and it is what they think is happening in middle-class homes today.

Their research, the most extensive piece of work of its kind ever to be conducted, has led the CELF researchers to believe, as they wrote in the final report, *Life at Home in the 21st Century*, that because of the "sheer numbers of artefacts" people today own, and because we are living in "the most materially rich society in global history, with light-years more possessions per average family than any preceding society", we are at a crunch point. We are at a point of "material saturation". We are coping with "extraordinary clutter". We, as individuals and as a society, are facing a "clutter crisis".

There are caveats, of course, to the study and these conclusions. Can we really consider 32 case studies in Los Angeles, for instance, and generalize for all middle-class families in the US? These case studies were chosen because they are average middle-class people, with typical jobs, incomes, home sizes, and family structures. They were picked because what goes on in their lives and homes reflects what others do. The CELF team spent months finding them and chose them for those reasons. So I think it is not only feasible but it is sensible to generalize for all middle-class families – in the United States, at least.

The clutter crises in other countries will be different, of course. But even if you think the Americans would "win" the clutter crisis, or at least elements of it, I am sure, as with the take-up of materialistic consumerism in the first place, the rest of the post-industrialized world is not far behind. Consider the homes and lives of people in Britain, France, Germany, Australia, or any other developed country.

Think of your own home and life, and those of the people you know. Is there lots of stuff? Spilling out? Messy? Are things in the wrong place? Would you ever call it "cluttered"? Do the kids have too many toys? What, would you say, are the average household counts for shoes, DVDs, and books and magazines? Is there any room left for cars in the garage?

Not everyone in the world, clearly, is at the mercy of this clutter crisis. There are hundreds of millions who do not have enough, and would love to have the problem of too much. But then, today, thanks to our materialistic culture, there are also many millions with far too much, who are running out of cupboards and closets and even space in the garage to store it all.

The clutter crisis, when you think about it, is likely to be worst in the US, where materialistic consumption began and is more fully developed than elsewhere. That is one reason why the simplest response to the clutter crisis and *Stuffocation* – minimalism – is so popular there. (Leo Babauta's blog, for instance, is read by more than a million people.) But the problem of too much stuff is not only an American problem. There is no doubt that there is a worldwide, rich-world, middle-class clutter crisis.

Perhaps, as you read this, you are wondering if "crisis" is too dramatic, too harsh a word. Shouldn't we, after all, only call a problem a "crisis" if it is bad for the physical and psychological health of a significant number of people? That, as it turns out, is exactly the problem with having too much stuff, and why the word "crisis" is so appropriate.

Because clutter, according to some groundbreaking and, till now, largely unnoticed research, has a number of specific, negative effects on every other person on the planet. The most worrying of those effects is that, as a psychologist would say, it increases your risk of mortality. There is another, less scientific, way of saying this that would make a good health warning or headline: clutter kills.

Clutter Kills

If you'd talked with Darby Saxbe, in summer 2013, she might have slowed down long enough to tell you a bit about the clutter in her life and how it was, if not killing her, certainly getting to her.

"We've got to get more space," she would have told you, most likely via her hands-free headset as she hurried from one side of the city to the other, driving her two kids to school as she juggled looking after them with her job, and looking for a new home. "At the moment we live in an incredibly small house – it's 850 square foot – and we are literally drowning in clutter. Both my kids are constantly taking toys out of the box and moving stuff from one side of the house to the other. There are always little pieces of Play-Doh under my feet."

Saxbe is Ivy League educated, with long brown hair, blue eyes, and bags of energy. She has the sort of enthusiasm for her subject, psychology, you would hope to hear in the voice of someone who has just started out – the sort of positive glow Jeanne Arnold felt when she started work on the Chumash all those years ago.

Saxbe had, in the summer of 2013, just been given her first tenured appointment, as assistant professor at UCLA. No doubt her work as a psychologist on the CELF team, alongside Dr Rena Repetti at UCLA, had helped. That work also means she, of all people, knows about the clutter problem.

"There are so many people out there today just drowning in stuff, they feel totally overwhelmed by it," she says.

"Drowning" and "overwhelmed", Saxbe would be the first to recognize, are not objective scientific terms. But then, the problem of personal, at-home *Stuffocation* is not objective either.

There is no blueprint to work out if your home is so cluttered you have a clutter crisis and you should do something about it – even if the amount of stuff you have and its wayward organization fulfils Jeanne Arnold's definition of clutter. There is no objective number, no magic formula that says "if you have more than x items per square foot in your home, it is cluttered", because some people can cope with more mess than others, some do not mind mess at all, and some, of course, view having things all around them as comforting.

There are only two ways to tell if someone has a clutter crisis. You either ask them how they feel or you measure their cortisol levels through the day. In the CELF study, Repetti and Saxbe did both.

They worked with 30 of the 32 families, and worked only with the adults. They gave each couple a camcorder and asked them to conduct a video tour of their home, describing their homes and talking about things that were important to them as they went.

They then gave each of the 30 men and 30 women a bagful of vials and asked them to spit in them at regular intervals. The first spit was right after waking up. The next three were just before lunch, leaving work and going to bed. What if you got nervous and your mouth went dry? "That's easy, we just tell them to think of something delicious to get their saliva flowing," says Saxbe. "Steak usually does it for most people, especially as it's a food you need to chew. But it could be strawberries or nectarines or chocolate – any food will do."

The idea was to compare the results from each experiment, to understand if how people felt about their homes – as indicated by what they said – could predict how well they were, or were not, coping with stress – the cortisol levels would show that.

The results were startling. They were so surprising, in fact, that Saxbe double-checked to make sure she had adjusted them, as is standard for psychological tests, for marital harmony, depression and neuroticism. But even after double-checking, the results were the same.

Saxbe and Repetti collected the camcorders and had the home tours transcribed. Each was, on average, 15–20 minutes long. The number of words the people said ranged from 89 to 9,164. The mean number of words was 2,024 words. How were they going to analyse all that?

After watching the tapes, they realized there were four main subjects that people talked about. They talked about things associated with nature, using words like outside, backyard, barbecue and hedge. They talked about their home as if it was a restful, restorative place, using words like relaxing, calming and homey. They moaned about all the unfinished jobs in the home, when they'd say things like unfinished, repair, redo and redecorate. And they complained about the state of their homes, saying things like messy, clutter, cluttered, unorganized, disorganized and chaotic.

Repetti and Saxbe used a computer program to count the number of times the participants said words that fitted into these four categories.

Next, Saxbe gathered the vials. In the old days, they would have taken all 720 vials of spit, and checked each one by hand for cortisol. There is a lab they can send them to now that does that work for them, so they sent them there to test for cortisol levels. Why cortisol? What would that indicate?

"Cortisol has a strong daily pattern that follows our circadian rhythm," Saxbe explains. "The optimal, healthy pattern is where it starts out high, drops steeply over the course of the morning, and continues to drop over the day. "

But if the fall in cortisol levels is shallow, it is considered to be a sign that the body is not managing stress very well. Shallow cortisol patterns are associated with people who have chronic fatigue, post-traumatic stress disorder, and who have a higher risk of mortality. In other words, if your cortisol declines slowly over the day, you are more likely to feel tired, depressed, and die.

The starkest revelation, at first, was the difference between men and women. Men, so the results said, were not stressed by clutter. The more interesting and far more worrying result was the discovery that women who found their homes stressful – those women who, as they had carried the camcorder round their homes, had used words like messy, disorganized, junk, unfinished and chaos – had a worrying cortisol pattern. Their cortisol levels followed the signature, less healthy, much flatter, slower fall across the day. Does this mean clutter causes stress?

It does not. "We haven't established a causal relationship," Saxbe explains. "But you don't need a causal relationship to get meaning. What the experiment has proven is this: that the more women feel stress and talk about their homes as being cluttered, the more likely they are to have a more depressed mood as the day wears on and at the end of the day."

So how does Saxbe explain the relationship between clutter and stress? There are, she says, three possibilities. One is that clutter causes stress because of something psychologists call "allostatic load". That is the wear and tear clutter puts on your system from watching out for it, picking it up, clearing it away – the sort Saxbe was struggling with in summer 2013 as she stepped around her children's toys and their Play-Doh. Two is that stress causes clutter, because it leaves the woman with less energy to clear up when she gets home. Three is that it is bidirectional: that clutter causes stress and stress causes clutter.

Whichever is the right explanation, clutter is clearly more than just a nagging problem. It is damaging to the psychological health of women. Through this study, Repetti and Saxbe have proved that more is not always better and that, beyond a certain point, less is more – for women, and for any man who cares about women. That suggests, at the least, that we should all, whoever we are, think about clearing up the clutter around us, by organizing our things better and getting rid of some of our stuff.

Is Getting Rid of Stuff Enough?

It is clear, then, that de-cluttering is a good idea. Beyond a certain point, less is more. But is knowing this enough to solve *Stuffocation*? As we saw in the previous chapter, it is clear that having less is making people feel happier. As we have learned in this chapter, there is now, as well as anecdotal evidence, scientific proof that shows that too much stuff is a serious problem, in your home and in society. Does that mean minimalism is the solution to *Stuffocation*? Does that mean that we should all become minimalists, and that, under the building pressure of *Stuffocation*, we are all set to become minimalists?

The evidence, at first glance, makes quite a compelling case for minimalism.

Consuming fewer things would solve many of the problems of *Stuffocation*, and align with some of the opportunities. By becoming minimalists, we would cause less environmental harm. Less burdened by things and the pursuit of things, we would most likely be happier. We would be happy in our downsized, smaller, urban homes. We would happily shift away from material objects to technological solutions: from having a library of books or a collection of CDs to a hard drive of e-books or songs.

But to forecast a minimalist future requires, of course, closer scrutiny. Is there, to begin with, a precedent for this sort of thing?

The sort of precedent we are looking for, to be clear, is a situation where the majority of people changed their values, attitudes, and behaviours. Has that happened in the past? As we saw in the story of how the captains of consciousness created a new throwaway culture in the 20th century, this is precisely the sort of change that happened.

Then, the attitudes, values, and behaviours of a rich, cultured, inquisitive, innovative few changed, and then the great mass of people in our societies followed. They sought happiness and status in material things. They found meaning in seeking better standards of living, for themselves and their children. So, to answer the question, is a sea change in attitudes, values, and behaviours the sort of thing that happens? The answer is an unequivocal yes. It happened in the 20th century.

That does not mean, of course, that the shift that is coming is from materialism to minimalism. Is there any evidence that minimalism is a long-term, growing trend? Have people been buying fewer goods for some decades?

Actually, when you look at the statistics, it is quite the opposite.

Americans, for instance, consume three times as much as their ancestors did fifty years ago, and they buy twice as many items of clothing as they did twenty years ago. In 1991, the average American bought 34 items of clothing each year. By 2007, they were buying 67 items every year. That's a lot of shirts, skirts, blouses, trousers, pants and socks too. It means Americans buy a new piece of clothing every four to five days. They are also buying a lot more of a lot more things.

In 1994, they bought 1.4 billion bath towels each year. They now buy two billion. That is more than three new bath towels a year. What on earth are they doing with them all? In 1995, they bought 188 million toasters and toaster-like devices – like toasted sandwich makers – each year. Now they buy 279 million. What are they doing with them? Probably not much, apart from storing them. Surveys suggest that the toasted sandwich maker is one of the kitchen gadgets people buy but don't use.

The British are similar. The amount the average Briton spent on clothing almost doubled between 1990 and 2004. The average British woman now buys 58 items of clothing each year. There are twice as many things in her wardrobe today than there were in 1980, and there are 22 things in there she has never worn. So minimalism may be an innovative way of living for a few pioneers. But it is very far from a long-term, mainstream trend.

Moreover, if you consider minimalism as an innovative lifestyle, and scrutinize it the way a forecaster using Everett Rogers's *Diffusion of Innovations* theory would, it starts to look far less appealing.

Minimalism, it is fair to say, is easy to understand, and also quite easy to try. Embracing total minimalism requires serious commitment, but there are many ways to give it a go, like Nicodemus and Fields Millburn's bin-bag experiment or Carver and Tuttle's "did you miss it?" game. It is also observable online, in social networks and through blogging.

Minimalists, remember, get a lot of kudos from their conspicuous anti-consumption. Why else would they announce how few things they have, and even post pictures of all their things online? But it is not observable in the real world. How could you tell that someone was a minimalist if they passed you on the street – unless you saw them every day and noticed they were wearing the same clothes?

But one of the other key questions we must ask of any innovation is: is it compatible with how things already are? On this, minimalism falls down. Since the idea is to have less, rather than more, it is directly opposite to materialism. It is about as incompatible as it could be.

And the final, and perhaps most important, question: is minimalism, compared to the way people live now, better? As proved by Repetti and Saxbe, too much can be bad for your health and that of society. But while that proves excessive materialism is not good for us, it does not prove that the answer is to get rid of all of your things. Getting rid of your excess stuff is very different from getting rid of most of your stuff.

Perhaps the final problem with minimalism is its knee-jerk negativity. It is defined more by what it is not than by what it is. More than anything, it is anti-materialism. If today's capitalist system – underpinned by a consumer culture which, in turn, is upheld by materialistic values – were a car driving along a road, and *Stuffocation* is the name of the crossroads at which it has just arrived, then minimalism would be like going along the same road, but pushing the brake pedal as hard as you can, and most likely with both feet.

If that is the case – and that seems to sum it up best to me – minimalism is not very aspirational.

Who, after all, drives a car with the brakes fully on all the time? That is hardly the type of lifestyle that the masses will aspire to and buy into. It is unlikely to be the sort of message that will spark a revolution in attitudes, values, and behaviours. Minimalism has its merits. But, in the final analysis, I think it will not appeal to enough people to replace materialism.

The solution to *Stuffocation* will not simply involve pushing on the brakes and slowing down the materialistic machine. The answer, I am sure, will be far more aspirational and positive. Perhaps the problem with minimalism, though, is not only that it is negative, but that it is not extreme enough.

Maybe, instead of just dragging our feet and slowing the system down, what we need to do at this crossroads is take a sharp turn off the path we are currently on, and get even further away from today's throwaway culture.

SIX

The Good Life and the Cage-Free Family

When Aimée LeVally decided that today's system was not for her, she jammed on the brakes, swung her family off the materialistic path they had been on, and hauled them – husband, children, dogs – from their smart suburban home in Texas, across the country, to the side of a rugged mountain in Nevada, to live, cut off from society, miles from their nearest neighbours, a life of voluntary simplicity.

LeVally is tiny. She is five feet tall. Her skin is porcelain white. It is flecked with freckles. She wears her fiery red hair in a shoulder-length bob or wrapped in a headscarf. She looks, from a distance, a little like a pixie doll.

She was sitting in a big leather easy chair in the lounge, her legs tucked under her, staring through the floor-to-ceiling windows of her suburban home, when her world shattered like a vase thrown hard at a solid floor.

It was July 2008, the wettest July anyone could remember. Rain fell morning, afternoon, evening. All day, every day, grey sheets came crashing down. Eighty inches fell in all. It turned the grass in the garden LeVally was staring at a green so bright and shiny it looked fake.

She did not dare move from that chair. The fibromyalgia which had haunted her for years had now, so it seemed, come back for vengeance. The pain was so bad she thought she might go mad. She was desperate to scream, to let go some of the pressure inside. But she was too scared to. She thought if she started again she might never stop. She couldn't even share the pain – not even with her husband, Jeff Harris, or her father, Ren LeVally, who was living with them to help out. Telling other people about it made them squirm. Whatever she did, she dared not move: any movement would invite in more pain.

Days before, doctors had told her they had given up. They had tried everything they could, they said, even the latest treatments. But, they had regretted to inform her, there was nothing more they could do.

"When I heard that, something snapped," LeVally says now. "And I just screamed, right there, as loud as my lungs would scream. And I kept crying for days."

Finally the crying stopped and she sat in silence, desperately trying to get used to the idea, to the fact that she might spend the rest of her life feeling that level of pain, and that deep despair. Then, as she sat there at the window, scraping along the bottom of what life could offer, she came across a speck of hope.

"Suddenly I realized that nothing could be worse than that moment," she says. "And as that thought came to me, I felt this very odd, very strange sense of peace. In that moment, I realized, if no one could help, the only person who could do something about it was me."

From then, whenever her energy levels would allow, LeVally would be researching – reading this, clicking that, connecting with people who had similar issues, looking for clues to solve her problem.

"I looked around for what I could change, and the first thing I saw was food," she says. "If I changed what I put in, would that change what came out?"

She experimented. She cut out meat. She drank raw milk. She brought back meat, but only meat from farmers' markets. She avoided preservatives. She made stock out of bulbs – it helps heal the lining of the stomach. She bought chickens and roosters and big bags of chicken's feet – good for collagen and gelatin – and made more stock. She stopped eating anything that, she decided, was not food.

"The more I looked at most things that come in a box or a bag or a can, the more I realized they contain things that are known to cause serious health problems," she says. "Most food that's available is covered in chemicals of all kinds. Once I discovered all that, it was obvious why I was sick."

It worked. Not perfectly, but it was at least a start. Most of her symptoms eased. Her strength returned. She got her life back. She could be a mother again. She revelled in every moment, playing with her children, making them food, going for walks with Harris and their fluffy, white, Great Pyrenees dogs. She sucked as much pleasure as she could out of everything she did – because she knew that the fibromyalgia and its agonizing pain were never far away.

Then LeVally got to thinking. If the system that she'd been taught to trust produced the food that had been poisoning her, what else was wrong with it? So she started to change more than just the food she and her family ate. She started purging every aspect of their lives. She cancelled the cable television subscription. She threw out the kids' plastic toys. She got rid of all the spare spatulas, spoons, dishes, pots and pans that were cluttering up the kitchen.

"I kept going and going," she will tell you now. "I went round the house like a crazy person with a sledgehammer."

The more stuff she shed, the better she felt. Then she wondered, if modern culture had made her sick, what if she lived outside of it? What if she lived in a different time and place?

That's when she realized that everything else – all the things Harris's career as a $120,000-a-year IT consultant brought them – had to go too, including the house. Her father suggested they put some of their possessions in storage "while they figure things out", but, to Aimée LeVally, all that stuff was exactly what was holding them back. Harris was right behind her.

They gave a few things to Ren, mostly family heirlooms, like a silver sugar bowl and a bone china cream pitcher, and a few bits of furniture. They donated the rest – vases, wood carvings, their oval, eight-seater dining table, the chairs and cabinet that matched it, their spare computers – to charity.

They kept only enough to keep them going, and that they could fit in a motorhome Harris found. It was thirty-foot long, the size of a small bus, painted brown and white, with aluminium panels.

The day the family left town is seared into Ren LeVally's memory. That day, he and Harris had filled up a truck with the last of their stuff and taken it to a charity shop, and Harris had helped him move into a new place in the city. The parking lot outside his apartment building was their last stop before they took off. After hugs and see-you-soons, Aimée LeVally, Harris, their kids Quinn and Nichola, and their dogs clambered, were carried, and jumped into their new home on wheels.

"I think the sun was setting but I wasn't really paying attention," Ren LeVally says now. "It was pretty emotional. Everybody was waving. Aimée and Jeff were waving. The kids were waving. I was waving. The dogs were barking. It was quite a send-off. I watched them go out of the parking lot, down the driveway, onto the street, and waved till they were gone. Then I went upstairs, opened a beer, and sat down on that big leather easy chair in the dark."

For the next year or so, Aimée LeVally and Harris, the kids, and the dogs toured the country. They visited 26 states. They went to Aimée's sister's graduation in Wisconsin. They went to a festival called the Rainbow Gathering in Wyoming. Finally, they stayed at the edge of a mountain community called Taos in New Mexico.

"We stayed on top of a mountain that first night," LeVally will tell you. "We watched the sun go down and the Sangre de Cristo mountains turn scarlet red, and then we saw the Milky Way."

When LeVally woke the next morning, she knew she had found the place she wanted to live. So they went out that day and found the home where they live now. It is a cabin, about a thousand feet above the main town of Taos, and a ten-minute drive away. It sits in 300 acres of woodland – ideal for Harris to chop logs for their fire, for their kids to play, their goats to graze, their dogs to roam, and for growing as many potatoes, tomatoes, chickpeas, black beans, green beans, and jalapeños as they can. It is about as far, in terms of lifestyle, as they could get from their old home and life.

"Back there, everything is so prescribed," says LeVally. "You get up in the morning, you go to work, you come home. If you're lucky and the traffic wasn't bad, you spend a couple of hours with the kids. Then you do the same thing the next day. You do that for five days and then you have two days to go out and spend the money you made. And the big reward for all that is a vacation once a year, when you get to buy things. And that's it. That's life."

"A lot of people can't see a problem with that," she continues. "But some of us aren't happy with it. Some of us need more from our time on this planet. I do. I don't think I would even know how to live that way anymore. Everything here, all of it, it's all so much more intense. Everything feels so real, and so much more rewarding and healthier and free and fulfilling."

And LeVally's fibromyalgia? The threat of its return will never leave her, but she does not have the symptoms anymore. She no longer spends her days curled up on a sofa, screaming inside. She is far too busy – with the kids, the kid goats, the vegetables, and her life outside the cage of the modern world – and far too healthy to do that.

Is the Good Life the Simple Answer?

LeVally and her family are not the first to reject the modern world and prefer a simpler life closer to nature. There were all the back-to-land movements of the 20th century, for one thing, whose frustrations were captured so well in the 1970s BBC sit-com *The Good Life*.

The series began with Tom Good, played by Richard Briers, realizing that he was just a "grotty little cog in a whacking great machine", and that his job of designing the plastic dinosaurs that went in boxes of cereal wasn't very meaningful – even if they were very well-made and very nicely designed dinosaurs, and even if he was very good at it.

The frustrations and the ideal go much further back than that. You can trace a line of people rejecting society from LeVally and her family, in fact, all the way back to the fifth century BC. Then a man who went by the name of Diogenes believed that modern life – modern for his time, at any rate – was rubbish.

Diogenes thought the world had become too sophisticated and that people relied too much on the things they owned – so he protested by living with as few things as he could and as simply as a dog. He begged. He slept rough, in a giant earthenware jar. For a time, he used a wooden bowl for eating. But when he saw a young boy scoop water with his hands, he smashed his bowl.

The most famous person to reject the modern world and advocate simple living was the 19th-century American author Henry David Thoreau. In 1845, frustrated by modern life – especially at the way people were no longer self-sufficient and spent so much time worrying about what was going on in far-off places – he escaped it and went back to nature. He did not go a long way, only to the woods at the edge of his hometown.

There, Thoreau lived a simple life in a wood cabin, ten feet wide by fifteen long, with a window either side. He grew vegetables. He gathered wild apples and chestnuts. He swam in the nearby Walden Pond.

He watched the sun come up and set. He listened to squirrels scuttling across his roof, foxes barking in the woods, and trains whistling along the far shore. He counted his belongings. They included one bed and one desk, one cup and one spoon, one jug for oil and one for molasses, two knives and two forks, three plates and three chairs – "one for solitude, two for friendship, three for society".

Thoreau had escaped modern life less to count, though, like today's minimalists, and more to question what life was all about. He decided that the best life lay in simple living. "Simplicity, simplicity, simplicity!" he wrote. "I say let your affairs be as two or three, and not a hundred or a thousand; instead of a million, count half a dozen, and keep your accounts on your thumb nail."

As well as famous, Thoreau is arguably the most influential advocate for simple living. His influence has been so strong that when a man called Duane Elgin set out to write what is considered the bible of the modern simple living movement, he felt he had to explain that, to live simply, you did not have to follow Thoreau's example.

"In the popular imagination there is a tendency to equate the simple life with Thoreau's cabin in the woods by Walden Pond and to assume that people must live an isolated and rural existence," Elgin wrote in *Voluntary Simplicity: Toward a Way of Life that Is Outwardly Simple, Inwardly Rich*.

The simple life is not like that, though, he explained. "While ecological living brings with it a reverence for nature, this does not require moving to rural setting. Instead of a 'back to the land' movement, it is more accurate to describe this as a 'make the most of wherever you are' movement."

In the book, Elgin was keen not only to explain what voluntary simplicity was, but also to show how popular it was becoming. Near the beginning of the 1993 reprint of his book, he demonstrated this with some compelling statistics from two magazines.

In a cover feature called "The Simple Life", *Time* had reported that 69% of Americans said they would like to "slow down and live a more relaxed life", and only 7% of them thought it was "worth bothering to shop for status-symbol products". And in an article in *Fortune* called "Is Greed Dead?", three-quarters of working Americans aged 25–49 had said they would like "to see our country return to a simpler lifestyle, with less emphasis on material success".

These statistics remind me of those in the survey I quoted at the beginning of this book, which said that "people in mature markets have had enough of excess", that they are "tired of the push to accumulate more", and two-thirds of people – almost exactly the same proportion as those in the *Time* survey – think they would prefer a simpler life.

Simple living, it is clear, is the sort of thing that has appealed to people and does appeal to people. It also, as proven by many years of research, makes people happier. Could it be the answer to *Stuffocation*?

Is Simple Living Plain Boring?

Thoreau lavished the highest praise he could muster on simple living. The answer to life, he wrote, was "Simplicity, simplicity, simplicity!" His readers, he thought, should "Simplify, simplify."

But, after a little over two years, Thoreau did not. Two years, two months and two days after he went down to live frugally, simply and next to nature in the woods, Thoreau came out and re-entered modern life. He had, as he wrote, "several more lives to live, and could not spare any more time for that one". He had had enough, in other words, of the simple life.

After that, he spent seven years living in the comfort of a friend's home, writing up his notes, and then published his hymn to the simple life, *Walden; or, Life in the Woods*. Later, he moved into his own regular home. He even ran the family pencil business, John Thoreau & Co, for a time.

Think about that for a moment. Isn't it odd that the man most famous for advocating voluntary simplicity gave it up after only two years? If he thought it was so great, why didn't he stay? More importantly, what does that tell us about simple living as a lifestyle choice?

I think it is a bit like someone telling you they love a restaurant and you really should go there, but, actually, they've been there a couple of times and they're not going back: if you heard that, would you eat there?

And contrast Thoreau's ultimate comment on voluntary simplicity with what Samuel Johnson said about England's capital, that "When a man is tired of London, he is tired of life." Isn't Thoreau, by saying he wanted to do other things, and by leaving after such a short time, effectively saying the opposite – that "when a man is tired of simplicity, fair enough, there are other, more interesting things to do"?

With that, I think Thoreau has damned simple living, especially for anyone living today. Because if simple living could not keep someone interested in the 19th century, how much more dull will it seem to someone in the 21st, when there are so many more exciting distractions and possibilities?

I think what we can learn from this is that escaping the comfortable cage of modern life is fun for a limited period of time, and it can help us put things into perspective. But voluntary simplicity is not stimulating enough to be a serious, long-term life choice.

There is another aspect of simple living, even more curious than the fact that it is not very stimulating: it is actually quite complicated.

The Complicated Side of Simple Living

Most years, there are 300 days of sunshine in Taos. In summer, the temperatures are balmy. They aren't in winter. On average, 305 inches of snow falls. For a family from Texas, unused to chopping down trees for firewood, who did not know how much wood they would need, or how often they would get snowed-in, that first winter was real tough. The second one was as well, and the third. Winters in Taos are always tough. If you had talked to Aimée LeVally one of those winters, she would have told you.

"We're in survival mode at this point," she'd say. "We're always learning new rules to get by. It's hard to reflect on what we're trying to do here. All we can hope for is that, at the end of the day, we're still afloat. It really hard right now. On a hierarchy of life, we're dealing with the foundation. It's almost impossible for us to consider higher levels. We're living on a day to day basis. When we've survived another day, when we've tackled another new problem, all I can think is, now I need to go to sleep."

Their first problem was Harris fixing enough fuel to burn and keep them warm, and doing it in a way that did not get him killed.

"It takes weeks of extremely hard physical labour to go out in the snow to bring the amount of wood we need, to turn into firewood. And Jeff had to learn how to do it – how to take a tree down without killing himself," LeVally would say. "In cartoons, they just shout timber and then stand and watch the tree arc towards the ground. But it isn't like that. It's incredibly dangerous. They can fall in any direction. That's why they call them widow makers."

Sometimes LeVally even thought about turning, and going back to the old life.

"When the rent's about to be due and we have to buy groceries because the garden didn't produce enough to get us through winter, I wonder, I really do," she would admit.

Here we have come across one of the thornier sides of simple living. When you first think about it, especially when you're daydreaming from your armchair or bed or sun-lounger, picturing what a rose-tinted simple life would look like for you, it looks, I think, something like this: the sun is shining, the vegetables are growing, your kids are playing safely nearby, and your partner looks rosy-cheek-healthy and rather sexy in that country get-up.

But, as you can see in LeVally and Harris's case, simple living just is not that, well, simple. It may seem, from a distance, simple because it is unencumbered with the stuff of modern life. But close up that simplicity is complicated by the practicalities of staying alive – which are precisely the sort of pressures that modern life is supposed to shield us from.

The odd truth of simple living is that it is a return to the way people lived before the Industrial Revolution. There are some potential benefits to that: like fewer chemicals, additives, distractions, and a greater sense of self-sufficiency. But there are also some terrible downsides.

By escaping the stresses and cage of the modern material world, LeVally and Harris have gone back to surviving the way people did in the 17th century. At least people who lived then had far lower expectations of life, and the legacy of generations who knew how to live on the land. Those skills have mostly been forgotten by most of us. Who today knows how to milk a cow, kill a chicken, make yarn, or plough a field? (I know how to do one of those. I think I do, at least, but I have never had the chance to try it out.)

There are, as you can see, some serious problems with simple living as a lifestyle, and with any notion that it might become mainstream, replace materialism as society's defining value system, and solve *Stuffocation*.

Consider the five key questions a forecaster would ask of any innovation before concluding that it will spread – is it observable, easy to try and to understand, compatible with how we live now and, crucially, better? – and voluntary simplicity falls down at most of those hurdles. It is as observable as minimalism – that is, not very observable. To try it properly requires commitment – though you could start by growing a few vegetables or herbs.

What exactly it is and what it requires is rather more complicated. At the very least, you need to be committed – especially as it is as incompatible with how most people live today as is possible. And, most damning of all, there is a real question of whether it is even better. Although, as I mentioned, people who live this life do tend to be happier, but rather than simply making life better, it makes many aspects of day-to-day living far more difficult.

Crucially, it also lacks the sort of challenges most of us want from life today. And, like minimalism, it is more defined by what it is not than what it is. It is a more intense version of anti-materialism even than minimalism. It sits, I think, somewhere between minimalism and asceticism.

So, if simple living is, in fact, such a disaster, why do so many people so often say they want a simpler life? Consider again those statistics that Elgin reported, that 75% of 25–49-year-old working Americans wanted to live more simply in 1989, and that 69% of the population said the same in 1991. How do those statements fit with the fact that, in the years following them, the amount of stuff that Americans consumed grew so quickly that, in the decades directly after, they bought twice as many clothes?

The way to make sense of this is, as behavioural psychologists have showed time and again, that people do not necessarily behave in a rational, logical way. It is perfectly possible for them to say they want one thing, and then do something entirely different.

People, in other words, like the sound of a less stressful, simpler life. But they are not prepared to give up all the benefits of the modern world, like Wi-Fi and smartphones and central heating and dishwashers, to get it. Besides, many are stuck in the deep ruts of materialism. They still believe that to be considered successful, by their peers and by themselves, they need the badges of success – and that still means a lot of stuff.

This makes sense of what happened before, but what does this all mean for the statistics I reported at the beginning of the book – that two-thirds of people would like a simpler life? Should we conclude that these statistics are just as irrelevant and that we should not listen to what people say they want? It is, I think, one more reason why simple living will not be the solution to *Stuffocation*.

The reason why so many of us think we want a simpler life with fewer possessions, at the same time as leading a more complex lifestyle with more stuff, can be found at the core of the system the captains of consciousness engineered. That system, to begin with, has provided us with a great many things that are enjoyable to wear, watch, drive, and play with – like J Brand jeans, HD televisions, the Mini Cooper, and the iPad.

But as much as the system provides these thrills, it also undermines them, by deliberately making us feel like we are behind the times and missing out. It does this by creating an endless cycle of new and improved things – like J Brand's new skinny jeans, 3D televisions, the Mini Cooper Coupé, and the next generation iPad.

No wonder, when you think about it this way, the system makes us wish for one thing but do another. It leaves us pining for the older, simpler version that did the job perfectly well yesterday and still works fine today. But, at the same time, it tells us about the next, new 'n' improved, better thing now available, and makes us think about it, lust after it, and buy it.

Not Simple, but Simpler Living

LeVally and Harris did not give up. They made it through their first winters. They learned fast. He learned to cut trees safely and to prepare enough firewood for winter. She has got better at growing vegetables and raising animals. But it was still not enough.

In February 2013, they came down from the mountain, and re-crossed the country, and went back to Texas, where Harris had taken a job. They moved into a complex with two swimming pools, huge flat-screen televisions, a dishwasher, central heating, air conditioning, and maid service. Had they given up?

Not entirely. They only stayed two months. The job is an IT role, so Harris can do it remotely, from their mountainside cabin. The money from that job will ensure the future of their simple life. They plan to spend it on a long list of things LeVally has drawn up, including: a new car, new fences, a barn, a woodshed, a cellar, an underground greenhouse, and to fix their wood-carrying truck.

With all these new things, winter will be much easier to manage. Life will not be so hard, nor will it be so simple. But they have not given up on their dream. They are just trying again, treading a fine line between the simplicity of plain living and the complications of modern life.

Rather than blindly following the road ahead of modern life or stick to the sharp turn of pure, plain living, they have found a compromise path somewhere in the middle. They do not have television. But they still have Wi-Fi. She writes a blog from her MacBook, called the Cage Free Family. He does his work from home. They have helped pay for their escape from materialism by going back in, if only remotely. This may be the only practical way that simple living might work in the future. A better name for this more realistic version of voluntary simplicity might then be *simpler* living.

This, I believe, holds the clue to understanding how voluntary simplicity will impact society and the world we live in. It is not going to replace materialism and become the world's dominant value system. It is too dull, and it involves too much of the sort of hard work people did in the 17th century.

But its appeal is likely to affect mainstream values. In fact, it already has. You can see it in the trend for people to grow their own and buy organic food. But while people in mainstream society have embraced many of the values of simple living, they have co-opted them into ever more complex, consumption-based ways of living. Growing your own has spawned an industry, for instance, in seeds and gardening equipment. Organic has become another marketing category. The impact of simple living, clearly, will not be large enough to solve *Stuffocation*.

And so, if we are not going to find the answer to *Stuffocation* by taking a sharp turn off the path we are currently on and learning from simple living, maybe it would be better to look for a solution not outside, but inside the system.

SEVEN

A Man Named Dave
and the Medium Chill

You may, by now, have thought about the way you currently live your life. You may have wondered about the attitudes and ambitions you used to have, about whether they really are ideal for your long-term happiness. You may have toyed with the idea of getting rid of some of your things or adopting a slightly simpler life.

But, even as your imagination went down that path, it probably wandered back to that bigger house, better car or more fashionable handbag – the ones Mr and Mrs Joneses have – and, deep down, you wondered if you really have the stomach for all the changes these new lifestyles require. And then you might have realized, as you read, that even though you would, genuinely, like to be happier and live a more meaningful existence, each of these ways of living sounded too much like hard work.

If that is the case, I have the perfect solution for you, the ideal easy-access pioneer lifestyle – the sort you could try at home today, without too much fuss, without doing too much. In fact, the less you do, the more you'll be doing it. To live this next lifestyle, you do not need to up sticks and head for the mountains or the countryside. You do not have to give up all the mod cons of modern life and start living like it's 1700. And you do not have to bag up all your shoes, shirts, and socks, and make each possession justify its existence in your home.

This way of living is less an angry, antagonistic struggle against the rat race of modern life, the way that minimalism or voluntary simplicity is. Instead, this lifestyle is more like a "no thanks, I don't think I'll bother with that" shrug.

Instead of an energetic battle against the one-way system of materialism, this innovative way of living is happy to chug along the same path. Instead of getting all het up about the bothersome parts of today's culture, it ignores them. Rather than fret about the competitive arms race that is conspicuous consumption, it consumes as and when it needs.

This lifestyle has an unlikely, and slightly reluctant, hero. He is a tall man with a bushy, black beard who goes by the name of Dave.

Most days, you'll find Dave – full name David Roberts – in regular blue jeans and a dark red plaid shirt. He grew up lower middle class, in an average backwater in Tennessee. It was the sort of monotonous town that is the inevitable result of mass production. It was based, if you can call it that, on the modern world's signpost to materialism: a suburban row of big-box stores. "It was very dull," Dave will tell you. "The sort of place where kids would drive up and down the strip and the parking lot for fun, and where you'd bump into people you knew in Walmart."

Dave now lives a regular, low-key life, in a nondescript neighbourhood, in a smallish house, in Seattle, with his two children and wife, Jennifer Roberts. He calls her Jen. She has long dark hair. Friends say she looks like a tall version of the comedienne Tina Fey. Jen works for a local coffee importer. She has been there more than 14 years. Dave writes for a website called Grist.org that covers environmental issues. He has been there nine years.

Dave and Jen take regular holidays, to go see family or spend time with old friends and their kids. They go with them to the three-day Pickathon Roots Music Festival in summer, for instance, and they ski with them in winter. They spend their free-time hanging out, watching television, teaching their boys to read.

Dave and Jen are very happy, and they had never really thought too much about how they lived, till Dave got talking, a while back, with a friend from university called Teyo. He wrote about that conversation in an article on Grist:

"I was visiting with an old friend of mine who lives in Portland now. He's helping to run a tech startup, working 80-hour weeks, half that on the road, with barely enough time at home to maintain a relationship with his dog, much less a romance. The goal, he said, is to grow like crazy, get bought out by Google, and retire at 40. 'It's the big chill, man!'"

That set Dave thinking. How come his old friend Teyo had turned out so hard working and ambitious – and he hadn't? Jen and he talked about it a fair bit.

"Teyo had all this money, he'd just bought a house for cash," Jen remembers. "He was going for the big chill – to burn hot and fast and get to a place where he could just relax and rest. We just didn't have that sort of energy, the sort of drive to put it all out there. I guess we just wondered: how come we didn't have that much money? And what did that say about our values?"

Dave answered that question in the article.

"If we wanted, we could both do the 'next thing' on our respective career paths. She could move to a bigger company. I could freelance more, angle to write for a bigger publication, write a book, hire a publicist, whatever. We could try to make more money. Then we could fix the water pressure in our shower, redo the back patio, get a second car, or hell, buy a bigger house closer in to town. Maybe get the kids in private schools. All that stuff people with more money than us do.

"But… meh. It's not that we don't think about those things. The water pressure thing drives me batty. Fact is, we just don't want to work that hard!

We already work harder than we feel like working. We enjoy having time to lay around in the living room with the kids, reading. We like to watch a little TV after the kids are in bed. We like going to the park and visits with friends and low-key vacations and generally relaxing. Going further down our respective career paths would likely mean more work, greater responsibilities, higher stress, and less time to lay around the living room with the kids."

In other words, when Dave and Jen thought about their life, in the context of a successful friend who was sacrificing so much to chase the all American materialistic dream, they realized that they were happy as they were. Since Teyo called his way of living the "big chill", it gave Dave a good title for his lifestyle. He called it the "medium chill".

Why the Medium Chill Matters

The medium chill may seem, at first glance, like a throwaway idea. Its message, after all, goes something like this: "Don't worry, be happy. Let other people speed past you on the highway to success, if that is what they want. Just because they are hurrying about, it doesn't mean you have to. You can just chill." If this, or some other version of "take it easy", is all there is to the medium chill, is it really worth bothering with?

The funny thing about the medium chill is that, in fact, it is that simple.

But just because it is easy to grasp, that does not mean that the medium chill is anything less than a radical and, I think, very important idea.

Imagine, for a moment, that you go into work, and your boss takes you into a meeting room, closes the door, sits you down, and offers you a bigger salary and a better title. What do you say? What do you do? Who is your first phone call to, to share the news of your promotion?

Now, run the movie again, but this time, instead of accepting, you say "thanks, but no thanks". You explain that while you appreciate the offer, you are actually quite happy with where you are, what you are doing and, as it happens, what you are earning. Think about the look on your boss's face, and what goes through her or his mind.

Consider, when you tell your partner, parents, friends about what had happened – the offer of promotion, you turning it down – how they would react. Wouldn't they think you were just a little bit mad? Wouldn't they think that, for some odd reason they had yet to figure out, you had lost sight of the system that we are all part of? Wouldn't they worry that you'd forgotten the point of work in the modern world: to get on and get up, to go out there and get more?

This is precisely why the medium chill is such a radical idea, why it is worthy of our time and consideration. Because at its heart, the medium chill offers a real alternative to the motorway of materialism. It is a signpost, if you like, to another way of living, one that is slower and gentler and more human than the ever-faster, never-happy pace of modern life.

That foot-to-the-floor pace is one of the consequences of the system the captains of consciousness set up in the 20th century. Since a core component of the current system is that status and happiness is predicated on material success, so the meaning of life has been reduced to the gathering of stuff. But since another core component of this system is that more is always better, there is no such thing, by definition, as enough.

One consequence of this – as Nicodemus and Fields Millburn found out – is that you can never, no matter how hard you work, fulfil your side of the happiness equation. Instead, you are always scrambling to get more, to keep up, to catch up, to overtake. No matter how much you gather, you can never feel like you've truly made it. Another consequence is that people sacrifice too much life to get more stuff. Yet another is that anyone who deliberately turns down the opportunity to get more success – as defined by the system – is frowned on.

"When you have big life decisions," Dave will tell you, "it's weird how you're not allowed to say, 'yeah, I could do that but I don't want to work harder. I don't want to sacrifice more time to achieve that. I would rather, say, lay around and read.' It's just not socially acceptable to do that."

In today's system, where materialistic values are dominant, you are supposed to always say yes to material success, no matter what. But in a system where medium chill values hold sway, you can make another choice. In the world of the medium chill, you can say no to the sort of success the current system deems worthy of your time and effort, and measure your achievements a different way. In that sort of society, you can turn off the super-charged road of materialism, and take a slower, more laid-back route, and not worry what people will say. You can say "thanks, but no thanks" to a promotion, and no one will look down on you for doing so.

This is one of the reasons Roberts has become – unwittingly, it must be said – something of a torchbearer for the idea.

"I want it to be okay to say no," he says. "I want it to be a positive good. I want it to be encouraged. So if you make that decision – to not work harder – you don't get called lazy."

Dave is not the first person to take it easy, of course, and he is not the only person who likes the idea of the medium chill. He has had more feedback from his post on the medium chill than any other he has written in his nine years at Grist, and the concept has been picked up by many other commentators and publications – by *The Economist* and *The Atlantic*, for instance.

By giving this lifestyle a name, Dave has clearly touched a nerve. He has also created a rallying point, and made many realize that they are not alone, that they, like Dave, are not happy with the current definition of success. By doing so, he may have already made the idea of openly saying "no thanks, I have enough already" more socially acceptable, and, at the same time, made it even easier to try out.

You already know how, of course. And when you do, if someone asks how come you've stopped getting up for the 6.23 express to Paddington and started taking the later, more leisurely, train that gets you to the office just in time, or why you no longer work so late but head home to spend more time with your kids or see friends, you no longer have to be embarrassed that you are not one of the go-getters on life's fast track. This isn't laziness, you can tell them. You are, as a matter of fact, taking part in a lifestyle experiment. You are involved in an emerging 21st-century trend, and it is called the medium chill.

Can Dave Save Us from Stuffocation?

The idea of Dave as a workaday, reluctant, modern-day hero – swooping down in his blue jeans and red plaid shirt to save us from the perils of working too hard and spending too often – is an arresting image. But is that really going to happen – by which I mean, will the masses follow his example? Can Dave and his medium chill lifestyle, in other words, save us from *Stuffocation*?

To answer, as before, we will ask the same questions any good cultural forecaster would ask of any new, innovative lifestyle. Is it the sort of thing that happens? Is there a long-term trend? And then, is it observable, easy to try and to understand, compatible with how we live now and better than materialism?

The idea at the heart of the medium chill has, to be sure, been around for a very long time. It has probably, I think, been a way of living since modern humans emerged. Back then, our distant ancestors would have lived a fairly laid-back existence.

Take, for instance, the life of your average Palaeolithic woman, about 40,000 years ago, as envisioned by the anthropologist Geoffrey Miller. She is a healthy mother of three in her early thirties. She lives in southern France. (There is a reason for putting her in this picturesque setting: the first discoveries of early modern humans in Europe were made there.)

"Every morning," Miller wrote, "she wakes gently to the sun rising over the six thousand acres of verdant French Riviera coast that her clan holds." She spends most of her day gossiping with friends, breastfeeding, watching over her children. She flirts with hunters to get free-range meat. She works, according to Miller's calculations, around twenty hours a week, gathering organic fruits and vegetables. Life in the Palaeolithic era, when you put it that way, sounds very much like the medium chill.

The idea of taking it easy has been with us ever since. From the birth of agriculture around 12,000 years ago until the Industrial Revolution, work was generally whatever was needed to keep everyone in the tribe alive. That meant, certainly, that there were times of hard work, especially during the spring planting season and autumn harvest, when the entire community would come together to sow seeds, gather crops, and muck in doing whatever had to be done.

Alongside those periods of hard work, though, there was plenty of time to do what we now call chilling. In summer, when the crops were planted and the sun was shining, and in winter, when the days were shorter and it was better to stay in, there was a lot less to do – except take it easy.

It was the Industrial Revolution that brought an end to what you might call the medium chill era. Then, the industrialists, with their machines and factories and clock-time, began the onslaught against anyone who was happy to take it easy. They made people work long hours, meaning there was less time to chill. They paid them handsomely for their work – relatively speaking, at least – making anyone who chose less well-paid work look bad, even if that did entail a more easy-going life.

Then, with the help of the captains of consciousness, they brainwashed the masses into thinking that society's and their ultimate goal should be ever-higher standards of living. Since that could only be achieved through hard work and constant consumption, anyone not working hard and consuming eagerly, like anyone we would today regard as living a medium chill life, was letting everyone else down.

The result was a society where people thought of quantity of stuff first, and quality of life as only an afterthought. That brought, as we now know, many benefits. But, as the appeal of more stuff wanes, we have once more become more interested in the sort of quality of life that the medium chill offers.

The medium chill, as we can see, and despite the hiatus created by the architects of our current system, is clearly the sort of thing that happens and appeals to people. Anyone who has ever lain out in the sun, who has put their feet up at the end of the day or ever lain in bed wishing they could stay there another ten minutes, or even hour, can understand its appeal.

It is interesting to think, given the aeons-long history of the medium chill, that those feelings are not just natural, but actually *more* natural than the get-up and hurry-up of the go-getting materialistic capitalist.

The medium chill has many more positives on its side. It is simple to understand and easy to try. It is almost perfectly compatible with how we live now. You simply work a bit less than you do now.

There is even some suggestion that this sort of behaviour may be on the rise. Other commentators besides David Roberts have written about the idea. They refer to it with terms like "enoughism", "satisficing" and "threshold earners" – referring to people who aim to have enough, who prefer to satisfy their needs rather than maximize their income, and who, once they have reach a certain level of income, do not do any more work.

But though some commentators, like the American political columnist Reihan Salam, for instance, have written about people who are choosing this way of working, and though I have come across a number of people choosing what looks to me like the medium chill, there seems to be, till now at least, no convincing quantitative evidence that the medium chill is on the rise.

There is no sign of the "social snowball" or "tipping point" that would suggest that it is set to make the leap along the adoption curve, from risk-taking, free-thinking innovator types like Dave and Jen, to all the other, more risk-averse later adopters who prefer to wait and see, and only try something if they hear about it from people they know well. For this reason, I do not think the medium chill will become the new dominant value system in the world.

This also brings to light another problem for the medium chill: if we only have a few pieces of circumstantial evidence, this suggests that the medium chill is, by its nature, not a very visible innovation. By talking about it openly, and by giving the lifestyle of taking it easy a new name, Dave has gone some way to resolving this. He has no doubt struck a chord with many. But there is a chasm between a lifestyle being socially acceptable and a viable alternative, and being aspirational and dominant.

If a large-scale shift to voluntary simplicity is like hauling society off the current way of living to a new path, and minimalism is like going along the same road but with the brakes jammed on almost to a standstill – then the medium chill is like going along the same road but taking your foot off the accelerator and cruising along in second gear. It is a far more pleasant pace of life. It is laid-back and relaxing. There is plenty of time to look out the window, watch television, play with your kids.

But who really wants to drive along in second gear? Isn't that like saying "okay, I'll play along, but I'm not going to try too hard"? This, in the final analysis, I think, is the problem with the medium chill.

Although it sounds nice, and although it resonates with almost everyone, it does not feel aspirational, and it does not provide a way for people to indicate their status. After all, "look at me, I'm in second gear" does not have much of a ring to it. So, regrettably, I do not think that the medium chill will appeal to the majority of people. It will not become a mainstream alternative to materialism. Although I think we will hear more about this way of living in years to come, Dave, sadly, is not about to save us from *Stuffocation*.

Lessons from the Medium Chill, Minimalism, and Simple Living

The medium chill, minimalism and voluntary simplicity – none of them is about to replace materialism as society's dominant value system. But, if you consider them closely, they each hold clues to the answer to *Stuffocation*.

The point of the medium chill, for Dave and Jen, is not merely to avoid the excesses of too many things, and to live life in second gear. It is, in fact, the opposite. Their aim is not simply to avoid getting caught in the work-hard, play-hard, spend-a-lot trap of consumerism. It is to step out of that race so that they can put life first – before money and material things.

"It's about having what we need to live," says Jen, "and what we need to enrich our lives so we can spend time together."

Instead of non-stop wanting, striving and wishing for something, and being dissatisfied with what they already have, Dave and Jen are perfectly happy with what they have, where they are, and what they are doing.

"We don't want to put it all out there and hope that someday we'll be able to relax and enjoy it," says Jen. "We'd rather go as we go, and enjoy where we are right now."

When you think of it like this, the medium chill is a very liberating philosophy. It frees you up so that rather than always thinking about tomorrow, the future and what might be, your focus is on today, the present and what actually is. That is a simple statement, but it changes everything. It changes how you view life. It changes what matters, and how you measure success.

"What matters are kindness and being good to people, and having good friends and love in your life," Dave says. "Life is not about having things. It's about having good experiences."

Compare that idea with the life choices Aimée LeVally and her family made. They gave up all the things that came with their comfortable, suburban life – big TV, big house, rooms full of toys, nice cars, private education – for experiences that made them feel alive.

As she said about her simple life in Taos, "Everything here, all of it, it's all so much more intense. Everything feels so real, and so much more rewarding and healthier and free and fulfilling."

Just as Dave and Jen Roberts have chosen to forgo material success for experiences, in other words, so Aimée LeVally, by swapping the material goods of modern life for intense experiences of scraping a simple living, has too. Now, compare this perspective with that of the minimalists, and you will soon see a common thread.

"Getting rid of stuff is like the first bite of the apple," Joshua Fields Millburn will tell you. "You can get rid of all your stuff and still be fucking miserable. Ryan and I didn't get rid of all our stuff for the sake of it. We got rid of it all to find out what was really important in life. And we decided, in the end, that there are five things: health, relationships, pursuing our passions, growth and contributing to society."

Tammy Strobel says something similar. "If we weren't in a tiny house, we'd be in a tiny apartment, but it isn't about that," she says. "Instead of buying more things now, we invest in things that matter – like experiences and community and family. We get to do things we couldn't do if we had a regular home with traditional jobs and the debt that comes with all that. If we want to hang out with our parents for a week, we do it. That was really useful when my Dad died. We were able to give my Mom a lot of real support. We could really be there for her."

So minimalism, for most minimalists, is more like a starting point, or, as Fields Millburn puts it, the "first bite of the apple". It is, when you think of it like this, really only a practice, rather than an all-encompassing philosophy. It is a reaction to materialism. It is, firstly, a way of doing things that is not materialistic. As such, it is only the first step that many people take on a new route to happiness.

When you look a little closer at these innovative ways of living, then, it is clear they each have something in common. They are, to begin with, reactions to the dominant value system. They are anti-materialism. But they are more than this.

In a world that has buried the idea of a healthy, fulfilling, intense life under a pile of material things, they are statements of defiance. Each one rejects the idea that life should be measured in terms of material possessions, and that, instead, it should be evaluated in terms of experiences. Each believes, in other words, that quantity of stuff comes second to quality of experience.

And what exactly is "experience"? It is, as distinct from a physical good, not something you can hold and touch. Rather, it is intangible, something you do, observe or encounter, like running, going to the beach, having a barbecue, or simply, as Tammy Strobel said, spending time with people you love. It could mean learning something new, helping a friend, or teaching your kids to read – which, Dave told me, has been one of best experiences of his life.

"In my head I thought it would be a long, slow process," he says. "Like it should happen in incremental steps. But it's not like that. A lot happens in a rush. Now they're both reading their own stuff."

By putting experience first, it makes anyone who lives a life of minimalism, simple living or medium chill, a lot closer to the final and, I think, most important, innovative lifestyle I will introduce to you in this book.

Till now in *Stuffocation*, we have met the lifestyle pioneers who are actively conscious of the fact they have had enough of materialism and the lifestyle that comes with that, and are rebelling energetically against the system. The minimalists and those practising simple living are, if you like, the anti-materialists. We have also met the medium chillers, who have had enough of stuff, but in a passive way. Rather than actively getting rid of possessions, they are simply not bothered about them. They are less anti-materialist radicals, more post-materialist revolutionaries.

There is another trailblazing movement of people like this. Like the medium chillers, they are just not that inspired or excited about material things anymore. Instead of spending their energy on what they do not want, though, they are positively engaged with finding status, meaning, and happiness elsewhere. That elsewhere is experience. I call these people "experientialists".

EIGHT

The Experientialists (part one): Escaping the Cubicle

By the 1950s, when you could see the Jet Age and the Space Race reflected in so many cars' chrome tail-fins, the work-hard, buy-now, throwaway consumer culture was in full swing. Towards the end of the decade, a man called Dirk Jan De Pree, but better known as DJ, set out to solve a problem. He wanted to see if he could do for offices what Henry Ford had done for factories a generation or so before. He wanted to design offices so that people could work more efficiently in them. Or, at least, that was his stated aim. He also hoped to see, truth be told, if he could sell more of the products his company, the office furniture maker Herman Miller, made.

After many years of research and one false start, his solution was a flexible, three-sided cube – called the "Action Office II", but which you and I know better as a typical office cubicle. The aim of this new cubicle was to make office workers happier and more productive. In these new cubicles, they would be shielded from sights and sounds that might put them off. They would have a private space they could personalize, a territory they could call their own. That, at least, was one point of view.

Another, as voiced by Herman Miller's director of design, George Nelson, who had stayed away from the project, was that office cubicles were the ideal way to cram as many "corporate zombies" into an office as possible.

In a typical cubicle in Silicon Valley, California, many years later, a telephone rang. A young man in a suit and a tie, with blond surf streaks in his hair, picked up the receiver. He had just come from one meeting. He had another to go to. It was a workday like any other.

Cliff Hodges, then 24 years old, was an entry-level manager in a technology firm, a subsidiary of the chip-maker AMD. This was his first proper job after five years at MIT, the Massachusetts Institute of Technology, in Boston. It was his first step towards the sort of success that seemed to grow, like so many magic beanstalks, out of the rich soil of Silicon Valley.

Hodges had always had two loves. One was computers. "Clifford was a natural," his father, Don Hodges, would say. "Ever since he got his first machine, an Apple IIe, when he only four years old, he just seemed to get it."

The other was the outdoors. "Some days," an old roommate of Hodges's from MIT, Kai McDonald, recalls, "I'd come back to the house expecting to see him working on his thesis. But he'd be out back trying to start a fire with nothing but sticks."

When his studies were complete, Hodges did what millions of other graduates do. He sent out some résumés, got a job and knuckled down.

"Hello, Cliff Hodges speaking," he said, in his best business voice.

"Clifford?" said a shaky voice at the other end.

It was his father, no doubt about it. But his voice didn't sound right. He was slurring his words, but it was still possible to make out what he was saying. He didn't want Clifford to worry, he said. He was fine. But something weird was happening. He was trying to write but couldn't hold his pen.

Hodges let his boss know and left the office, and never came back. When he arrived at hospital, his father was in a hospital gown, slumped in a bed. There were tubes dripping things into him and, by the looks of it, taking things out. There were pads on his chest, with wires coming out of them. When his son walked in the room, Don did his best to look up and smile.

Hodges spent the next weeks in the hospital as his father gradually recovered from the stroke. As the wires came off and Don got better, they got talking about what he was going to do next. He could not go back to work full time. He had to take it easy from now on. Life was precious. You had to look after yourself.

The more they discussed it, though, the more Hodges realized that while they were talking about his father's life, he was also thinking about his own.

"Seeing that happen to my Dad," he says now, "made me think: life is short. If you don't love what you're doing you need to figure out another way."

And Hodges did not love what he was doing.

"My job was going to meetings all day," he says. "I'd go to meetings with the engineers to understand what they were doing. Then I'd go to meetings with the business people to explain what the engineers were doing, and hear what they were doing. Then I'd go to meetings with the engineers to explain what the business people were doing."

He was working Saturdays more often than not. He spent half of his Sundays asleep, trying to get some energy back. He always seemed to be staying late for conference calls with the company's office in Japan.

"I was 24 but I felt like I was dead inside," he recalls. "I was getting up in the dark, getting home in the dark, driving three hours a day."

Yet the commute was one of the highlights of his day. "I always prayed for traffic," he recalls. "I had too much of a conscience to leave late. But if I left early enough and there was a bunch of traffic, it wasn't my fault. I always prayed there'd be traffic so I could stay longer in my car."

Those conversations with his father made him realize he had to quit. His parents weren't sure if that was a good idea.

"Why did you go to MIT if it wasn't what you wanted to do?" his mother asked. "Why don't you build up a career and some money, so you've got something to fall back on?" Don suggested.

But it was too late to worry about any of that.

"You can't measure your life by money – or at least I realized I couldn't anyway," he decided. "You measure your life by the experiences you have."

For Hodges, he wanted those experiences to be outdoors, as far from those conference calls and that cubicle, and as close to wildlife, as possible. He started working outdoors, taking people on wildlife adventures, and he now runs his own adventure company, teaching surfing, climbing and stone-age survival skills.

His "office", if you like, is the wilderness where he runs his courses. He shows people how to survive in nature, how to light a fire without matches, how to make a bow and arrow, how to catch and skin a wild animal. When he has no classes on, he makes sure the techniques he teaches work – like the time he went elk hunting with his friend, Bill McConnell.

"We drove out to a friend's house in the middle of this 500-acre property," Hodges will tell you. "We're standing on the deck of the ranch house, and he points, across juniper and pine forests, and cedar swamps, and dry grasslands, to the mountains in the distance, and he says: 'See that? That's still not the end of the property.' There are elk, antelope, black bear and mountain lions here. But we were here for the elk. We got up the next morning before sunrise and headed out."

By now, his gaze has gone hazy. If you ever hear Hodges talk about this sort of thing, by now you know that he is more there than here.

"With elk they move so much you try to pick them out from a distance and guess where they're going to go. They cover many miles each morning, and you have to get there silently and invisibly."

That morning was misty. There was an eerie feeling, like the mist might part at any moment to reveal something special, or dangerous. It carried the fresh smell of morning and juniper. McConnell and Hodges were each carrying their trusty weapons: bows and arrows they had made themselves. At one point, they saw some animals move. Were they elks? They both thought so.

"So we creep through a cedar swamp. We crawl up a grassy hillside. Then Bill comes real close and he whispers in my ear: 'I'm sure they're out there.' As we approach a clearing at the top of the hillside, he goes one way, I go the other. It's lighter now, but it's still misty. You can't see them, you can't hear them, but you can feel them. You can feel the energy of these enormous 1,000-pound animals.

"I crawl through the brush, trying to control my breathing, to hold my breath. I get to a small stand of juniper trees, to hide in their shadow. I'm looking into the clearing.

"Then, suddenly, ten, maybe fifteen feet away, there's this huge bugle call, like something in between a brass instrument and a primordial scream but it's louder and clearer, and it almost knocks me over through the fog, and then two, full-adult bull elks come out of the mist in the middle of this dominance battle – they're running at each other, they're screaming, they rear up on their hind legs, they crash into each other, one hits a sapling and just knocks the tree over – and one falls on its side, crashes to the floor, and it makes the ground beneath me shake, and my heart is beating at a million beats a second and I'm watching this elk slam down into the ground and right then I look down at my hands holding a wooden bow and arrow, these sticks in my shaking hands and I think – 'no fucking way!' And I did not shoot any arrows that day."

You have probably heard a story like this before, apart from the bit about the elks, anyway. They usually go like this: someone goes through a traumatic experience, an illness, say, or the death of a loved one, something like that. Then, as a result, they realize that life isn't about working hard and having lots of money and possessions. Enlightened, they throw it all in and start a new life that is more meaningful.

From that point of view, Cliff Hodges's tale is a cliché. But it is also a true story. And, more importantly, I chose Hodges as I chose Tammy Strobel, or the way the CELF researchers selected the families in their study. He is a typical example of this emerging group of people I call experientialists.

His story represents what many other experientialist innovators have been through: they have realized, for whatever reason, that they no longer believe in the system, that they are not motivated by materialistic values, and that they find the idea of experiences more meaningful and exciting.

There are similarities between the experientialists, the minimalists, and all the other case studies in this book. But there are also important distinctions. Compare Ryan Nicodemus with Hodges. As a case-study minimalist, Nicodemus experienced *Stuffocation* from the material objects he had gathered. He did give up his job as well. But the principal way he rejected materialism was by getting rid of most of his stuff.

As a typical experientialist, Hodges, on the other hand, felt *Stuffocation* because of the life he was leading, the one that came with the current system. The primary way he rejected materialism was not by getting rid of his possessions: he didn't have that many in any case. It was by trading in the job and life that the materialist value system necessitated, and upgrading to a new, liberated lifestyle that measures success in experiential rather than material terms.

I think there are many more making that choice today – like, for example, a thirty-something Australian in London called Marianne Cantwell.

Marianne and the Free-Range Lifestyle

The realization of *Stuffocation* comes to people in many different ways. For some, like the minimalists Tammy Strobel and Ryan Nicodemus, for instance, it is not a sudden thing. The feeling builds up slowly, like steam in a pressure cooker. Then, when they make the change, it is like they have twisted off the lid to let the steam out.

For others, like Aimée LeVally, say, or Cliff Hodges, *Stuffocation* comes crashing out of the mist like a bugling elk. This is how it hit Marianne Cantwell a few years back. *Stuffocation* exploded into her life, not far from the Houses of Parliament in London, England, about 200 feet below ground.

It was a London morning like any other. Outside, grey clouds. Inside, in the apartment Cantwell shared with her boyfriend in north London, the alarm on her Blackberry went off. She stopped the noise, checked for incoming emails. She did not want any surprises when she arrived at the office. "I wanted to make sure everyone was happy, that nothing was going to bite me," she recalls.

She had, as she will tell you now, her dream job. In her late twenties, she revered her boss. She loved her work. She was a gung-ho marketing consultant, thinking up smart ideas for blue-chip clients with big problems. She was well respected. In the office she was hailed as a member of the Heroic Boys Club.

"That meant you were so busy," she says, "you wrote the presentation in the car on the way to the meeting and presented it without any preparation."

Mornings were the only time she did not have to hurry. After checking her emails, she would do everything she could to put off the moment when she had to leave for work. In the kitchen that morning, she turned on the radio, made toast, looked out the window at the gardens below. She stroked Elvis, her ginger tabby cat. As usual, he had jumped onto the sideboard and into the sink. He was in there now, licking drips of water from the tap. Back in the bedroom, rubbing her temples, she opened her wardrobe and surveyed the things success had bought her.

"Working in the city, you're always buying new shoes and handbags," she says. "They're a reward for all the hard work. Working as hard as I was, I deserved them too."

She picked out clothes that said smart-but-not-too-sexy. With her pretty face, blue eyes and blonde bob – "She looks like Gwyneth Paltrow," says her friend Katherine Tickle – Cantwell always made an effort not to look like a secretary. She paired a grey shift dress by a hip Australian brand called Cue with a black leather belt and black patent heels by British fashion brand Ted Baker. All three, of course, would go with her designer accessories – a fawn-coloured handbag by Longchamp, and a pair of tortoiseshell glasses by Prada which, when she deliberately, delicately removed them in a meeting, helped her hold a room.

Kissing her boyfriend goodbye, checking the time and her emails one last time on her Blackberry – she definitely did not want any surprises when she got to the office – she left.

Instead of the fast route to the tube, she turned the other way, ambling past picturesque Georgian and Victorian houses and the green parkland of Highbury Fields. At the station, she took the escalator down into the ground and the busy tube south, changing, along a tunnel packed with commuters at Green Park, from the Piccadilly to the Jubilee line.

Most of London's tube lines carry a multicultural mix of people from many lines of work. The Jubilee line heading east at rush hour is different. It heads to one of the world's most important financial centres, so at this time of day it is crowded with two types.

"The bankers and corporate lawyers wear blue and white checked shirts, too-wide ties, and iPods. They turn them up so everyone else can listen too," Cantwell remembers. "Then there's the secretaries. They carry designer bags and wear too much make-up. Their nails are manicured in the French style, natural to the end of the finger, and then white to the sharp ends."

They all herd at the points on the platform where the train doors open. They seem to be busy reading, but really, Cantwell says, they are watching, waiting.

"It feels really aggressive," recalls Cantwell. "Everyone's overhyped on adrenalin already. It's like they're already in the office. They think of it as a point of honour if they can get to a seat before you. If they got the chance, they'd push you over to get to a seat."

There was no chance of getting a seat that day. The pack Cantwell squashed herself into couldn't squeeze into the first train that stopped. When the next one screeched into the station and its doors opened, it surged forward again. She heaved herself forward, shuffling her shoes, shimmying her shoulders, and managing to get a hand on a rail.

Now, hopefully, her body would not press too intimately onto whoever was in front, behind and beside her. Her face was in a man's sweaty-but-not-smelly armpit. Someone else's was in hers. Had she put deodorant on? She could not remember. If she had forgotten, she was not the only one. She made a note to check before she went into the office.

She closed her eyes, held her breath. She tried to push current reality from her mind. She daydreamed about being outdoors, walking free in the park at Highbury Fields, or, better yet, in the Hunter Valley where she had grown up.

At the next stop, a few more squeezed on, pressing everyone even closer together. Hanging on to the rail and her spot, she turned her head forty-five degrees, to breathe and take in her surrounds. Just as before, the suits and the secretaries were doing their best to ignore everyone else, engrossed in their mission-critical emails and news.

Now, though, they were trying even harder, as they were pushed up even closer to each other, like animals herded into a pen.

"And that's when it hit me," she says. "We were supposed to be the best and brightest people of our age, we were meant to have it all. And we were standing in each other's armpits, trapped in a metal tube hurtling hundreds of feet beneath the street. We couldn't even breathe.

"That's when I realized – we were just like caged animals. And if we had actually been animals, this would not be OK. This would not be allowed. There'd be animal rights protesters protesting. And in that moment, it just hit me. I just suddenly realized I couldn't take it anymore. I couldn't be in that cage any longer. I had to get out. I had to live a cage-free life."

Cantwell started plotting her exit that moment. A few months later, she walked out of her career, and started living as far from her animal-cage commute as possible. She still travels, but not every day as a commuter. Instead, she moves every few months, switching between her favourite places around the world, like Thailand, Italy, Australia, and the UK. She still likes possessions, though she has fewer than before.

"I don't collect material possessions, but I don't avoid them either," she says. "I like nice things around me – and that could mean a fun experience, a countryside view, or a beautiful dress."

She still works, but not in a nine-to-five, Monday-to-Friday job that, with a Blackberry and a demanding boss, had felt more like a five-to-nine, Monday-to-Sunday sentence.

Now, as a career and life-coach, she thinks up smart ideas for everyday people with real problems. She helps others escape their Blackberry-enabled, caged existences, so they can, like her, live what she calls a free-range life. And she still, when in London, takes the tube. But not, ever, at rush hour.

We have all, at some point in our lives, been through rush hour. Who hasn't wondered if there's a better way? After moaning about the hell of it all, though – the heat, the sweating, the smell, the dirt, the delays, the lack of seats and, worst of all, the other people – most of us accept it as part of life.

Cantwell didn't.

After one close encounter with a stranger's armpit and one tube journey too many, she decided that she and her fellow commuters were being treated worse than animals, and she vowed that enough was enough. She didn't walk away that day. But the seed was planted that morning. In the weeks and months after that, how she was going to get out became the only thing she thought about.

She suddenly looked at the people above her in the system in a whole new light. Before she had envied their bigger homes and more expensive handbags. But now she realized all those things had not made them any happier. So, like Cliff Hodges, she chose to put life experiences before the traditional, material markers of success. And it has worked. Like Hodges, Cantwell has told me a number of times she is now far happier than before.

There are many more people who, like Hodges and Cantwell, are finding happiness, meaning, and status in experiences rather than material possessions. (We'll meet more in the next chapter.)

Is there something odd or different or special about them? What I mean by that is: will this way of living only work for a few anomalous people? Or should we all follow their example? Is there, in other words, a general rule or even scientific proof that says: "if you want to be happier you should choose experiences rather than material possessions"?

To Do or to Have? That is No Longer in Question

There was a time, not so long ago, when you couldn't say categorically whether it was better to choose experiences or material possessions, whether one or the other would more likely lead to happiness. Some thought it was obvious that experiences – like relationships, say, or cycling or dancing – were more meaningful and made you happier.

Others said if you thought that, you were buying the wrong things. After all, they said, getting new clothes or shoes or a handbag or a car always made them feel great. Stuff like that was key to their happiness. The sceptical observer would have considered the opinions of one or two or even a dozen of these people – and dismissed them, the same way she or he would have considered the anecdotal evidence of the minimalists. Perhaps one or the other was better. But, since there was no scientific proof, you could not say for sure whether experiences or material possessions were better.

What you could say, though, was that the virtuous circle of materialism that the captains of consciousness created was not as great as it had first seemed. Richard Easterlin made that clear in 1974, when he showed that higher income, above a certain point, did not lead to higher happiness. In the decades after, researchers noticed another truth: that more materialistic people tended to be less happy. That was interesting, but it created a new riddle, because no one knew which way the relationship worked.

Did being materialistic cause people to be less happy? Or, was it the other way round, that unhappiness made people more materialistic? Or, could it be, as Darby Saxbe suggested for the relationship between stress and clutter, bidirectional? Or, lastly, did neither cause the other, and were the two only loosely connected, in what scientists call a correlation? Understanding this relationship is not just an academic question. It is key, if you care about people's happiness.

Then, in 2003, two psychologists, Tom Gilovich and Leaf van Boven, collaborated on a landmark study that answered this question. In their paper *To Do or To Have? That is the Question*, Gilovich and van

Boven began with a simple query: "Do experiences make people happier than material possessions?"

To find out, the first thing they did was establish the difference between the two concepts. The simplest way to think about this, as we saw in the last chapter, is that an experience is something you do, and a material possession is something you have. In some cases, the difference is black and white: hosting friends for a barbecue, for instance, as opposed to a chair.

But, as you may have already realized, there is also a lot of grey area. Most objects provide some sort of experience. Even a chair provides you with a, hopefully comfortable, experience of sitting. There are objects even more closely associated with the experiences they provide. So how do you count those? Is, for instance, a pair of skis or a 3D TV or a Porsche a material possession, or an experiential one?

The solution, Gilovich and van Boven decided, lies in the intention of the individual. If you buy something with the aim of acquiring experience, that is, the event or events it will provide, that is an experiential possession. But if you buy something with the primary intention of having a physical, tangible object that you keep in your possession, that is a material purchase.

This may sound complicated when you first consider it, but it has been shown, by Gilovich and van Boven and by other psychologists, to work. It also allows for people to choose. Some people, when they think about their television, for instance, think about the big thing on the wall in their living room that looks good with the furniture and impresses their friends. Others think first about the movies or sports games they will watch on it.

Now that they had clearly defined the two key concepts, Gilovich and van Boven conducted a series of experiments where they asked people to think of experiential and material purchases they had made. Then they asked questions like: when you think about this purchase, how happy does it make you? How much does this purchase contribute to your happiness in life? To what extent would you say this purchase is money well spent? To what extent do you think the money spent on this purchase would have been better spent on something else that would have made you happier?

The results were clear, the conclusion simple: experiences do make people happier than material possessions.

That meant that van Boven and Gilovich were able to answer the other question that had vexed researchers for so long, and confirm how the relationship between happiness and materialism worked. By showing that experiences – things you do – make people more happy than material possessions – things you have – they were able to solve the riddle of the relationship between materialism and unhappiness. Materialism, they concluded, causes unhappiness.

To do or to have, in other words, is no longer in question. The answer is unequivocal. If you want to be happy, you should spend your money, time and energy on experiences rather than material possessions. They are more likely to help you be happy.

Why? Why is it that experiences are better than material goods at making us happy? A small band of pioneering psychologists – people like Ryan Howell, Travis Carter, Elizabeth Dunn, as well as van Boven and Gilovich – have been trying to work that out ever since. So far, they have found five principal reasons.

Experiences, for one thing, are more prone to what psychologists call "positive reinterpretation", and what you or I might call "looking through rose-tinted glasses". In other words, if you make a mistake and buy a bad material good, like shoes that hurt or a coat that makes an odd swishing noise when you walk, for instance, that is it. It was a bad choice. You are stuck with it.

But with experiences it is different. Even when experiences go badly wrong, our rose-tinted reinterpretations give them a positive spin. That camping holiday when all it did was rain, the bus trip when someone in the seat behind you threw up all the whole journey, the time you got laid off – somehow, those things, so awful at the time, never seem quite so horrific in the re-telling, do they?

Material possessions are not as good as experiences because they are more likely to suffer from something psychologists call "hedonic adaptation". Think of a new game or toy or mobile phone. You are, to begin with when you walk out of the shop, or just after the delivery man has been, very excited to have your shiny new thing. You play with it constantly, press buttons, learn how to use it, show it to friends. But as the days, weeks and months pass you get used to it, until, eventually, you do not even notice it anymore. You adapt to having it and, as you do, you get less and less pleasure from it.

Experiences are also better, psychologists say, because it is harder to compare them than material goods. Consider the difference between a car and a holiday. If you own a Nissan and your neighbour has a Porsche, no one would doubt who has the better car. But even if you go camping in West Wittering and your neighbours go to a five-star resort in the Seychelles, there is no doubt that they went to a swankier place. But that does not mean they had a better time.

Does sunset look better when you are drinking a beer on the beach on England's south coast, or sipping a daiquiri in your resort's beach bar in the Indian Ocean?

This fact, that experiences are harder to compare, matters. Because if it is harder to say which experience is better or worse, it is less likely that you will regret your choice, or think that yours is less good and suffer the indignity of lower status. This, psychologists have found, makes it easier to be happy with what you chose and, therefore, more likely to be happy.

As well as being more prone to positive reinterpretation, less likely to be dulled by hedonic adaptation, and harder to compare, experiences are also better because we are more likely to view them as contributing to, and part of, our identities. That is, we are more likely to think of them as part of what makes us who we are.

Think of the last time you went to a fancy-dress party or climbed to the top of a hill or went to a sporting event. Hasn't each one contributed to who you are in some way? Hasn't each one contributed more to who you are than the last things you bought? And if you had to give up a thing or an experience, which would you be more likely to let go – to wipe the memory of a stag party or a wedding you went to, or hand back a toaster or a crystal vase someone bought you?

And, as well as being more prone to positive reinterpretation, less likely to be dulled by hedonic adaptation, harder to compare, and more likely to contribute to our identity, the fifth reason experiences are better than material goods is that they have, as social scientists say, more social value, that is, they bring us closer to other people. Since we humans are sociable animals, being close to other people makes us happy.

Experiences are more likely to bring us closer to people in three key ways. By doing something, rather than having something, you are more likely to be doing that thing with other people.

Also, while material purchases are more likely to separate people, experiences are more likely to bring them together. Think of cars and camping. If you have a Nissan, having that Nissan will not make you feel part of the same car-owning group as the person who owns a Porsche. There will be no close connection between you. Instead, you are more separated. If you go camping, however, it makes you part of the camping social group. It puts you, in some way, in the "camping club". Even if you only go to a campsite on the south coast, you have something in common – stories to share, experiences that are similar – with the person who camps halfway up Mont Blanc.

Or consider camping alongside holidaying in the Seychelles: although they are oceans apart, you are both still part of the "holiday club", and could talk about beaches, swimming in the sea, what the locals were like, and the food you ate. Experiences also bring people closer because, quite simply, they make better conversation. If you do something rather than have something, you are more likely to have something interesting to say.

Research has even shown that people prefer people who talk about experiences rather than material goods. Would you rather hear someone talk about their new Nissan, or their camping trip?

Psychologists, then, have found five main ways to explain why experiences are better than material goods at making people happy, that is, why it is better to do than to have: experiences are more prone to positive reinterpretation, less likely to be dulled by hedonic adaptation, harder to compare, more likely to contribute to identity, and they bring you closer to people.

I would add a sixth reason. The unintended consequence of being materialistic for an individual is that they are more likely to have cluttered homes, which is likely to bring them, and those around them, stress and unhappiness. And the unintended consequence for a society where having is rated more highly than doing is the same: stress, unhappiness and *Stuffocation*.

That problem, I think, can be solved by a shift in society's values. If more people put experiences before possessions, if more preferred doing rather than having, we would have less clutter, less stress, and a happier society. There are a few innovative pioneers already living this way, like the people you have just met, Cliff Hodges and Marianne Cantwell. Their examples illustrate the difference between a life lived based on materialistic values, and one grounded in experientialist ones. But, to be fair, they also leave the idea open to debate.

Choosing experience over material possessions may work for them, and it may work for everyone *in theory*, as the psychologists have shown, but does that mean it will work for us all *in practice*?

Making the choice was easy enough, from a certain point of view, for Hodges and Cantwell. After all, they were single, in their twenties, and they had minimal commitments when they decided to drop everything and try something else. But what if you are not young, free and single – could you still, even then, become an experientialist? And, if you did, would you have to up sticks and leave your job? Is that the only way to get the proven benefits of experientialism?

NINE

The Experientialists (part two): Hippies with Calculators

Not long ago, during a normal Saturday lie-in, Sue and Bertrand Lenet, who are now both in their early fifties, woke up in their three-storey Victorian home in Clapham, London, and wondered aloud what life was all about.

Sue and Bertrand are a classic Anglo-French couple. She is pretty and prim and wears her dark hair short. There is something of the school teacher, or perhaps Maggie Thatcher, about her. Though she is the sort who says "thank goodness", she has a steeliness that suggests she is not to be trifled with. He is from a seven-sibling family in Brittany. He has a big, bull's head. He keeps his grey hair cropped, right down to his wide sideburns. To look at, he could be a soldier in a foreign legion. But talk to him for a moment, and you will instantly recognize the bon viveur's appreciation of good food, fine wine and company. He is as friendly as Yogi Bear and has a smile to match.

That morning, they were propped up in bed, sipping coffee as the sun shone through the open window. Their daughter, Solen, 10, and two boys, Anton, 9, and Jude, 3, were bounding in and out. It felt, as Sue says now, "like one of those bright mornings when anything is possible". They had a great life. She ran her own textile business. Bertrand had his own restaurant. Their kids were in private school. But what was the point of it all?

Not much, they decided. So they started picturing what an alternative life would look like. That weekend, they started planning, and they kept on, even when Bertrand was diagnosed with cancer.

As soon as the cancer went into remission, and five years after the idea had first come to them, they put their plans into action.

They rented their house. They divided their stuff into two piles: junk and things worth keeping. They threw the junk out. They gave their eight favourite paintings to friends to hang on their walls. They put a few other bits in storage.

They gave it all up to live with nothing but the things that fitted in their backpacks, and they went in search of the kind of life-affirming experiences that they decided, would make life worth living – even bad ones, like the time they got stranded in a snowstorm in Peru for two days, wearing nothing but t-shirts, shorts and flip-flops.

They had decided to go to Machu Picchu by taxi because, as Bertrand said, Jude's little legs would not cope well with the Inca Trail. When they started off, it had been warm and sunny, a typically tropical day. But as they climbed into the mountains, the weather came in.

Before they knew it, as they neared a high mountain pass, the air, and then the road and everything around them, was thick with snow. The busy road now clogged up in both directions. Lorries got stuck trying to turn around. They were stranded. The taxi driver shrugged his shoulders, turned to look at them and said there was nothing to do but wait.

"You're in Peru!" he said. The Lenets were not sure if he was trying to explain the situation or cheer them up. As day turned to night, they shared round the only food they had – a few Snickers bars. They huddled like penguins to keep warm, Sue with Solen, Bertrand with the boys. They shivered through that first night.

Sitting upright in the dark, Bertrand resolved that as soon as it was light, he would go down the mountain, find the next village and get help. At six the next morning, Bertrand stuck his head out and went looking. He found a village, asked some locals where the nearest town was: three hours down the road, on a good day. On a bad day, they shrugged, who knew? There was a short cut, though, they said, pointing. So he wandered for a few hours, but snow had covered the way and, besides, it was far too steep and dangerous –

especially in flip-flops. He gave up and trudged back to the cab. There, things were getting worse.

"The cold had got into their bodies, into their bones," Bertrand recalls. "One by one, Solen and then Anton started to be really cold. Sue couldn't move her jaw. It was like she was paralysed. That's when I thought we were in big trouble."

As night came in, there was nothing to do but sit and shiver through. And at first light, Bertrand rallied his troops.

"We walked for three, maybe four, hours, until we got out of the traffic jam, and till a bus came along. We squeezed in, got to a town, got a taxi back to our hotel and went straight to bed."

They have had other bad journeys, like the 24-hour bus ride across Bolivia when the toilet was out of order, the air conditioning was broken, it was 35 degrees outside, the road was really a dirt track, and the journey took twice as long as advertised: two whole days.

Just as the nightmare was coming to an end and they arrived in the Bolivian capital, La Paz, 3,650 metres above sea level, the temperature plummeted, they all started shivering with cold, got altitude sickness and stomach cramps and started vomiting. It took them a week to recover.

The Lenets would not, of course, swap any of it. "We'd worked so hard all those years to build our businesses," Bertrand will tell you now. "I'd worked 18-hour days. The kids had grown up in the restaurant, those years went by so quickly. But that wasn't life. Life is about spending time with the family. That's what matters: our family having experiences all together."

Sue agrees. "Modern children grow up too quickly, they're ever more materialistic, and we weren't seeing enough of them," she'll say. "Now we are sharing this adventure together. What we see and what we experience together is definitely what life is all about."

When they originally went, the plan was to go for a few years, and "see what happened". Last I heard, they had settled semi-permanently near a beach on the island of Bali, in Indonesia. They surf. Friends visit them. Their children go to the local French lycée. They cannot remember what they put in storage, and they do not know if they will ever come back for good.

Many of us have daydreamed about throwing it all in and going off travelling. Most of us accept, though, that gung-ho trips are a thing of the past, something we did during a golden period of our youth, before mortgages, commitments, children, work, and all the other excuses that come with growing up. So we accept the few weeks' holiday we get each year, and take that as our lot.

The Lenets didn't.

They had plenty of stuff, they had all they wanted, and they had worked very hard for it. But now they had it all, they realized that the rewards for success in the consumerist system weren't enough for them.

So Sue and Bertrand meticulously planned their exit, got rid of most of their things, rented their house, and escaped the system, as an intact family unit, to travel the world and do something that meant more to them. By doing so, in my view, they prove that you do not have to be young or free and single at least, to be experientialist. They show that experientialism is also possible for people who have commitments and children.

Why Don't You Just Call them Hippies?

There might be a part of you thinking, "I'm really happy for these so-called experientialists, but there's nothing new going on here. Didn't the hippies do all this back in the '60s?" And you would have a point. The hippies did reject the establishment. They did criticize the more-is-better values of mainstream materialistic society. They did look for meaning elsewhere, and especially in experiences. They did pass up lucrative careers, like Hodges. They did reject the commute, like Cantwell. They did go live on beaches, like the Lenets. But when they turned on and tuned in, they also dropped out. They turned their backs on society.

The people I call experientialists are not doing that. These pioneers are rejecting materialism. But that is not their focus. It is less that they are reacting to the materialistic values of modern life, and spending their energy on that, and more that they are evolving beyond those old values. They are quite happy to have things, if they need them. But they are not hoping to find meaning, status, or happiness in material things. And, unlike the hippies, they are not turning their backs on society.

The experientialists' minds may be focused on a new set of values, but their feet are very firmly planted in mainstream culture. They have not given up, dropped out and turned their backs on society. Instead, they are very much participating in it.

Cliff Hodges did not give up his big money, Silicon Valley career to wear a flower in his hair. Just because he wanted to spend his time outdoors does not mean he has given up on society. Leaving the tech world and setting up his own business were not decisions made for financial reasons, of course. He even gives free classes to children whose parents cannot afford to send them, for instance. But he does still make money and he still wants to make money.

"I give 1% of my profits away," he says. "But I also save a lot. My goal is to buy a large piece of land so I can have my own wilderness that I can use and protect." He is also, last I heard, getting married and is planning to buy a house.

Sue and Bertrand Lenet have given up their straight life of working long hours, owning a big house, and sending their kids to private school. But, although it was impractical for Sue to keep her textile business going, Bertrand still runs his restaurant.

Sometimes, when they come to a place with an internet connection, he logs on to see how things are going – to check the stock, look at the webcams, and speak with his managers. In March 2013, he came back to London and spent a month with his staff, overseeing the running of his restaurant.

And Marianne Cantwell still works. She has simply exchanged the hemmed-in, buttoned-down experience of commuting, an office job and the caged hopes and dreams that come with those, for a life that is on her own terms.

Like the hippies and the counterculture movement before them, Cantwell, the Lenets, and Hodges have rejected the mainstream model.

But, unlike the hippies, even though they have dropped out of conventional materialistic society, they are still turning on their computers and tuning their minds in to running functioning businesses. They are still making money. They may prefer doing things to accumulating stuff, but they still have their computers and their calculators, their spreadsheets and their profit and loss accounts to hand. I call them experientialists, but you could, if you wanted, think of them as "hippies with calculators".

Although each of the "hippies with calculators" we have met so far still earns money like the rest of us, every one has also, it must be said, made big, brave decisions – the sort that most of us, locked in to mortgages and comfortable routines that, for the most part, work, would not make. Does this mean that experientialism is still a closed shop to the rest of us? Does it mean that if you want to get the sort of happiness that researchers say this life promises, you have to give up your job and your home, and abandon the life you live now?

Part-time Hippy, Full-time Professional

You wouldn't say *Stuffocation* really ever quite hit Jim Whyte. It was more something he has always felt somehow. He grew up with plenty of stuff, in a listed building in East Sussex, in the green, south-east corner of England. He slept in a four-poster bed that, so he told his friends, Anne Boleyn had once slept in. At school, he carried a rabbit's foot, called Oscar, with him – "For luck," he used to say.

Now in his forties, he has a ready smile, dark hair he pushes back, a cropped salt-and-pepper beard, and an encyclopaedic mind.

"He has an incredible memory," says an old school-friend, Hector Proud. "He can remember obscure details about all sorts of things, like lines from Blackadder and Blaxploitation movies he watched twenty years ago. We call him the Jim-ternet."

Whyte holds an MBA, and is a retail analyst. He is old enough, successful enough, and earns more than enough to own plenty of things, but he is almost possession-less. All his worldly goods fit in the dingy room he rents in Earls Court, London.

"I could fit all my stuff into four large suitcases," he will tell you, waving a hand at the things in his room. "Actually, probably three, as I'd throw things away while I was packing."

Whyte, you see, does not look for meaning in material possessions, or in what people tend to think of the typical markers of success.

"If someone asks 'how would you characterize the last 40 years?' most people talk about family, friends, career, money," he says. "But for me, it's not like that. For me, it's the places I've visited, and the experiences I've had there. Some people remember who won the cup in '82, or what car they bought in '95. I don't remember any of that. My life is defined by where I went each year, and what I saw and did there. It's like I have an album in my head of snaps and smells and memories."

"There's a picture in there of the monkey I saw in a temple in Kyoto," he will tell you, "on my second to last day in Japan in 2004, and one of an elephant waddling down a side road in India in 1990. There's a video, if you can call it that, of an angry crowd gathering round me and the guy I was travelling with, Rob, in a square in Marrakech in 1991, just after the first Gulf War.

"Then there's the smell of Tahiti in 1999. I'd gone to French Polynesia and was sailing to Tahiti. I'd been told you could smell Tahiti before you could see it – which sounded pretty implausible. But I was on watch just before dawn in the middle of the vast Pacific and could suddenly smell flowers. The island didn't emerge over the horizon for another couple of hours – by which time the air was almost technicolour with perfume. Paradise is a very overused word, but now I can see why the crew of the *Bounty* decided to mutiny rather than leave.

"These trips, and the experiences they hold are like markers for me. They're how I measure things. In twenty years' time, I'll only remember one thing about 2011, for instance. Everything else will have just faded away. For me, 2011 will always be the year I drove to Iran in a Citroen 2CV."

Driving to Iran was not the first cross-continent road trip Whyte had made. He had previously driven from London to Ulan Bator in Mongolia, in the same 2CV with the same driver, a friend called Rupert. So when he was wondering how best to celebrate his 40th birthday, he already had a starting point. He decided, after some research, to re-enact a rally that had begun in 1971, two days before Whyte was born. It was a hippy era trail from Paris to Persepolis, in Iran.

A few weeks into their trip in August 2011, at the eastern end of Turkey's Black Sea coast, Rupert was driving along the smooth modern road between the inky sea and the rainforest. Whyte was gazing out the window. Suddenly, he spotted a section of the old road, and a rare turn-off.

"So I yelled at Rupert – above the noise of the engine – to take the turn-off," he says now.

Rupert pushed the brakes, yanked the steering wheel. The car slowed, lurched to the left, and the whine of engine over tarmac was replaced by a rougher sound, as the car bumpety-bumped along the forgotten road as it gradually broke up and turned back to dust.

"The original road!" Whyte says. "It had been snaking along side us for miles, heading out here and there to headlands on its own. We had to have a look."

They drove down it, a half-mile or so, to the furthest point, forty feet or so above the sea, and got out. Standing there, Whyte says, on an abandoned, crumbling road next to the Black Sea, was one of the journey's highlights, more special even than seeing the ruins of Persepolis or meeting a mechanic who remembered the rally forty years before.

"It was almost a spiritual experience," he says. "Seeing the old 1971 road like that… to think, they'd been here, forty years before. And now it was silent, forgotten, overgrown with grass and creepers and vines. It was slowly turning back into rainforest."

Isn't it funny how, as many of us get older, we still want to be happy, but somewhere along the way we forget what truly makes us happy, and our spending shifts? We used to blow our money on extravagant adventures and genuinely memorable experiences, but we don't have the time or energy for that anymore.

So, instead, we reward ourselves for all that hard work by splurging on material consolations, on clothes, gadgets, and jewellery we don't need, have room to store or time to wear. But, hey, we think, *we've earned it so we might as well spend it.*

Whyte doesn't.

At the end of the week, he doesn't buy things to make up for the time he spent working. He can fit all his goods into three or four suitcases. Even his favourite possession is run-down.

"My laptop is old and it's crap and it gets a bit worse everyday," he will tell you. "If I try to watch a video on it, it overheats and shuts down. I give it a moment, start it up again, and make it suffer a bit more. One day, and probably soon, it'll die. I guess then I'll have to get a new one."

Instead of buying things, Whyte spends his money on experiences. At the weekends, instead of shopping, he goes to the latest pop-up event or Secret Cinema screening. In his holidays, rather than take a "fly-and-flop" holiday, he does something eventful and meaningful.

Whyte shows, in my view, that you don't have to leave your job and your home and your friends and the life you live now to live a life based on experientialist values. As such, he is a good representative of this growing tribe of people – the "hippies with calculators" – who are carrying on life as normal, still taking part in the current system, but whose values are shifting from materialism to experientialism.

The Rise of the Hippies with Calculators

In the past, people who rejected the mainstream system tended to downshift or drop out completely.

Where else could they go? Today, though, in our connected world where the barriers to starting a business are lower than ever, people no longer need to make the black or white choice of tearing along in the hamster wheel of materialism or moseying around like a hippy. Now, it is not so clear-cut. There are many more alternatives.

In the past, Deborah Richmond in Berkshire in the UK, for instance, would have quit her corporate marketing job and become a hippy. But instead, she launched a business consultancy that means more to her called BrandYoga.

And Olga Sasplugas might have just had a job as a dance therapist. But, thanks to her computer, the internet, and Skype, she chases debts, deals with distribution, runs spreadsheets – and everything else her New York-based business requires. But she does not do this from there, or even a regular office. She does it from Barcelona or Bali or India, or wherever she happens to be.

"This way of life feels so normal and fun, and it's so easy to do it," she will tell you. "I don't care about things, I don't care about possessions. Whenever it's cold outside and it's winter in the city I'm in, I just pack my bags and go and live, and work, somewhere else." (We'll hear more from Sasplugas, and taking showers in the kitchen, in a later chapter.)

Today, there are many more experientialists like Richmond, Sasplugas, Cantwell, and the Lenets. There are, for instance, the 120,000-plus professionals who have joined a London and New York-based organization called Escape the City since it launched in 2009. It works as a supportive social network and marketplace for people who are fed up with the sort of corporate life that did for Cantwell, and would prefer to, say, develop a beach lodge in Ghana, work for a children's charity in Uganda, or run the marketing for Tough Mudder.

Then there are the thousands in the social media scene in California's Silicon Valley. They, according to a four-year study by a researcher called Alice Marwick, eschew "typical status symbols like clothes and cars". Instead, as she wrote in her PhD dissertation, they spend their money on "acceptable conspicuous consumption" – activities like rock climbing, cycling, and yoga, and going to events like TED, Sundance, Coachella, South by Southwest and New York Internet Week.

It is now not only socially *acceptable*, but also socially *expected*, in some, innovator, walks of life to prefer experiences over stuff. The ideas and values these hippies with calculators hold dear are already starting to spread from experientialist innovators like these people to the hundreds of millions in the mainstream, especially, I believe, because of one of the 21st century's most important innovations: Facebook.

TEN

Facebook Changed How
We Keep up with the Joneses

If you ask them, most experientialists laugh at the idea of keeping up with the Joneses. Conspicuous consumption is something other people do, you see. It is what materialistic people do when they want to show off that they have newer, shinier, or more stuff than their neighbours. Ask Sue and Bertrand Lenet, or Marianne Cantwell, or Jim Whyte, or Cliff Hodges, or any number of experientialists, and their first response will be the same – that they do not do conspicuous consumption.

Talking to them, and hearing how little they value the traditional status markers of the 20th century, like fancy watches, cars and clothes, it is easy to understand why they would say that.

And yet one of the most counterintuitive things about experientialists in general is that, although they want nothing to do with keeping up with the Joneses, many consume more conspicuously even than the most status-conscious materialists.

I blame Facebook.

Remember how people used to tell you about their holiday in the last century? They would invite you round for dinner, and, as the After Eights were passed round, pull out their holiday snaps, and bore you for a bit. "There's Jean at the Acropolis, Jean in front of the Parthenon, Jean eating a souvlaki…"

Then, they would have other friends over, and do the same. It was hard work telling everyone about their trip, but if they got the dates booked in before they went away, it was possible. They could usually do it within a couple of months.

It is not like that anymore. Now, since so many are on social network sites – more than a billion are on Facebook, and more than a 100 million use Instagram each month – you do not have to wait till you get home to get them back.

Now, using Facebook, Instagram, Twitter, and all the other social media sites, you can bore all of your friends, including the ones who visited the Acropolis, in an instant. You can let everyone know that, right now, you are watching the sunrise over Angkor Wat or the sunset from the rooftop of your riad in Marrakech, or that you are on a chairlift in the Alps, or just that you have finished packing and cannot wait to go.

You do not, of course, have to confine your updates to holidays either. Why not share that you have just run the Sydney marathon, that you are at a Rolling Stones concert or a TEDx conference, what you think of the film you just saw or how happy you are because someone bought you flowers?

Now, where you are, how you are feeling, what you are doing, and what you have done, have suddenly become valuable social currency – just as they were before the 20th century.

Then, most people lived in small communities. Everyone knew everybody else in the village. That meant everyone would just as likely know what you did with your time as how many possessions you owned, and how expensive and how good those possessions were. They would be as aware of the days you spent drinking in the local hostelry or chasing foxes from horseback, as they would be of the horse-drawn carriage you owned.

That meant, for signalling your status to others and establishing your place in the village's social hierarchy, what you did was as important as what you owned. In those times, to signal status, the conspicuous consumption of leisure – that is, experiences – was just as good as the conspicuous consumption of goods.

It was the arrival of cities that changed all that. The mass migrations of the 20th century, from small communities where everyone knew everyone else to large metropolises where you barely knew your neighbour, meant that what you did with your time became virtually useless as a way to signify status.

In the relative anonymity of urban and, to a lesser extent, suburban life, your neighbours, friends, colleagues at work, and the people you passed on the street were much more likely to see what you owned than know what you did. They could admire the BMW you parked on your drive, the Breitling watch on your wrist, the Prada handbag on your arm, or the Louis Vuitton wallet you used to pay.

But how would they know what you did with your time? How would they be aware that, last weekend, you had been to the opera, the Ivy, or the coast?

There were exceptions to this rule, of course, like the suntan, the ideal way to turn an intangible, and therefore, for status purposes, invisible purchase into a status symbol everyone could see. Consider the statement of the panda-eyes ski tan. And why else did people waste so much of their summer holidays sweating under a burning sun, if not to show off that they had been away?

Generally, though, and suntans aside, a material possession could deliver far more status than an experiential purchase. And so, in the 20th century, the conspicuous consumption of leisure was not nearly so good as the conspicuous consumption of goods at telling others who you were.

Social media has turned this on its head. Now, only a few people, relatively, might see your car or your handbag. But with all your friends and followers on Twitter, Facebook, Pinterest and Instagram, many more will now know you are partying in Ibiza, playing golf on the roof of Selfridges, or that you have just completed a Tough Mudder course. And rather than absolute strangers, these people are more likely to be in your peer group, the people, in other words, whose opinion you are most interested in.

Social media sites have also made experiences more important than material goods, thanks to the role they play in the rarity principle. According to this idea, the bigger the difference between the number of people who know about something and the number of people who have it, the rarer and more valuable we think the thing is. Anyone, after all, can go and buy most material goods, but not everyone can be at the event you are tweeting or Instagram-ing a picture from.

This explains the social kudos, for instance, of the principal TED conference. TED's videos have been watched more than a billion times, but there is still only one grandstand event, and only 1500 or so can attend.

Of course, it is worth noting that, as well as update your followers on what you are doing, you could post pictures of your new possession. But if you did that, I think you would soon lose followers. Remember the insight from the happiness researchers: we prefer to listen to people talk about things they did – like the camping weekend they went on – than possessions – like their new sofa.

And you could argue that limited edition material goods could be as effective at leveraging the rarity principle as limited capacity events, and therefore offer similar amounts of social currency. But, once produced, even if the production run has finished, the material goods are still theoretically available. All you have to do is afford them.

But experiences, because of the nature of time, have a built-in feature that makes them even more rare. If you were not there – in Berlin when the wall came down, in Myanmar before the masses came, at Wimbledon when Murray won – you were not there.

So, whether it is because more people now know about the experiences you are having compared to the material things you own, or because, as per the rarity principle, the difference between those that know about it and those who are doing it is ever greater, there is no doubt that, thanks to social media, experiences are now more visible, more tangible and more valuable, and they are more likely than material goods to contribute to status.

This matters, because status matters. If you have high status, people laugh at your jokes more, you earn more, you get invited out to more parties. You are also more likely to live longer, feel more important and loved, and have a more attractive partner. So status matters, and it matters more now than at any previous point in history, because of some of the other hallmarks, besides urbanization, of our modern society: in particular, meritocracy, social mobility, and the Snakes and Ladders game of status that comes with it.

In the old, materialistic consumerist system, where people played the game through the regular purchase and ritual display of their possessions, they tried to keep up with what the Joneses had, and they worried that they might not have as many and as nice possessions as they did.

Now, the game's rules have been given a 21st-century, digital twist. Now, thanks to social media, we want to keep up with what the Joneses are doing. Are we going to enough pop-ups, conferences, and concerts – like all our friends and acquaintances seem to be?

This concern has already become so widespread social commentators have given it a new name: fear of missing out, better known by its acronym, FOMO. Now, at the beginning of this experiential era, four in every ten aged 18–34 in the USA and UK say they sometimes worry that they are missing out. Facebook, you might say, is giving us a new way to keep up with the Joneses, and a new way to worry we might not be keeping up with them.

Is Experientialism the Answer to Stuffocation?

As well as giving us FOMO, social media sites are also supporting the diffusion of experientialism, because they are making it much easier for other people to notice it. If you consider, in fact, how often people check their social media feeds and post status updates, you could say the practice of experientialism has become hyper-observable. After all, people spend more time on social media than any other activity online and, of course, increasingly do that from the smartphones they carry with them.

The fact that this new lifestyle is so observable is important because, as you may recall, it is one of the five considerations the forecaster would ask of any new idea, to decide whether it is likely to pass from the innovators to the early adopters, and on to the majority.

How does experientialism hold up under interrogation by the four other key questions? Is it, in other words, the sort of innovation that is likely to catch on? It is. To begin with, it is simple to understand. It is also easy to try. And it is compatible with how we live now. After all, we already go to concerts, conferences, dinners, parties, events. There is just a shift of attention: less having, more doing.

So you could try experientialism this month, simply by spending the normal amount you would spend, but making sure you did not end up having anything new at the end of it – except for the memories and stories from the things you did. That would, I am sure, convince you of the final point, that experientialism is better than materialism – for status, happiness, identity, and, as we have seen, many more reasons besides. It is, I believe, the sort of innovation that is likely to spread.

If you also consider the problems causing *Stuffocation*, you can see still more reasons why experientialism is better, and why it is likely to appeal not just to a few pioneering hippies with calculators, but to the majority of those in the rich, currently materialistic world. Since, in a world underpinned by experientialism, status and happiness and meaning are no longer based on material goods, it is likely to cause far fewer environmental problems.

Many experiences, to be sure, require material goods and do create a footprint. Consider the carbon footprint of an experiential purchase like a holiday to Borneo, for instance. But since experiences are, by definition, less predicated on material possessions they are likely, overall, to cause less damage to the environment.

Since in an experientialist system we are less likely to accumulate possessions, we are likely to have fewer things, less clutter and less of the stress that comes with all that stuff.

Experientialism should be better able to cope with the growing population and the rise of the global middle class: since we are less interested in things, resource cost will be less problematic. Since accommodation tends to be smaller and more expensive in cities, so there is room for less stuff, experientialism will make far more sense there.

Experientialism could even restore some belief in the system. Since experiences are harder to compare, for instance, fewer people will be aggravated that some have more, in material terms at least, than others.

Experientialism, then, clearly has a lot going for it. But if I am to claim, and you are to believe, that experientialism will replace materialism and solve the problem of *Stuffocation*, there would have to be some indications that materialism is waning and experientialism is spreading. Is there any evidence that this is happening? There is, and lots of it, if you know where and how to look.

In a perfect world, we would have clean, clear information and know what all people are thinking and doing. In that world, spotting trends and forecasting the future would be simple – and I would not have a job.

In the real world, though, trend forecasters like me have to make do with noisy, imperfect information. Some trends, like colour blocking or animal prints, are easy to spot, especially if they are seasonal and if you wait until they have come out into the open, when they are in the mainstream press and everyone is wearing them.

But if the trend you are tracking is a cultural change – like a shift in the values that underpin the world we live in – and you are trying to authenticate its existence at an early stage of its development, that will be far harder to detect and describe. At those early stages, cultural trends rarely appear clearly, with many examples and evenly distributed proof.

Instead, we have to identify the trend through the shadows it casts and the footprints it makes.

Fortunately, experientialism has been casting plenty of shadows, and is making what I think are unmistakable footprints.

There is the clear trail, for a start, in the work of the political scientist who I mentioned in the introduction, Ron Inglehart. His research shows that we have been becoming less materialistic for more than forty years. And think, for a moment, about the changing make-up of our economy.

"If you look at items on those first national income accounts in 1934," the late economist Robert Fogel told me. "Eighty per cent of the things on it, like food, clothing, and shelter – you could touch them. They were material. Now, though, those things make up less than a third. We have a lot more money to spend on other things. Today, most of what is entered into the national income is immaterial. You can't touch it."

There is a long-term shift in our economy, in other words, away from material goods.

There is now new evidence that not only is the relative importance of material goods in our national income accounts falling, but the absolute level of material goods is falling too. We have reached, as the man who discovered this, ex-McKinsey consultant and environmental analyst Chris Goodall, says, "peak stuff".

Goodall's detailed analysis shows that Britain has been consuming less water, concrete, paper, cars, and clothes since 2003 at least. And he has also seen signs that other countries, including France, Sweden and the

United States, are consuming less as well. Remember that most of this reduction in material use happened during a time when our economies were rising. We were spending more, in other words, but not on goods that were material.

We may have reached the apex of our (over) consumption on clothes as well. After decades of going up, perhaps we have reached "peak clothes". In 2007, the average American bought almost twice as many items of clothing each year compared to 1991. But by 2012, the number they were buying had stopped rising, and had even fallen slightly, from 67 to 64 items.

I have found more evidence throughout our society and economy – in surveys I conducted that show people in the UK and Ireland prefer experiences to material goods, in the demise of the hardback and the rise of e-books, in the plummeting sales of recorded music and the boom in live music and festivals, in the fact that people in their sixties spend more on holidays than any other age group, in the emergence of extreme sports and challenges like Tough Mudder, in the doubling in the number of people working part-time in recent years, and in the expanding healthcare market.

"In 1929, we spent 3% of GDP on health," Fogel told me. "Today we spend 16%. Forecasts suggest that by 2040 we could be spending 30%."

There are also indications of the rise of experientialism in the luxury market. In 2011, luxury consumers – who, with their high economic status, tend to be ones who try things first and who the rest of society emulates – spent more, for the first time, on experiential luxury goods, such as holidays, than any other sector, according to research from a company called the Boston Consulting Group. The trend for what the company calls "experiential luxury" has continued.

"In an era of over-consumption, people are realizing that there is more than just buying products," Jean-Marc Bellaiche, a senior partner at the Boston Consulting Group, said in a newspaper interview. "Buying experiences provides more pleasure and satisfaction."

There are other signs of the shift in what the next generation of consumers, people in their twenties today who marketers call "Millennials", are doing, and in what they are not doing. They are no longer buying cars like their parents did, and they are choosing to live in small, city-centre apartments – which, by the nature of their size and location, offer less room for stuff and more possibilities for experience – since one thing cities do is offer a far greater variety of experiences than the countryside.

Rather than owning a thing – whether that's a piece of music, a movie, or a car – Millennials prefer access, through services like Zipcar, Spotify, and Netflix. Rather than show off through physical goods, like previous generations used to, they are expressing their identities and getting status through experiences they can share through social media.

And as we've seen, they are not the only ones: there are 140 million people sharing their experiences on Twitter and one billion posting theirs on Facebook.

There are, as you can see, and even if they are unevenly distributed, a lot of signposts that suggest the practice and values of experientialism are spreading. Before we conclude, though, that experientialism will be the answer to *Stuffocation*, we should also bear in mind that the last time the underlying value system of our world changed, the ones who chose the path we would all follow were those who held power: the captains of consciousness in government and big business.

While there has been a shift, in terms of the structure of power, from the pyramid to the pancake, the government and big business are still exceptionally powerful. Before we can be sure which way the world will turn, we should know what they think about experientialism.

ELEVEN

Are You Experienced?
Your Government Wants to Know

On stage at the Monterey International Pop Music Festival, in July 1967, in a yellow frilly shirt, a black waistcoat and red trousers, Jimi Hendrix set light to his guitar, held it aloft, smashed it down, threw the burnt leftovers into the crowd – and announced his arrival in America. His songs topped the charts all around the world. Everyone, it seemed, was going wild for him – except for those in power. When he asked "are you experienced?", governments everywhere shuddered at the thought.

Governments did not care, then, about whether their citizens were "experienced", and they did not care how their experience of life was. What they cared about was whether they were working and shopping or not. They wanted them to do what governments had always, in peacetime and since the materialist era began, at any rate, wanted their citizens to do: be good workers and work hard, and be good consumers and buy lots of things.

After the terrorist attacks of 9/11, for example, the leaders of the free world encouraged their citizens to keep calm and shop. "This great nation will never be intimidated," George W Bush declared. "People are going about their daily lives, working and shopping and playing, worshipping at churches and synagogues and mosques, going to movies and to baseball games." And Tony Blair told the British people "they should go about their daily lives: to work, to live, to travel and to shop".

There is a good reason why they did this. It is that the key way governments and the countries they run are judged is the size and, hopefully, rise of the economy and the number that measures it, gross domestic product, better known to most of us as GDP.

Counting, the Economists' Way

As the problems of overproduction ran into other headwinds in the 1920s, the US economy collapsed in the crash of 1929. Farmers lost their farms. Workers lost their jobs. Families lost their homes. The homeless wandered the country in search of work. When they found some, they settled in shanty-towns made out of scraps of wood and cardboard. When they had no money to eat, they stood in breadlines and outside soup kitchens. By 1932, 25% of the working population was unemployed.

The economies of other countries crashed too, devastating the lives of millions more. Unemployment soared to 25% in the UK, for instance, and to 30% in Australia.

Politicians and their advisors around the world scrambled for solutions. How could they fix their economies and get people working again? Some, as we know, thought the government should introduce "death dates", to force people to throw out the old and buy in the new, to re-start the virtuous circle of materialism. Others thought the best idea was for the government to step in and start spending.

But, if the government was to do this, where should it spend its effort and money? And how much was needed in each case? Till that time, there were statistics from individual businesses. There were indications from particular industries. And everyone could see the shanty-towns and the people queuing for food.

But there was no way of getting a clear, overall perspective of what was up, what was down, and by how much. It was like asking a general to deploy his troops without knowing the lay of the land or where the enemy was, or where reinforcements were needed, and how many. How could any leader make plans when he could not see the whole picture?

So the US senate commissioned a private enterprise called the National Bureau of Economic Research (NBER), which had been collecting records for some time, to create a set of national income accounts. The lead researcher on the project was a man by the name of Simon Kuznets.

Born in Pinsk in what was then Russia in 1901, Kuznets had briefly served as a statistician in Odessa in the Ukraine. He had arrived in the US in 1922. He had distinguished himself, so far, only at Columbia University. He was about to create his magnum opus.

It is hard for us to imagine economics as anything other than what it is today – a central consideration of our lives. But as recently as the late 19th century, economics was considered of such little importance that at Oxford University, for example, there was only one part-time lecturer, and at American universities it was merely one section of one segment of an entire course – moral philosophy, which was then only taught by ordained ministers. One standard economics textbook of that time, which was written by one Reverend Francis Wayland, proclaimed that its aim was "to set forth God's law regarding the production and distribution of those products that constitute the material wealth of the nation".

By the beginning of the 20th century, though, times and economics were changing. Some more empirically minded economists had begun collecting information on the agricultural, manufacturing and transportation sectors of the economy, as well data about how much industrial workers were earning. It was their foundations that Kuznets built on.

Kuznets had, as the final report noted, a team of four: Miss Lillian Epstein and Miss Elizabeth Jenks of the NBER, and Messrs Robert F Martin and Robert R Nathan of the US Department of Commerce.

Imagine the task before the five of them, in the days before computers, email and Google, in a country of 124 million people. They gathered information about wages and tips, salaries and commissions. They found out how much bituminous and anthracite coal had been mined, and the value of the "quarrying" and "non-metallic" that had been produced. They aggregated the amounts spent on water transportation, street railways, amusement and recreation, as well as the value of professional service, personal service, domestic service, business service and, I suppose so they didn't miss anything, "miscellaneous" service.

They spent three years working on their first report. Published in 1934 as *National Income, 1929–32*, the report was, as you can imagine, neither light reading nor very upbeat. It listed the means of measuring the economy and explained that, for many of its calculations, the information was scanty, imprecise and subject to a wide margin of error. "The national income total is thus an amalgam," the report concludes, "of relatively accurate and only approximate estimates rather than a unique, highly precise measurement."

Still, despite its flaws, the publication of Kuznets's report was a watershed moment. Its methodology, as the economist Robert Fogel observed, raised economics from a speculative and ideologically-riven discipline into an empirically based social science.

The government could now make, for the first time, a reliable estimate of the size and rise – or fall – of the economy, and of its constituent parts. That meant the government now knew which sectors of the economy were working and which were not, and by how much. It could now act like a clear-sighted general, one who could see where his army was doing okay, where it needed reinforcement, and how many troops to send. If demand was particularly low in one area, for instance, the government could help stimulate that demand.

The national income accounts proved indispensable throughout the 1930s as the government sought to solve the problems of the Great Depression, and again in the 1940s when economics and economists proved vital to the war effort.

Through information gleaned from the income accounts, economists assessed the country's capacity to produce the military goods that were essential in arming the US and its allies. They also designed the financial instruments that paid for them, and they planned the air force's bomb strikes on Germany, in order to cause the most damage to the Nazi war effort. Their input proved so valuable that the economist Paul Samuelson would later claim that World War II had been "the economists' war".

That may have been overstating the case, but by the time peace returned, the discipline of economics, and its practitioners, had arrived. In 1946, Congress established the Council of Economic Advisers to the President, cementing the role of economics at the heart of government. And by the late 1950s, with backing from the International Monetary Fund, Kuznets's method was adopted by all countries.

Since then, national income accounting – which includes GDP in its reports – has become the principal method by which a country measures its economic performance. The logic for that is simple. But also in the years since then, national income has become the de facto way that politicians measure a country's general progress. The logic for that is not nearly so simple.

What Have the Economists Ever Done for Us?

It is Palestine, sometime in the early part of the first century AD. The Roman empire stretches from Hispania in the west to Judea in the east. Or rather, strictly speaking, it is Tunisia, 1978, and we are on the set of Monty Python's Life of Brian, in a dusty room with ragged curtains.

Sitting at a table, addressing a handful of followers who sit cross-legged on the floor, are the three angry leaders of the People's Front of Judea, the PFJ – not the Judean People's Front (JPF), mind you, or the Popular Front (PF), or even the Judean Popular People's Front (JPPF). That lot are all splitters. No, these men are the People's Front of Judea, and they are pretty worked up about the Romans.

"They've bled us white, the bastards," says one of the PFJ's commanders, Reg, played by John Cleese.

"They've taken everything we had, and not just from us, from our fathers, and from our fathers' fathers."

"And from our fathers' fathers' fathers," Stan – another terrorist chief, Eric Idle – chimes in.

"Yeah," agrees Reg.

"And from our fathers' fathers' fathers' fathers," says Stan, getting into this now.

"Yeah. All right, Stan. Don't labour the point," Reg answers. "And what have they ever given us in return?!"

"Sanitation?" one of the recruits pipes up.

"Roads?" says another.

"Irrigation."

"Medicine."

"Education."

"Wine."

"Public baths."

"Yeah. Yeah, that's something we'd really miss, Reg, if the Romans left," says the third PFJ leader, Francis, played by Michael Palin.

"And it's safe to walk in the streets at night now, Reg," adds Stan.

"Yeah, they certainly know how to keep order," says Francis. "Let's face it. They're the only ones who could in a place like this."

Reg grudgingly admits all these, and he tries one last time.

"All right," he says, "but apart from the sanitation, the medicine, education, wine, public order, irrigation, roads, a fresh water system, and public health, what have the Romans ever done for us?"

"Brought peace," one of the recruits says.

Reg, exasperated, gives up.

Given everything the captains of consciousness – the industrialists, economists, and politicians – have done for us, sometimes the people who complain about the system can seem a little like Reg, the leader of the Judean People's Front – sorry, People's Front of Judea. They are so focused, in other words, on what is wrong, they forget about what is right.

Now, though, in an era when we have more than enough and are feeling *Stuffocation*, the rest of us are also losing patience with the captains of consciousness, especially with the economists and their way of measuring progress – GDP.

The Limits to GDP

National income accounting was never perfect. Of all the figures in Kuznets's report, two, in particular, stand out. Between 1929 and 1932, the economy, as calculated by the amount of income paid out, had contracted by 40%. When calculated by income produced, it had shrunk by 53%.

Consider those numbers for a moment. In 1929, income paid out and income produced were roughly the same. Yet, just three years later, they were worlds apart. In that time, income produced had fallen by 13 percentage points more than income paid out. That is a disparity of 33%. Where had all the money gone? In the report, Kuznets tried to make sense of that missing 33%. He made some good suggestions. But even then, as he admitted, he could not be sure. Think about that. Imagine if your expenses, the profit and loss report for the division you run, or the accounts for your entire business not only featured a small discrepancy you could not fully explain, but one that was a whopping 33%. What would your boss or your accountant or your shareholders say?

Still, those numbers were better than anything the US government had had before, and they were useful in pinpointing problem areas. Even if, in other words, they did not give the general a perfectly clear view of the land and his army and the enemy, at least they raised the fog of war enough that he could do something useful. Besides, Kuznets spent the next thirty years improving the national income accounts. They became better and more useful every year.

Beyond any counting concerns, though, there are other, more serious accusations made against GDP. The principal charge is not that it is inaccurate. It is that it has outgrown its role. The unintended consequence, it turns out, of creating a useful way of calculating economic progress is that, in the absence of any other agreed measure, it has become the definitive way to benchmark the progress of society. Why?

The simple answer is that, to begin with at least, it did tell us how well our societies were doing. By focusing on GDP, the economists solved the huge, debilitating problems of scarcity that had plagued humans since people first settled down into complex societies. So in terms of solving the problem of scarcity – which also happens to be the stated goal of the discipline of economics – a rise in GDP, and especially GDP per capita, did mean progress.

Moreover, increases in GDP per capita do improve wellbeing, up to a certain level. So, up to that point, a rise in GDP per capita does measure progress, but after it – which research suggests is around $75,000 or £50,000 in today's money – the returns are vastly diminished, if they exist at all.

Many, like Richard Easterlin, for instance, or Australia's foremost wellbeing champion, Bob Cummins, believe that level was reached years ago.

"Mature markets," says Cummins, "arrived some decades ago at the point at which there was no further benefit in increasing material wealth, as far as the majority of citizens are concerned at any rate. Increasing wealth has done nothing to make people happier in America, Australia, and the UK."

There are two other reasons why GDP has become the benchmark for progress. It is relatively easy to count and it is simple. To understand why these are so compelling, consider two insights from social science called substitution and the drunkard's search.

The drunkard's search, which some now call the streetlight bias, was first described by another

American by way of Odessa in the Ukraine, the philosopher Abraham Kaplan.

In his 1964 book *The Conduct of Enquiry*, Kaplan told the tale of a drunkard searching under a street lamp for his house key, which he had dropped somewhere else. Asked why he was looking there and not where he had dropped it, he replied "It's lighter here!" Is measuring GDP like the drunkard looking for his keys? Does it really measure, in other words, what matters to us? Or are we just looking where it's lighter?

Substitution is the sort of mental short cut – psychologists call them heuristics – that people use to avoid the time-consuming hard work of making complex decisions. Instead of answering a difficult question by the long, rational route, instead, we look for a simpler version of the original question.

Perhaps this is what we are doing at a societal level, swapping an easier question for a demanding one. Instead of answering a tricky question like "Are we making progress?", we prefer to answer a simpler substitute: "Is GDP going up?"

The simplicity of GDP makes it a very attractive measure for progress. It is, after all, only a number, one that tells us three essential facts about the economy. How big is it? Is it getting bigger or smaller? Is ours bigger than yours?

The simplicity of GDP is its power, and also its Achilles heel, as a measure of general progress at any rate. It counts goods and income, but it has no opinion of them. It counts quantity of stuff, even when all that stuff does is pollute the air and blot the landscape, or helps us keep up with the Joneses but does nothing for our wellbeing. But GDP does not measure quality of life. It has nothing to say about better health, living longer, or sledging on a school day.

Remember those days when you'd wake up and the snow was so thick the roads were blocked, the trains would not run and the weatherman said stay at home? You'd put on some warm clothes and get hold of a sledge – ideally your kit would include ski gloves and one of those wooden sledges Austrians use, but you would have just as much fun wearing woolly gloves with yellow Marigolds to keep them dry, and a sledge made of red plastic. Then, wrapped up warm, you would go sledging for a stolen day of magic.

Then the next day the paper would scream that the cost to the economy was billions. *The economy?* you'd think. *Who cares about the economy? We were sledging.*

When the problem we faced was scarcity, GDP made sense as a measure of progress. Today, though, expecting GDP to reflect the health and direction of society is like looking at your reflection in one of those wobbly fairground mirrors to work out if you look good. GDP, in other words, has a distorted view of progress. How could it not, when it counts business and busyness, but has nothing good to say about sledging?

Economists, ecologists, psychologists, and others have been trying to right the wrongs of GDP, and work out more appropriate measures of progress, since the 1960s. They have come up with many alternatives. There is the Environmental Sustainability Index (ESI), the Environmental Performance Index (EPI) and the Genuine Progress Indicator (GPI). There is the Index of Economic Wellbeing (IEW), the Measure of Economic Welfare (MEW) and the Sustainable Measure of Economic Welfare (SMEW). There is even an Index of Sustainable Economic Welfare (ISEW).

Each of these has its merits. Each has fuelled the debate. But there is something about them that sounds, to me at least, a little like the People's Front of Judea (PFJ), the People's Front (PF), the Judean People's Front (JPF), and the Judean Popular People's Front (JPPF).

Meanwhile, GDP and the materialistic system it measures and promotes, like the Roman empire, has marched on unchallenged – until now.

Nicolas Sarkozy Has a Problem

Towards the end of 2007, less than a year into his presidency, Nicolas Sarkozy had a problem – the financial crash, which, as it ran into other headwinds, like overconsumption, stagnating wages, inequality, and rising resources costs, was fast becoming the Great Recession. The fall in GDP was hardly his fault.

The whole world was feeling the effects of the meltdown. But that did not matter to the people who had put him in the Élysée Palace, the French voters, who would also decide if he would remain there after the next election. And they were rapidly falling out of love with him. His popularity rating was nose-diving – from a high of 65% approval just after the election in July 2007 to only 41% in February 2008, and his party was floored in local elections the following month.

This was the issue vexing him as he stalked the vast halls of the Élysée Palace: how could he regain his people's support? The problem was not only GDP, he decided. It was, as he would later write, that "our world, our society and our economy have changed, and the measures have not kept pace".

The French people, he thought, would not only judge him on GDP and standards of living, but on how good, happy and satisfied they felt with life. They were not only bothered, in other words, about quantity of stuff, they were interested in quality of life.

So Sarkozy decided to construct a measure of progress that would do a better, more accurate job than GDP – and be acceptable to the wider community. He gathered a team of public intellectuals, like the behavioural psychologist Daniel Kahneman, and economists like Jean-Paul Fitoussi and Joseph Stiglitz. They produced a report and a book of their findings, *Mismeasuring Our Lives: Why GDP Doesn't Add Up*. And Sarkozy implemented the ideas almost immediately.

In 2010, France became the first leading nation to measure not only the size and rise of its economy, but the wellbeing of its people. It became the first major country, if you like, to not only be concerned with the material wellbeing of its people, but to also ask what their experience of life was like. Its government asked a version of the question Hendrix had asked all those years before. Were the people of France happy with their experience of life?

The next year, 2011, the UK government started asking its citizens about their experience of life too. Other countries are now following suit: Germany, Australia, Canada, and the USA are now all working out better ways to measure wellbeing and track progress.

Like the national income accounts when they were first introduced, the wellbeing measures are not perfect – nor are they universally accepted. Some question whether it is possible to measure happiness at all. Others say it is simple. "You just ask people," says Bob Cummins. He thinks you can determine someone's mood happiness with just seven or eight questions. (Try them on page 236 and 237.)

Some worry about substitution. So when the government asks "How happy are you with your life nowadays?", most of us are likely to substitute that hard question with an easier question, some version of "What is my mood right now?"

Others worry that there is a difference between the person who answers those questions, the "remembering self", and the person actually doing the living. (Does this explain why the Lenets treasure the memory of the 48-hour bus trip across Bolivia even though it was deeply unpleasant at the time?)

How will we solve these disagreements to find a methodology for measuring wellbeing that is acceptable to everyone? And how will we agree on a system for measuring progress? Because at present there are as many methods as there are countries.

The new, official system in Canada, the government's Indicators of Well-being in Canada (IWC), contains ten domains, like work and family life, and more than sixty indicators, like weekly earnings, marriage, divorce and age of mother at childbirth. The citizen-backed Canadian Index of Wellbeing (CIW) is based on fewer domains – eight – including the quality of the communities people live in and what people do with their time, but a similar number of indicators. Australia's system, called Measuring Australia's Progress (MAP) contains even more indicators – 80.

Not to be outdone, the United States' new way to measure progress looks like it will contain as many as 300 different indicators.

If these sound like another set of Judean terrorist groups, that is because, at this point, they are. They are all a bunch of splitters – because not only do they not agree with each other, they have all bypassed the other, internationally sanctioned challengers of GDP as measures of progress, like the Organisation for Economic Co-operation and Development (OECD)'s Better Life Index, based on eleven topics, the UN's Human Development Index (HDI), featuring three dimensions and four indicators, and the granddaddy of all wellbeing measures: Bhutan's Gross National Happiness (GNH), which was coined by Bhutan's Dragon King in 1972 and is based on four "pillars".

It is all, as you can see, a very long way from the simplicity of GDP's headline figure, a simple number that tells us if things are good, bad, up, down, and better, or not, than our neighbours. And we are still a long way from finding a dominant method for measuring society's progress, as GDP does for economic progress.

It is easy to poke fun at the current state of the debate on measuring progress. But at least it is a step in the right direction. There is already broad agreement, for instance, about the essential elements of progress, like wellbeing, the environment, and quality of life factors like how safe people feel.

More importantly, it is not only the captains of consciousness in the government who will debate and decide this time: the US and Australian governments, for instance, are asking their citizens for input.

"This is the beginning of the debate, not the end of it," says Chris Hoenig, who is CEO of the US government's attempt to find a new measure of progress, State of the United States of America (SUSA). "We want to find out: are we creating a world full of the sort of experiences we want in our lives? Are we progressing? The answer isn't only about wellbeing. It's also about the environment, safety, biodiversity. It's about structural inequality, the kind of cities we want to live in, and how we want to live. Till now, that has been the debate of the elite. But now, with our system, everyone can get involved and have their say."

Besides, it may be easy to laugh, but this is how the economic measures began. It was not when Kuznets created national income accounting, that amalgam of relatively accurate and only approximate estimates, that there was a single method of measuring material progress. That did not happen until the late 1950s, a quarter of a century later, when it was accepted by all members of the International Monetary Fund.

Today, we are a long way from solving all the disagreements. And that is perfectly okay. You could argue that what economists and psychologists are doing today for the measurement of wellbeing and progress is exactly the same as what Kuznets and his team did for economics in the 1930s – transforming them from speculative and ideologically-riven disciplines into empirically based social sciences.

Given this shift from material to experiential progress, psychologists are also likely, at some point in the near future, to become as important in government as economists are today. Barry Schwartz recently proposed a psychological parallel to the Council of Economic Advisers that was created in 1946: a "Council of Psychological Advisers for the US President".

Does all this mean that, just as Kuznets's paper in 1934 led to the acceptance of a global benchmark for material progress, that we will have a new internationally agreed standard for measuring wellbeing and experiential progress in the same time frame? That we will have one a quarter of a century from now, that is, by 2038? I believe we will.

This will be an important breakthrough, but even as things stand at present, even if there is yet not one agreed measure, and even though the measures are not perfect, governments can use the new measures today to improve the progress of society – just as Kuznets's measure, despite the fact its headline figures were out by 33%, raised the fog and helped governments work out where to apply their efforts.

They can use happiness surveys, for instance, to raise the general level of wellbeing. Bob Cummins offers some useful examples.

"When we do national surveys we can identify groups of people who have lower levels of mood happiness than they should have," he says. "They might lack important resources of some kind. That could be financial. That might be to do with relationships. It might be safety. Once we identify the group, we can do something to help.

"For example, there's an informal crisis of people looking after disabled family members. They have some of the lowest levels of mood happiness in Australia. But knowing this means we could provide them with more resources and get them functioning normally. Another example is middle-aged men living alone. They have perfectly adequate salaries but many of them are pretty bad at forming non-sexual supportive relationships."

This, then, is why measures of wellbeing matter. Just as the introduction of the national income accounts enabled the government to do a better job of caring for its citizens in a time of scarcity, so these measures are helping today's governments do a better job of caring for its citizens in a time of abundance. Armed with information from the wellbeing surveys, governments can help their people avoid unhappiness, and increase the general level of wellbeing in society. That, to me, and to a great many people today, sounds a lot closer to human progress than working to increase GDP.

So Sarkozy was right. People today, in rich, developed countries at least, are far less bothered about standards of living and the quantity of things. Now they have them, they take them for granted. Now, they are far more interested in quality of life and the experiences we have.

Just as the creation of the national income accounts in 1934 reflected, signalled and encouraged the age of materialism, so these new wellbeing measures are doing the same for this new era of experientialism. As we know from the law of unintended consequences, it does not matter whether the people in charge realize it or not: by measuring experiential progress they are not only reflecting the emergence of experientialism, they are encouraging it – because, as Joseph Stiglitz says, "what we measure affects what we do".

ARE YOU HAPPY?

Answer each of the following questions on a scale of one to ten, where one is not satisfied at all, and ten is completely satisfied.

1. How satisfied are you with your standard of living?

2. How satisfied are you with your health?

3. How satisfied are you with what you are currently achieving in life?

4. How satisfied are you with your personal relationships?

5. How satisfied are you with how safe you feel?

6. How satisfied are you with feeling part of your community?

7. How satisfied are you with your future security?

If you are spiritual, you can also answer the next question:

8. How satisfied are you with your spirituality or religion?

Add the scores and divide by seven (or eight) to estimate your happiness.

This scale, called the Personal Wellbeing Index, is primarily for you to find out how happy you feel about different parts of your life, not for you to compare yourself with other people – as, in terms of rating feelings, one person's seven is another person's nine.

Anywhere between six and nine is considered healthy. However, if you score five or less, you are probably not very happy at present, and should do something about it.

If you want to compare yourself with others, take the tests at BeyondThePurchase.org, from the director of the Personality & Well-being Lab at San Francisco State University, Ryan Howell.

TWELVE

Scenes from the Experience Economy

At the end of a long, dark corridor, in a warehouse somewhere in central London, a few years ago, I found myself, like Alice when she first arrived in Wonderland, rubbing my eyes with surprise. I was in a square room, a bit smaller than a squash court, with wood-panelled walls.

On each of the wood-panelled walls were deep recesses. In each of the recesses were the sort of collectibles you would see in the country home of a gentleman traveller: carved statues, tusks, the skulls of hunted animals.

On my right was a floor-length, blood red, gold-braided velvet curtain. In one recess, that was almost as high as a human, on the far side of the room, a small painted man was doing a slow motion ballet dance or, perhaps, some version of Tai Chi.

As I stood watching him, I felt a hand on my arm.

The hand hauls me sideways, pulls back the red curtain, moves me out of the square room and into a cubby hole that looks like a gypsy caravan. There is a wooden writing desk, covered with knick-knacks from a life on the road in a horse-drawn wagon. Sitting at the desk, gazing up at me with plaintive, intense, green eyes, and a bandana holding her dark hair back, is a woman in her early twenties. She tells me about the wasp.

The wasp, she says, it had a good life. It had been happy. It had travelled far. Oh, how she had loved that wasp!

She seemed to be saying this, at any rate. I was struggling to keep up, to be honest. I was frantically trying to take it all in, to work out what was going on, and keep up with her tale, but it was all a bit too much and my head was spinning. It sounds odd now but it felt like I was listening to her from the bottom of the sea.

As she went on, telling me more about this wasp she had loved – too much, I think she said – she stretched her bare arm out, setting it free from her shawls and silks, and in her hand was a small, mottled egg, or half of it anyway. It was cracked. It had a jagged edge.

"Look!" she said. "Take it."

Mesmerized, I took it. I held it. Inside, in some kind of frozen gel – glue, I suppose – like a mini, insect-equivalent of a Damien Hirst cow in formaldehyde, was a dead wasp.

Then I think she must have stopped talking, because it was at that moment that I turned back to look at her and she was still staring straight at me, but now she had thrown open the rest of her shawls and silks, and I think she must have had a bra on but what I really remember, more than anything, was her big, swollen belly, and thinking, "Oh, she's pregnant."

Then, I felt a hand on my arm again, and I was pulled out of the cubby-hole caravan, and I was back in the other room. By the time I had blinked and turned to look, the curtain was already still.

The Pilot and the Pig's Ear

Not long after the encounter with the gypsy, I met a man who looked like a pilot who told me something very odd indeed. It happened in a room that had no windows, and felt like the sort of place they sacrificed people.

The floor of that windowless room is a mosaic of black and white marble squares. The ceiling is painted cyan, and criss-crossed with gold stars. In the middle, overseeing all proceedings, is a light in the shape of a five-pointed star. Golden metal rays reach out towards all the corners of the room, by way of other lights that hang from the ceiling and look like the scales of justice.

The walls are various hues of marble. Their backgrounds are white, cream, pink. Their veins are grey, black, red. Dark wood benches line two sides of the room. At one end is a throne. This, by the way, is not a movie set. It is an old masonic temple, lost for decades, rediscovered a decade or so back.

I'm sitting in the centre of this room, at a heavy, antique, mahogany table. On my left is an actress with long, wavy hair like Jessica Rabbit's. She is best known for her role in a tasteful porn movie. On my right is a man with a pencil-thin, 1940s Spitfire pilot moustache. He is, he says, Commander of Special Operations.

Dinner is served.

The first course is pig's ears soup. I sloop around in the bowl. Yes, there, and not quite swimming, is, as advertised, a pig's ear. I had been warned. As I descended the steps on the way in, a young man called Sam Bompas, the impresario of this event, held my arm for a moment.

"Gird your loins," he stage-whispered. "The first two courses are rather savage."

The menu continues to raise the hackles on the back of my and most of the other diners' necks – though the Commander of Special Operations, I notice, seems quite calm. After the pig's ears soup, we have veal, snails and blood marrow pudding. I would have said we were eating dinner but, truth be told, it is hard to focus on the food.

On a makeshift screen, opposite the throne, they are showing a surreal movie from 1973. It was made by a man who took LSD to prepare for the filming, and had the actors take magic mushrooms for some scenes. It is called *Holy Mountain* and the makeshift screen is so big, and the scenes so compelling, it is impossible to avoid. A limbless dwarf and a gang of children attack a man who looks like Jesus. A woman says she makes mystical weapons for Buddhists, Jews and Christians. After faeces are cooked, the stern narrator says: "You are excrement. You can change yourself into gold."

It is a little after that scene, I think, that the Commander of Special Operations leans in to tell me something. "I have seen this movie many times," he says. "I like to make love as I watch it."

"Everyone is an autobiographer nowadays"

Do these sound like nightmares to you? The opening to surreal David Lynch movies, perhaps? They are, in fact, neither. They are scenes from the experience economy. They are real-world examples of the sort of experiential marketing event that hints at a future where experientialism has eclipsed materialism, but whose aim, at present, is to sell stuff.

The first, where I met the gypsy who told me about the wasp, was created for the luxury brand Louis Vuitton by a theatre company called Punchdrunk. At a Punchdrunk play, instead of sitting down in seats and watching actors perform a play on the stage, members of the audience wander corridors, go upstairs, downstairs, are pulled into random rooms, never quite sure what is happening or where they should be going.

As you do, you come across what seem like impromptu, slightly surreal mini-plays. Actors whisper and shout, wander in and push through, argue and fight, tell stories and kiss and caress, each other and even, sometimes, you. There is an overarching story, but it is less linear than a formal, regular play.

To understand what that is like compared to a normal play, think of the difference between seeing a concert and going to a festival – except this festival would be one where the bands did not play on the stage but among the crowd, and where you would never be sure if the person next to you was, like you, a punter, or in on the act. Part of the magic of a Punchdrunk play is that every member of the audience goes to different places, sees different things and has a different experience. Everyone has different stories to tell at the end of the night.

Since its first event in 2000, Punchdrunk has won awards on both sides of the Atlantic. The company has also, now and then, created events for brands. It has launched a Playstation game, a premium beer, and, like the night I met the gypsy, a new store. That night, Louis Vuitton was opening on London's New Bond Street. They staged this event for their biggest spenders, for A-listers like Jerry Hall and Gwyneth Paltrow, and for journalists like me.

The question is: why?

If Louis Vuitton wanted to let people know about its new shop and entice people to visit and buy from them there, why not just let people know about it by having a launch party at the store, telling the press about it and advertising in luxury magazines?

The second scene, with the pig's ears and the pilot, was a far simpler, smaller event. There were no actors pretending to be somebody else. There were no gypsies. There was no arguing, no fighting, and, sadly, no caressing. It was, in many ways, just a regular night of drinks, dinner, and movie. It was, clearly, very different and far more memorable than an ordinary evening's entertainment, though. It was what people today call an "experiential dinner".

Created by a company called Bompas & Parr, it was supported by a hotel chain called Andaz, and a gin brand called Hendricks. The question, again, is: why? Why do these brands bother to stage an experiential event at all when they could be simply advertising the way brands used to?

Perhaps Sam Bompas, the man who warned me about the savagery of the courses on my way in, and his partner Harry Parr might have some ideas.

Going to see them in their office, on the south side of the Thames, near Borough Market, in London, is a little like going down a rabbit hole and arriving in a real-world Wonderland. You go down a narrow lane, turn right into a car park, and there, round the back, inside a boxy, unremarkable, two-storey building, is their bat cave of half-baked ideas-in-progress.

The main room is dominated by a colossal, green, friendly dinosaur's head. It pokes through one wall like a hunting trophy. Its nostrils are flared. There is a small horn on its nose. Its lips are pursed, as if, at any moment, it might whistle. Next to it a banner proclaims "the four horsemen of the oesophagus". On shelves nearby are the sort of plastic trophies you would win on a night of ten-pin bowling, and jelly moulds in shapes you might recognize – the Reichstag, the Empire State Building, St Paul's.

Bompas and Parr are both turning thirty. They are old friends from Eton. If someone cast him in a movie, Parr would be a quiet, English, and not-at-all-evil version of the Joker. He has salt-and-pepper hair and a wide grin. He does not say much. You get the sense, when you talk with him, that he is saving his energy, that behind his polite smile far more important work is being done. In there, an army of mad scientists are figuring things out, putting potions in vats, and doing odd things with Bunsen burners, test-tubes and Victorian bicycle parts.

Bompas is the front man. The glint in his eye is the glint of a Barnum, or a Willy Wonka – the Gene Wilder version. When you see him, he might be wearing a military greatcoat, or a floor-length bear-style fur cape. He will most likely be sporting one of his 40 bow ties, and a pair of bright blue, red or yellow Turnbull and Asser socks.

Going to see Bompas and Parr, in other words, is quite an experience, especially when Bompas starts talking about their latest plans. He might tell you how they want to give people religious experiences at will, to make roses that flame and change colour as you hand them to your date on Valentine's, and to create a way for people to not only talk at, but really communicate with, plants.

These are not just hopes and dreams. Bompas knows how to whip up a bit of PR just as well as he knows how to make a jelly, a cake or a 12-course Victorian breakfast, but there is also substance behind the talk.

When I last saw them, Bompas and Parr had found a physicist who had a solution for those flaming roses. They had just commissioned an environmentalist and programmer to write an algorithm that would turn human words into the sort of piezoelectric signals that plants understand. They were going out that afternoon to meet a neuropsychologist at a haunted house, to find a way to induce religious experiences. They often turn their fantastical ideas, you see, into real events.

There was the time Bompas and Parr made a nine-hole crazy-golf course on the roof of Selfridges. Each hole featured a London landmark, made to look like a giant, pastel yellow, pink, blue or mauve cake. Players teed off by hitting their ball around a six-foot-tall mauve version of the Gherkin on a giant cake stand. To complete the par-two third hole, players putted their way across a water feature in the shape of a four-foot-high, pastel-blue Tower Bridge.

Another time, for the brandy maker Courvoisier, they made a punch that weighed four tonnes and was enough to serve 25,000 people. It was so large that not only could you go across it in a rowboat, people did cross it in a rowboat.

On another occasion, for Unilever's Magnum ice cream brand, they worked with neuroscientists to make a shiny metal helmet that, while it looked like a prop from a 1970s sci-fi film, contained bio-sensors to measure the wearer's skin tension, facial expression, deglutition (swallowing) and heartbeat data – as she or he ate a Magnum ice cream. The helmet then passed that data, via black, white and red wires, to the rest of installation, which turned it into a piece of personalized art.

Why did Selfridges and Courvoisier and Unilever commission these events? And why are so many brands – like Louis Vuitton, Stella Artois, Heinz, Intel, and Mercedes-Benz – rather than simply advertising as they used to, now staging experiences?

It certainly is not only for fun. The people who control big marketing budgets have to justify everything they do just as much as people did in the past. In today's digital era where everything is more trackable, in fact, it is even more imperative. They still have to show they are getting a decent return for their investment. They are still trying to sell stuff.

The answer, I think, lies in *Stuffocation*. We live in a cluttered time of too much information and too much stuff. How should a brand cut through the noise and get some stand-out? With the same old marketing clichés – by shouting louder and saying it more often than their competitors, by offering more for less, free gift with purchase, two-for-one, buy one get one free?

The problem with all these, to begin with, is that they have all been done. But, more importantly, they no longer work as well today, especially with the more discerning, ahead-of-the-curve consumers that so many advertisers want to reach. They, like the first farmers to plant the new hybrid seed in Neal and Gross's 1941 study, and as all innovators and early adopters on Rogers's *Diffusion of Innovations* S-curve, tend to be richer, more connected and more influential.

These people, then, are not only important in terms of influencing what others think and do – and buy – but they are also the ones most likely to be busy, and have more than enough material possessions already. The last thing they want, in other words, is more information competing for their limited attention spans, and more stuff clogging up their finite homes. They are not bothered about quantity of stuff anymore, but they are excited by quality of life. They do not want more material possessions, but they still want status.

And they increasingly know they are more likely to find that not in material possessions, but in experiences that tell them who they are and that give them a story to tell.

"Everyone is an autobiographer nowadays, it's like everyone is actively writing their own biography all the time," says Bompas. "So stories are becoming even more important. In the '80s, people wanted a fast car. Now they want a good story to tell."

At present, of course, businesses are creating these experiences in order to get people to buy material things – like handbags, beer, and cars. But, as we know from the law of unintended consequences, it does not really matter, strictly speaking, what they mean to do.

Although they are using experiences to get people to buy their products, what they are also doing is teaching them to value the experience more than the stuff the experience was designed to sell. As they do so, they are encouraging the shift from the material to the experience economy.

THIRTEEN

The Experientialists Who Love Stuff

The modern economy is predicated on growth. We need it for stability. Without it, the system would creak to a halt – as it does in recessions and, especially, depressions. Since the modern economy is, largely, the consumer economy – consumer spending makes up around 65% of the British, and just above 70% of the US economy, for instance – we really need people to keep buying more.

But what if tens of millions of people gave up materialistic ways and became experientialists – and started buying a lot less stuff? What if more people followed the experientialist example set by Jim Whyte and his three suitcases of possessions? Or the Lenet family, with their lives stuffed into backpacks?

If millions followed them, there would be far fewer material possessions needed. That could be damaging, devastating even, to many industries.

Consider the impact on the shoe business, for example. There would be less leather and rubber required, so fewer people needed to herd the cattle, tan the hides, tend the rubber plantations, transport the rubber to the factory, work in the factory, make the packaging. We would not require so many people to import, distribute, market, make adverts for, and sell the shoes. If millions of people gave up their materialistic ways, there would be far fewer jobs.

As Bernard Mandeville explored in the *Fable of the Bees*, and the architects of our system realized, those things we all buy create a lot of work, a lot of wealth, and a lot of material wellbeing. And as Christine Frederick pointed out in what she called the American paradox, we have more when we spend more.

Seen this way, a few becoming experientialists and buying fewer goods is clearly okay. But if experientialism became the dominant value system it would be little short of a disaster. Supporters of the materialist system – especially those old grumpy men who benefit so handsomely from the system – are quick to turn to this reasoning to explain why the current materialistic way is better than any alternative.

But is that not just a lack of imagination? This, after all, is what some people always say about progress. This argument often appears when an innovation threatens a person or an industry. This is exactly why textile makers were protesting in the early 19th century, for example.

Back then, they were so worried about the new labour-saving machines taking their jobs, and giving them to less-skilled, low-wage labourers, that they smashed wool-and cotton-making machines, and burned down mills. They called themselves after a man who had, in a pique of anti-machine rage, smashed one to pieces. His name was Ned Ludd. They were the Luddites.

Where do you sit on this issue?

I do not mean, by asking this, to imply that if you worry about the shift to a new way of working you are a Luddite. The stability of society, after all, is a good thing. And just because there is a new way of doing things does not mean it is better – though it could be. There is no point rocking the boat we have just for the sake of it.

But if the problems are coming in waves, and already threatening to overturn our system – as I think is happening in this time of *Stuffocation* – it seems like a good idea to at least consider an alternative that looks, in many ways, like it might be better. The question is: is materialism the only value system that can give us stability and growth – or could experientialism provide that too?

The Secret Loot in the Experience Economy

My wife and I brought the papers the email said to bring, so when we arrived at the venue, an old dance hall called the Troxy in east London, we had no problems with the soldiers of occupied France.

They wave us through, and we wander down a deserted corridor, past the sort of potted palms you might see in North Africa. We enter a vast auditorium.

"Rick's Café Américain," says an electric blue sign. Beneath the sign, a man plays the piano. Everywhere, people are in trilbies and suits, and vintage dresses. It is like a huge 1940s fancy-dress party.

There is something about it, too, that reminds me of the BBC comedy series *'Allo 'Allo!* – especially when, a little later, a French policeman with a false moustache comes to our table, tells us not to cause any trouble, but if we come across any letters of transit we are to tell him. I tell him he is a Nazi stooge and that he should be ashamed of himself, helping them like that. A minute later, as I sip my beer, the policeman is back, and this time he is accompanied by the Nazi Major Strasser – the chief baddy in the movie *Casablanca* – and his two henchmen in SS uniforms.

"Zis is the ze man!" the French policeman says, pointing at me.

"Vot is the meaning of ze zings you said," Strasser demands.

"You'll never win this war!" I say.

(This is fun. I've always wanted to tell a Nazi that, to be honest.)

"Take him," he says, and his two SS henchmen grab me by the shoulders, haul me off my seat, push me to my knees.

"Vot did you say?" one SS man demands.

"You'll. Never. Vin. This. Var," I say. It is all I can do not to laugh – yet at the same time, pushed to the floor, my knees on old carpet, two ruffians in uniform holding me by each shoulder, I'm kind of scared.

Strasser stares at me with hatred, his face turns puce.

"Bring him viz you," he stammers, turning on his black-booted heel and goose-stepping through the amazed crowd.

And the two men frog-march me after him, until we come to a small table. They rough-house me into a big chair.

"Vill you," the major says menacingly, "svear allegiance to Heil Hitler?"

"Never," I vow.

"Zen you vill drink zis as your punishment," he declares, pouring a shot of Jack Daniels into a glass.

I take it.

"Churchill!" I declare, and down the drink.

"Go," he says, dismissing me. And I wander off back to my seat and my wife.

By the time the movie starts, an hour or so later, more actors have appeared, played out more scenes from Casablanca around the room. I have attended an impromptu rally where Victor Laszlo has stood on a chair, roused the crowd to pledge our allegiance to "free France!", and, with hand on heart and tears in his eyes, sung the Marseillaise: "Aux armes citoyens, Formez vos bataillons, Marchons, marchons!"

Rick and Ilsa have talked by the piano. Sam has played 'As Time Goes By'. He has played it again. I have, with another man who brought some silks to swap, obtained letters of transit and passed them surreptitiously – keeping a keen eye out for that policeman and those Nazis – to Laszlo.

By the time the curtains open on the screen, the suspension of our disbelief – an essential ingredient in the enjoyment of any piece of fiction – is complete. We, like Laszlo and Ilsa and Rick, are sitting in Rick's café in Casablanca in 1941. We hate the Germans. We understand Ilsa's torment. We feel the nobility of Laszlo's struggle. We know how important those letters of transit are.

One Secret Cinema event, and you are hooked. If only every time you saw a movie it could be as immersive, engaging, memorable and, quite frankly, amazing, as this. It is not just seeing the movie, it is a complete experience.

No wonder people treat it as if their favourite band has come to town. They cross the country to attend, they stay in hotels near the venue, they take the day off work the next day.

Secret Cinema is a prime example of how the experience economy might work in the future, and how it is already working. Besides *Casablanca*, Secret Cinema has staged many other movies including *Anvil! The Story of Anvil*, which featured a live set from the real band, and *Shawshank Redemption*, where the audience were transformed into convicts – as they swapped their civvies for regulation uniforms, and prison guards shouted at them and locked them in cells. The formula – pick a movie, find a venue and stage an experience based on that movie – is proving very popular.

When the company hired 40 actors and 40 crew to turn a London warehouse into a spaceship, and made 25,000 people over 28 days become boiler-suited crew members of Ridley Scott's *Prometheus*, the company took more money than London's biggest Imax cinema. Secret Cinema, as its founder, Fabien Riggall once boasted, is a very good way to get people to pay £50 each to see a film. Was someone at the back worrying whether there was money – and jobs – in the experience economy?

Ben: the Experientialist who Loves Stuff

One bright, sunny, Sunday morning some years back, Sarah Howell found herself at the edge of a cliff in the Morialta falls area of Adelaide, Australia, trembling like a gum tree leaf in the breeze. What the *bloody hell* was she doing here?

"I'm just not the sporty type," she says now. "I love food markets, finding new recipes and testing out menus with chefs. I'm used to feeling like I'm in charge! Standing at the top of that cliff, I was petrified.

Adrenalin was pumping through me. There was *no way*. I just did *not* want to do it."

At least it was different from the usual dates she went on. Most guys who fell for her pale skin, ruby red hair and English-rose looks would take her for drinks and dinner. Since she was a restaurateur, that was a bit like going to work.

But when a cocky DJ called Ben had said he would pick her up Sunday morning, and that she should wear sneakers and sports kit, though, she thought he might be different. She soon realized he was. He did not seem to care too much about clothes, for instance. He always wore the same khaki pants and some sort of pineapple print surf shirt. Also, he never tried to impress her with money. And instead of talking about *having* things, he would talk about *doing* things: skiing, kiteboarding, climbing – and taking her abseiling.

"Ben was great that day in Morialta falls," she remembers. "He talked me through it, told me I'd be alright. I felt really vulnerable, but he knew what he was doing." Looking back, it is clear he did. He and Red – as he calls Sarah because of the colour of her hair – got together, got married. They have a five-year-old called Poppy. They haven't changed much since they met all those years ago. She is still a restaurateur. She runs a Spanish restaurant, an Italian osteria, and, in 2013, opened a pop-up place called Ruby Red Flamingo. He still prefers doing to having. He owns as few possessions as he can get away with.

"Don't own a watch, never have," Ben Howell says. "I only have three pairs of shoes – a pair of leather work boots, a pair of sneakers for jogging, and a pair of smart shoes in case Red makes me dress up to go to an awards ceremony with her. Actually, I have four pairs, if you count my thongs."

(For the non-Australian reader: those thongs are not a G-string. Ben really is not that type. It is the Aussie term for flip-flops.)

The Howells are a typical 21st-century experientialist family. "We put experiences first," says Sarah Howell. She fulfils her passion for food and hospitality at work and in her spare time. Whenever they pass a food market, they stop. Their overseas trips often include foodie elements, like visiting the fish markets in Tokyo, or finding great foie gras in Paris. Ben Howell, meanwhile, spends his money and spare time mastering sports like surfing, kiteboarding and, his latest hobby, dirt biking.

And here, we have come across one of the counterintuitive aspects of experientialism. Because, while Ben Howell prefers experiences to things, and is not someone you would describe as materialistic, he likes some things very much.

If you were to visit the Howells in Adelaide, you would soon see what I mean. You would notice, first of all, that they are not materialistic. Their house is simple. It is not cluttered up with physical possessions. But take a walk out back, though, yank up the creaky garage door, and you would realize there is a very different material story in there.

Inside, the garage is bursting with kit. There are surfboards and wetsuits. There are windsurf boards, sails, booms, and masts. There are kiteboards, a power kite, a foil kite, a kite harness, and sets of flying lines. There is a rock-climbing harness. There is a dirt bike and a motorbike helmet. There are also lots of shoes. But these are not fashion items, that look good one season but you cannot wear the next. This is technical footwear, like motorbike boots, windsurf boots, and climbing shoes.

Though Ben Howell cannot see the point in accumulating ordinary material possessions, he loves things that give him experiences – and he does not hesitate to spend on them.

"I spent $12 on a pair of shoes the other week, and it really annoyed me – they should have cost $10," he once told me. "But then I went out the next day and blew $1700 on a great new kite."

And here, we have come across another typical aspect of the Howells, and most experientialists. They are not materialistic, but they have no problem with, and therefore pose little threat to, the overall system we live in. They fully intend to keep working and earning and spending. As Sarah Howell says, "You can't have all the experiences Ben has without all the stuff, and the money to buy that stuff."

Given the chance, the Howells and most experientialists will continue to play their part in "have more by spending more" consumerism, and do their bit for growth and stability. But they will increasingly do that by spending their money on experiences rather than objects.

"Red and me, we still see ourselves as capitalists," Ben Howell says. "A lot of things we do cost a fair bit of money. But rather than buy some pointless thing, like a fancy shirt or a black BMW, we invest our money in experiences – like jumping out of a plane or going skiing."

Graham: the Minimalist who Loves Stuff

It was Olga who opened Graham Hill's eyes.

Olga Sasplugas, who we met earlier, is a hippy with a calculator. Now in her mid-thirties, she is originally from Andorra, the mountain principality between France and Spain. She has brown eyes, olive skin and long legs. She is a ballet dancer and a dance therapist who teaches orphans. She was the first Andorran to win a Fulbright scholarship to study for a master's degree in the US. She took a course in performing arts in New York. It was there she met Hill.

After they had been dating three months, Sasplugas's visa ran out and she had to leave the country. Hill did what any sensible man would have done. He followed her.

First stop was Barcelona, and Sasplugas's student flat, a run-down place about a million miles from the loft Hill – a technology millionaire – had in Manhattan. Getting to it was bad enough. It was like going to a petty criminal's lair: you went down a car park's narrow ramp and, just as you came to the yellow chevrons pointing to the car park on the right, there, on the left, was the entrance. The flat was just as ramshackle. Sasplugas had filled it with things she had found on the street: people leave their unwanted furniture outside on Tuesdays in Barcelona.

"The couch was a bed, the table was a wooden door – nothing went with nothing!" says Sasplugas. "And here was Graham coming from his fancy apartment in SoHo – I was absolutely scared!"

Hill did not mind, though. They had a dream summer. They cycled to the beach. They ate *pimientos del padron* – spicy green peppers, deep-fried and served with salt. They had dinner parties on the roof. Sometimes, when it was cool, they would work up there too: to make the Wi-Fi reach, Hill strung a wire out the window, up the side, and onto the top, of the building.

Sasplugas was soon off again, to northern Cambodia, to teach dance therapy in an orphanage. The internet connection was terrible, so Hill went as far as Bangkok. At least they could see each other on Sasplugas's few days off each month.

Then they went to Mysore, India for Sasplugas to learn yoga. They rented an apartment in an old colonial house. It had three bedrooms, two bathrooms, a meditation room, a kitchen – but no hot water, no internet and not a single piece of furniture. They borrowed a mattress from their neighbours. Hill worked from the local internet café. Next stop was Buenos Aires. Sasplugas learnt tango. They stayed in a tiny top-floor apartment, far above the cobbled streets and jacaranda trees of a district called Palermo Viejo.

By the time they got back to New York, the last thing they wanted was the complications and hassle of a designer loft. So they rented a 300-square-foot, sixth-floor walk-up.

"The toilet was in the back, the shower was in the kitchen," Hill recalls.

"At least it had a curtain round it though," says Sasplugas. "One of us could shower while the other cooked."

Then Hill ran into a problem, one that most people dream of. When he sold his business – an eco-site called Treehugger.com he had set up from Sasplugas's place in Barcelona – he made the sort of money that would buy a loft in SoHo, gut it, fix it up and fill it with brand new stuff. Luckily, though, he had faced this problem before.

That time, he had bought a vast, 3,600-square-foot house and, because he was too busy working, hired a personal assistant to buy all the things it needed. At first, Hill had loved it. He had filled the house with friends, renting out rooms and hosting barbecues and dinner parties. But he soon realized how much hassle the house and everything that came with it was, and he had sold it all. This time, then, he was older and wiser.

"When I'd been with Olga, I'd been working really hard, but always in a different place and always having cool new experiences," he recalls now. "And I guess I just realized – that was a really great way to live, and that I just didn't need that much stuff."

Hill did not want a big house this time, but he did want a place to call home. The obvious solution was a small apartment, like all those places he had shared with Sasplugas. But then, he had loved having people over for dinner and friends to stay at his old place. Could he, he wondered, have both – a really small place with almost no stuff and no hassle, but also somewhere he could have friends over?

To answer that question, Hill posted a challenge on a crowdsourcing website called Jovoto. He detailed the parameters and requirements: he wanted someone to create a design for a 420-square-foot apartment he had bought that would allow him to live and work there, host a sit-down dinner for twelve, and have a couple of friends to stay, while still giving them some privacy. To excite people to get involved, he offered $70,000 in prizes.

It worked. The Jovoto community responded with three hundred designs, 70,000 people voted on their favourite, and Hill found a design he liked. He now lives there, in an apartment that has been called a "Swiss Army apartment" and a "transformer home" – as every one of its 420 square feet shape-shifts and multi-tasks from morning to night. Everything seems to double up as something else, and hides away until it is needed. There is a pull-down bed, a pop-out desk, and, for when two friends stay, a pull-out wall. There is an extendable table so ten – not twelve, but who's counting? – can have a sit-down meal.

Hill cannot bear having too much stuff. He lives in a tiny house. He calls himself a minimalist. His brand of minimalism, though, as you can see, does not look anything like deprivation. It does not mean he is missing out on anything. And it does not come cheap. The push-out table that telescopes out to seat ten? $3,950. His pull-down queen-size bed? $15,000. The overall cost of creating his apartment – just the renovation, not the cost of the real estate – $315,000.

Hill is not the only one practising this type of minimalism. This is the minimalism favoured by the social media scene that Alice Marwick wrote about in her dissertation, and the one practised by the wider tech community.

Consider Colin Wright, for instance, an entrepreneur from Los Angeles who gave up a six-figure salary and thriving user interface business to live with only 51 things.

"If you're only going to have one of something, it should be your favourite of that thing – and that means upgrading to higher quality whenever you can," he says. "It's important to recalibrate and not to get stuck with one brand. At the moment, I have a Mac computer, an Android phone, and a Canon camera. But I won't always. I always try to make sure

I have the best from each category for me, the thing that makes me happiest."

This point of view, the one that Hill and Wright, for instance, advocate, is fascinating when you think about it. It is a perspective that manages to marry two ways of thinking that seem, at first glance, diametrically opposed. First, they are committed minimalists. They are not interested in accumulating material possessions. Things, they believe, weigh them down. Things do not bring happiness. Stuff cannot confer status.

But, at the same time, Hill and Wright are enthusiastic consumers. That makes them, if you think about it, similar to the materialists of the last century. But the difference is that their way of consuming feels far more discerning and sophisticated. Instead of gathering more, they only want the best. While the materialists, you could say, are interested, principally, in quantity, these "consumer minimalists" are interested in quality.

These people matter, because Silicon Valley matters. We live in a far flatter world today, but there are people and places that wield far more influence. The bright ideas that originate in Silicon Valley, and in all the other Silicon Somethings around the world, in particular those that come from the consumer technology and social media scenes, influence what people all around the world think. If they are more interested in getting status by having fewer but better things – and conspicuously consuming, as Alice

Marwick showed, experiences – then more people will think and behave this way.

Besides this, I also think the consumer minimalists are more proof that a value system other than materialism could still deliver stability and growth. As you can see, the consumer minimalists – who, like all minimalists, are ultimately interested in experiences rather than stuff and are therefore what I would call experientialists – would deliver stability and growth by buying fewer goods, but ones that cost a whole lot more.

The New 'n' Improved Experience Economy

The idea of the "experience economy" was popularized in the late 1990s by a pair of business consultants called Joe Pine and Jim Gilmore. In an article for the *Harvard Business Review* and then a book, Pine and Gilmore set out a persuasive case that every business – including yours – should use experiences to sell more to more people. They also proposed that, after the agrarian, manufacturing, and service economies, the experience economy is the logical evolution of capitalism.

By that, they meant that, just as the creation and delivery of food and drink was the hallmark of the agrarian system, and the people who owned the means of production were the wealthiest – and just as the creation and delivery of material goods was the pillar of the manufacturing economy, and the people and businesses which owned the factories were the most successful, and so on for the service economy – so the creation and delivery of experiences will be the essential characteristic of the experience economy.

The difference between the output of the agrarian and manufacturing economies is obvious, but perhaps the difference between a service and an experience needs explaining. Both are intangible, that is, you cannot touch them. But whereas service is only that, an experience is also designed to be memorable, to touch you, if you like, on an emotional, physical, intellectual, or even spiritual level. As with the other aspects of the economy, there is often some overlap, but with a little consideration you can see the difference.

Food is a useful way to illustrate how each sector is distinct. When you shop for ingredients, some courgettes, potatoes and steaks for dinner, say, this is part of the agrarian economy. When you buy prepared food, like a ready-made pizza, you are purchasing a manufactured good. When you buy dinner in a restaurant, you are supporting the service sector. And when you eat at an event – in a masonic temple while watching a shocking movie, say, or at a pirate-themed dinner – you are spending money in the experience sector.

It is worthwhile understanding this difference, because the experience economy – where businesses make the staging of memorable, engaging events their priority – is the sector growing fastest. In the past fifty years or so, it has grown, according to

Pine and Gilmore's calculations, 38% faster than the manufacturing sector.

In the future, in a world responding to *Stuffocation*, it is likely to accelerate even faster. And if that happens, as I believe it will, who will be the winners and the losers in this new system? What will be the features and benefits of this new and improved world? What, in short, will the experience economy look like?

It will not, as is clear from the stories about Ben Howell and Graham Hill, spell the end for the other sectors of the economy. We will still need and want services. We will still buy, use and use up products. We are not about to give up the goods and live like a bunch of cave-dwelling, ascetic hermits. The stuff of our modern lives is not about to disappear.

We have always used tools and bought goods, not only to keep up with the Joneses, but for their practical value and the experiences they give us. What is a tennis racket for if not to play tennis? And the dishwasher saves us the experience of washing up, and gives us time to spend on other, more meaningful experiences. Even if that experience is "only" watching *The Sopranos* box-set or playing Sims or reading this book, it is still better than washing up.

To sketch out what the experience economy will look like, there are three ideal places where the forecaster should look for clues. They are: the list of factors causing *Stuffocation* today, the reasons why experiences make us happier than material goods, and the pioneering businesses, brands, and even cities, that are successful today because of the experiences they provide.

The new and improved experience economy will, as it responds to *Stuffocation*, be a world of goods – products, services, experiences – that are far less bad, or even actually positive, for the environment. They will require fewer material resources.

Rather than cluttering our homes with yet more monotonous, commoditized stuff, companies will sell us goods that are customized and 3D printed, so that they give each of us more engaging, relevant experiences. They will provide goods that take up less room, or no physical space at all.

Instead of focusing on tangible objects we can have and hold, companies will sell us solutions we need or, better still, activities we can do. More of the goods we buy will be temporary, and easy to update – with new apps or software, for instance, or with re-use in mind – so that we avoid the waste of hedonic adaptation. They will be more egalitarian, and designed for sharing. They will promote activities that bring us closer to others, and make us feel part of a social group. They will deliberately provide us with better stories, with shareable conversational currency. They will contribute to our identity.

Does this sound like a utopian, idealistic dream to you? It shouldn't. While projections of the future you have come across before may have sometimes felt like wishful thinking, often involving an enlightened, post-paranoid race of people who have given up the status game of Snakes and Ladders, this forecast does not ignore our need to express status.

The experience economy – which will be the commercial expression of our new culture of experientialism – may well help solve the problems of *Stuffocation*, but it will not do so by hoping we forget all about establishing our position in the social pecking order.

"People still want to keep up with the Joneses," says Jim Gilmore. "Before, they wanted goods that were shinier, faster, more powerful. And they still want to keep up in the experience economy. But now they want things that are different – more durable, say, or more egalitarian, or more participatory."

Moreover, the experience economy should not feel like hopeful idealism because, even though it is still unevenly distributed, there are many signs that it is already happening. Consider, for instance, the rise of experiential events, e-books, TOMS shoes, the Common Threads Initiative, Puma's Clever Little Shopper, collaborative consumption, the runaway success of Apple, and why London is one of the most visited cities in the world. These are stellar examples, the pioneers, if you like, of the experience economy. Here is why.

Even if you do not read on a digital device, you already know how e-books help solve the problem of *Stuffocation*: fewer trees cut down, lower carbon footprint, instant access so no need to actually go to the shops, and, best of all, fewer books cluttering up the house, bag, or suitcase when you go on holiday.

Instead of the "buy one get one free" offer – known as BOGOF by retailers – of the old economy, TOMS shoes come with a "buy one give one away" offer: BOGOA, you could call it. For every pair of TOMS shoes you buy, rather than hand you something tangible, they give another pair to a child in need, and, by doing so, they give you the feel-good sense that you have helped someone out. Instead of getting your attention by giving you more stuff, in other words, the TOMS brand connects with its customers by helping them share with those less fortunate.

In its Common Threads Initiative with eBay, the outdoor brand Patagonia asked people to buy less, or, as the company's founder, Yvon Chouinard said, "to not buy something if they don't need it". This is, if you think about it, a revolutionary statement. It is the antithesis of all the "more is better", "spend more to have" ideals of the past. Imagine, for a moment, taking that idea to your boss: "let's ask our customers to buy less from us". Yet it is the sort of statement that makes sense in a world suffering *Stuffocation*. By actually caring about the environment, Patagonia is far more likely to connect with people concerned with the state of our planet and feeling *Stuffocation*.

To understand the magic of some of sportswear brand Puma's recent work, think about your home for a moment, just after you have got back from shopping, and that time when you look around and all you seem to see is bags and packaging. To solve that, Puma created a bag that, rather than add to the clutter in your home when you stash it away, or the guilt you feel when you throw it out, would simply disappear. Put the brand's Clever Little Shopper bag in hot water for three minutes and it harmlessly dissolves, so you can pour it safely down the plug.

The social accommodation brand Airbnb, the car-sharing service Zipcar and music-streaming site Spotify are all examples of what is variously known, from slightly different angles, as the new trend for dis-ownership, the sharing economy and collaborative consumption.

Now, thanks to these trends and the technologies that make them possible, you can enjoy the experience of a room, a house, a car, a CD, a handbag, a lawnmower, a musical instrument or even a dog – without all the hassle that comes with owning them.

The success of Zipcar, for instance, reflects the space and cost that comes with keeping a car in a city, and the fact that, if you live in a city, you just do not need a car so much anymore. With Spotify, why own a CD or even a download, when you can listen to it whenever you want?

Airbnb goes one better. As well as giving people the chance to borrow other people's goods, it also lets them share a good they already own: their own home. Beyond the obvious financial reward, there is also a participatory, social good that comes with Airbnb. It provides the people who let their rooms and their homes, and the people who stay there, with real connections. As a result, they tend to feel part of the new, innovative sharing economy, they feel more connected to other people, and they have more stories to share.

Apple has become the world's leading brand because of its ruthless focus on experience. Think, for a moment, how easy it is to operate an Apple device, and how slim the operating manual is. How different is that to the manual that came with, say, your VHS recorder in the 1980s? Do you remember how complicated it was to record a TV show back then? Jonathan Ive and his designers at Apple do not only consider the experience of using their product, though. They make everything pleasant, from the stores to the moment you open the box.

"Not only do the guys at Apple make sure their products are products people love to use," says Joe Pine. "They even think about the packaging, about the 'box opening experience', so even that is unique and engaging."

Finally, why is London one of the world's most visited cities? It is a city, to be sure, that is steeped in history. So it already has many of its own stories.

But it also provides people with their own tales, like the time you: watched the sunset from Waterloo Bridge, went to the latest pop-up shop or underground bar or skyscraper restaurant, met some crazy people in a dingy little pub in Covent Garden, danced all night in a warehouse in Hackney or all day at the Notting Hill carnival, ate a Dead Hippy burger or confit of duck with maple syrup on a waffle, played golf on the roof of Selfridges – or any of a thousand and one things.

London may be expensive, loud, dirty, and frustrating to get round, but it offers, in short, experiences that give the people who come here, and those who live here, the kind of exciting experiential and conversational currency that you are unlikely to get in Madrid, Stockholm, and most other cities you could mention.

As people suffer *Stuffocation*, their values are changing. What they want from the goods and services they buy is shifting.

As a result, today's captains of industry – who may be lazy, greedy or frightened, or all three, and who are certainly looking for easier, more profitable, and safer ways of ensuring the success of their business – are re-imagining and re-working their products, services and business models.

They are reducing their resource requirements and their impact on the environment. They are creating less clutter and producing more happiness. Rather than give people a material object they can touch, hold and have, they are selling them an activity they can do, that gives them identity, makes them feel part of a group, and gives them stories to tell others.

Inspired by pioneers like Bompas & Parr, Zipcar, Secret Cinema, Puma, Punchdrunk and Apple, they are putting their material offer in the background, and instead making experience the star. As they do, they, like the government, are not only passively reflecting the change in values, and they are not only encouraging it. Whether it is their intention or not, they are actively creating the shift from the material to the experience economy.

FOURTEEN

What About the Chinese?

How do you say "keeping up with the Joneses" in Mandarin or Cantonese? In Hindi, Urdu, or Brazilian Portuguese? In Tamil, Thai, or Bahasa Indonesia? Not so long ago, no one needed to know. Except for a tiny minority, conspicuous consumption was a Western phenomenon. Now, though, that is changing, and fast.

When twenty-something Liu Dandan and her husband Zhou Zhou wake each morning in their apartment in Beijing, they are surrounded by designers. Philippe Stark designed the gold AK-47 lamp on the table in their lounge. Paul Smith made Zhou Zhou's shoes. They have handbags, wallets, watches by Louis Vuitton, MCM, Cartier, Burberry, Fendi, Prada, Tod's, Hermès. They keep the pristine boxes each item came in. They drive a Mercedes-Benz. They dress their baby in designer clothes.

If material goods could talk – and social scientists say they do – Liu and Zhou's possessions would scream conspicuous consumption.

So would the shoes that another Beijing resident, Richard Lu, has accumulated. His multi-coloured collection features around 50 pairs, by brands like Valentino, D&G, Prada, Tod's and YSL. What pair will he wear today? The spring green suede ankle boots? The white bowling shoes with black laces? A pair of suede loafers, perhaps, but which colour to choose: red, burgundy, mustard, cornflower blue, French navy blue, imperial purple, deep purple, or ivy green? Or the metallic blue and silver loafers, or the ones in the cheetah-patterned pony skin? Or the metal-studded black high-top trainers, or the brown high-tops with fluorescent green trim and Louis Vuitton scrawled across them in orange? Or perhaps keep it simple with a pair of leather brogues – in tan, black and white, brown and white, or brown, green and red?

Liu, Zhou and Lu are influential. They are trendsetters, and not only because of Lu's shoes. Zhou, for instance, works at the Chinese version of *Esquire* magazine. Lu runs a public relations agency. They represent the future of China, and the future of a vast swathe of the rest of the world. Because their lifestyle, and the labels, logos, handbags, and shoes that come with it, is one many others now aspire to. It is also a lifestyle, or an approximation of it, that many millions will soon have. Because in the next few decades, more than a billion people in countries like India, Indonesia, Vietnam, Nigeria, and Brazil will be joining them as middle-class, conspicuous consumers.

As that happens, those billion or so people will afford, for the first time, to not only live but enjoy a lifestyle that you and I would recognize. As they make the march, from country to city, from hardscrabble poor to having some spare money to spend on life's little luxuries, these millions upon millions of people will get their first chance to buy a television, a car, a mobile phone, a week's worth of shirts, and a washing machine to wash them in. In other words, there will be a lot of people getting their first taste of materialism. A lucky few million may even get the chance to buy the sort of shoes that would fit in Richard Lu's collection.

As the new middle classes enjoy the sweet side of materialism, they will also experience its sour twist. They will feel the status anxiety that comes with the Snakes and Ladders game of conspicuous consumption.

From Lima to Lagos, Kolkata to Jakarta, Chongqing to Beijing, they will look across the corridor or fence or street. They will take note of what their neighbours have. They will want something a little newer, fancier, and better, and they will buy it sooner than they strictly need it. They will try to stay ahead or, at least, keep up with the Silvas, the Kapoors, the Wangs or the Lius – or whatever those pesky Joneses next door are called in their country.

Is Stuffocation Middle-Age Angst?

As conspicuous consumption becomes the global norm, so we will see a similar surge in standards of living in the developing world to the one that came with the rise of consumerism in the West.

At the same time, the rise of the global middle class over *there* will make the sense of *Stuffocation* we feel over *here* even more acute, especially since two of the most pressing problems causing *Stuffocation* are resource scarcity and the environment. These are going to become much worse with a billion more people asking for their piece of the materialist pie on our finite planet.

This growing tribe of eager, first-time materialists is like the proverbial bull, elephant, and eight-hundred-pound gorilla in any meaningful discussion about *Stuffocation*.

This billion-strong group gate-crashes its way in by calling into question whether we should even bother trying to solve problems like overconsumption and our impact on the environment. Because just as fast as we wealthy few try to curb our collective footprint and reduce our consumption, there will be a billion or so others queuing up to take our place and make their mark on the world by gobbling up its resources with their new cars, motorbikes, microwaves, washing machines, shirts, and blue suede shoes.

Does that suggest, therefore, that *Stuffocation* is merely the middle-class, middle-age angst of a waning

Western society worried about its place in the world – and that we may as well just get over it?

The Next Great Leap Forward

Stuffocation may well be the middle-age angst of a maturing society on the downturn today. But if we take into consideration our learnings from the past and knowledge of the present, I think we can make a realistic forecast about China and the other emerging nations. That forecast is this: that they will follow similar development curves to those we did in the West, only their curves will be steeper, and their revolutions will come quicker.

In the West, it took 150-odd years from the start of the Industrial Revolution to lead to overproduction. After that, it took just under 80 years or so in the West for the consumer revolution to lead to overconsumption and *Stuffocation*.

A similar journey – from industrial revolution to mass production and overproduction, from consumer revolution to mass consumption, overconsumption and *Stuffocation* – is likely to happen in the emerging nations. But it is likely to happen far, far quicker.

Industrialization in the West happened, of course, in fits and starts and incremental steps, as new discoveries were made over decades, and then those innovations took time to spread. The emerging economies have evolved from agricultural communities to industrial societies far more rapidly.

Over there, they have benefited from all the dead ends, wrong turns, and blind alleys that the pioneers over here made – and been able to avoid them. At the same time, they have been able to treat all the knowledge, inventions, and scientific advances like useful signposts that point them to the best way forward. Internationalization has also meant ready markets for all the goods their new factories can produce.

But, despite these advantages, as China has rapidly industrialized and production has increased, it has started to face problems that sound very similar to those the US confronted in the 1920s: the twin spectres of overproduction and underconsumption. In 2012, for instance, there were overproduction problems in industries ranging from coal, cotton, and ship-building to clothing, solar cell, and construction.

And this problem, of overproduction, is compounded by the fact that people in China today share some strikingly similar traits with the people in America in the 1920s. Famine and austerity have taught generation upon generation of Chinese to be careful with their possessions and thrifty with their money. They are just not – yet – used to mass-consuming in the manner that the country's new mass-producing communist-consumerist-materialist system requires. But that, as we know, is rapidly changing.

As in America in the 1920s, commentators have been weighing in with their worries, and a set of solutions that sound very similar.

"Can China's famously thrifty workers become the world's big spenders?" asked a journalist called Bill Saporito in an article in *Time* magazine.

"Chinese Consumers Are Still Not Spending Enough" wrote a journalist called Dhara Ranasinghe in an article for newscaster CNBC.

Economists have similar concerns. For stability and growth – in China as well as the rest of the world – The World Bank and the International Monetary Fund both want the Chinese to become, like the bees in Mandeville's fable and like their counterparts in the West, high-spending consumers.

Just as the captains of consciousness, the government and business leaders, in the US solved overproduction by deliberately turning their country's once thrifty citizens into wasteful, conspicuous consumers, so China's captains of consciousness are doing the same. Advertising, the industry most likely to engineer consumers rather than products, is exploding. In 1976, there weren't even ten advertising agencies in the whole country. By 2001, there were 70,000. By 2010, 234,000. And by the end of 2012, that had shot up to 377,000.

The Chinese government is explicitly intent on creating consumers as well, and borrowing ideas from the American experiment of the 20th century. The government plans to improve wages, so people spend more. It is making credit easier to come by, so people spend more. It is improving the welfare system so that its people worry less about the future, so they save less and spend more. It is also improving the country's parcel delivery system, so people spend more on e-commerce.

Are these policies working? Consider this: the value of e-commerce in China in 2012, from a standing start a few years ago, was almost the same as the entire economy of the Republic of Ireland.

As those hundreds of millions of Chinese, and the new middle classes in India, China, Indonesia, and all the other emerging nations become better off, and buy more things in stores and online, all the factors that have caused *Stuffocation* over here – the safety net of affluence and a functioning welfare state, the move to cities, ageing populations, environmental degradation, equality, and overconsumption – will concern them too. They will also feel *Stuffocation*.

The early signs, in fact, are already there. There are the frequent demonstrations and riots as people put their environment and quality of life before growth. There is the problem of stalling levels of happiness: since 1990, the average Chinese person's material living standard has increased by four times, for instance, yet happiness has not increased at all.

There are the young who are already evolving away from materialism. "China in general is in a grossly materialistic phase," Ron Inglehart told me. "But post-materialism is already beginning to emerge in a young, significant minority."

And then there are the wealthy, who already have enough. They are already beginning to prefer experiences over material goods. In China, the experiential luxury sector – which includes days out at spas, playing golf and going on holiday – is growing around 25% faster than the personal luxury goods sector.

Once the Lius and Zhous and Lus have got enough, and had enough of their, LV wallets, Prada bags and Paul Smith shoes, they, like the rest of us, will veer towards experiential, rather than material, goods. Once the hundreds of millions in China, and all the other emerging nations catch up, and once they not only satisfy but also sate their basic material needs, their preferences will also shift, I believe, from material to experiential goods.

Since the emerging economies are on steeper development curves, it is likely to happen soon – within the next few decades. It took China around a third of the time to go from the start of its industrialization to overproduction – around 60 years. If it continues to follow a similar accelerated path, it will reach overconsumption by 2037.

As materialism builds up, as consuming turns to overconsumption, and as they run into all the other problems and opportunities that make up *Stuffocation*, today's new materialists will make the next great leap forward, and become tomorrow's experientialists.

CONCLUSION

Why You Need Experience More than Ever

On 27 January 1940, it was a quiet night in London. The blackouts were in place. There was snow on the ground. In the north of the city, near where Tottenham Hotspur play football, a man in a suit and dickie-bow stepped out of a dance hall leading a woman by the hand. He leaned in and kissed his new bride, Pam.

"Come on," Jack said, squeezing her hand. "Let's go home."

With that, he led her to their first home, a two-room flat on the ground floor of a two-up, two-down house with an apple tree in the garden. They shared the kitchen and bathroom with the owner of the house, a spinster called Miss Burt, who lived upstairs.

A few years later, they had a son, Alan. When Alan was too big to share the bedroom with them, they gave it to him.

Each night at bedtime, Jack and Pam would open out a camp bed and make it up for themselves in the living room. Every morning, before Alan left for his paper round, he would wake to the smell of bacon, eggs, sausages, and fried bread. Jack cooked that for him every day, until the one he left for the Liverpool University in 1962.

Alan was the first person in the family to reach higher education. (His Aunt Lulu had been offered a place at Oxford in the 1930s, but the family had been far too poor to send her.) He made the most of it. He played football in the university team. He saw the Beatles and the Rolling Stones before they were famous. He graduated with an engineering degree. After, he joined IBM, got promoted, married, had kids.

Jack was my grandfather, Alan is my father. This is my backstory. Why am I telling you all this? Because Jack and Alan are typical.

Just as the families in the CELF study are characteristic of the middle class today, and the case studies in this book exemplify others, so Alan and Jack are representative of their generations. And because, like Ryan Nicodemus's story, the shift in circumstances from Jack to Alan to me reflects our society's journey from scarcity to abundance, and illustrates the effect that has had on our attitudes, values, and behaviours.

In our ordinary family tale, in other words, you can trace the story of this book: the rise of materialism, its subsequent demise, and the emergence of experientialism.

As an archetypal Baby Boomer, my father, who people say looks a bit like Harrison Ford, measured success in material terms and looked for happiness in material things, like the house he lived in or the car he drove.

I recall how happy he was – we all were – every time he got a new one. At the sound of an engine on the anointed day, we would all rush to the front room, my brother and I on tiptoes at the window, our mother following us, looking for the latest symbol of our Dad's success. I remember them all: the boxy, blue Triumph Toledo and the curvy, caramel Mark I Cavalier in the '70s and, in the '80s, the silver Mark II Cavalier SR, the gold Opel Senator, the red Porsche 911, and the gold Porsche 944.

My father does not only value material things, of course. Over the years, he has spent a great deal of his money on experiences, like watching Spurs and seeing the Stones play live.

But he and the rest of the Baby Boomers were brought up believing in the materialistic consumerist system, as it offered the straightest route from the poverty they had been born into, to the plenty they were helping to create.

Like millions of us who came after the Boomers, I grew up believing in that system too. But then something happened. Or, rather, many things did.

They all added up to this problem I call *Stuffocation*. And so I, like millions today, started questioning the benefits of materialism. You can see that in the work I have done. I have bounced between materialistic jobs, like tele-selling in a boiler room similar to the one in the movie *Wall Street*, and experiential ones, like ski-guiding and travel-writing.

One Sunday in January 2002, my father brought Jack and Pam over for a pub lunch in south London. We talked about the past: the tangy taste of the apples from the tree in their garden, days out on London's red buses, the holiday when Jack got everyone lost in Lisbon. We talked about the future as well, in particular, my dreams for success in advertising, the career I was then pursuing. Just before they left, Jack handed me an envelope. Inside was a £5 note – enough for two pints of beer in those days – and a message on a scrap of paper.

"27-1-2002," it read. "This date in 1940 Nanna & I tramped through snow to our first home. Memories live longer than dreams. Treat yourself to a nice momento [sic]. Good Luck."

Ten minutes later, as they were about to drive across the River Thames, Jack gasped, like he was choking, my father told me later, and slumped in his seat. His aorta had burst. My father did what he could. He roared through traffic, jumped the lights, got pulled over, and was then escorted by the police and their flashing blue lights in a race to get my grandfather to hospital. They tried their best, but Jack died that day.

I have thought a lot about that note since then, especially since I started thinking about and researching the ideas in this book. Did my grandfather somehow know he was going to die that day? And what did he mean by "memories live longer than dreams": did he mean that the past is more important than the future? Or was he saying, as I have come to believe, that *material* dreams have their place, but that life is made up of memories, which come from *experiences*?

He might, he might not have done. Perhaps this is just a reading that suits me. At the very least, it was quite a parting shot. In that note, he addressed, and gave advice on, one of the most important questions a person can ask, the question, in fact, which is at the heart of this book: how should we live in order to be happy?

Thou Shall *Covet Thy Neighbour's Donkey*

For most of the past two millennia, the answer to that question was defined by circumstance, and, in the West at least, controlled by the church. Circumstance remained fairly constant. Life, for most people, for most of those years, was a matter of scraping by, not much above the subsistence level.

The church's message did not waver much either. Happiness, it said, would come in the next life, in heaven. To get there you had to live a good life of moderation, thrift, and poverty – after all, it was easier for a camel to pass through the eye of a needle than for a rich man to get into heaven. And you had to follow a set of rules. One of those was explicitly anti-materialistic: thou shalt not covet thy neighbour's house, wife, manservant, maidservant, ox, donkey, or, if you really thought about it, any of his material possessions.

The church's – and therefore society's – version of the good life remained the same for most of the next two thousand years. It shifted, slightly, for a couple of centuries. During the Crusades, when the church needed Christian solders to protect the Holy Land, you could also be good and happy by fighting for Jesus.

After the wars were over, though, the definition returned to the older, simpler message: that you should be moderate, thrifty and poor, and, while you were about it, no coveting anything your neighbour had.

That ideal made a lot of sense when society was static, when, if you were born poor, as most people were, you would stay poor. What was the point, after all, of wishing for something you would never have?

But, as circumstances changed, especially from the 16th century onwards, that version of the good life and happiness did not make nearly so much sense. Thanks to mining, banking, and trade, at first, and, later, the machines of the Industrial Revolution, Western society became increasingly prosperous.

That created a new problem.

For the first time, for large numbers of people, there was tension between church and circumstance, between the version of the good life they heard being preached from the pulpit each Sunday, and the life they were living the other days of the week. Did material success in the here and now really mean they were not living a good life, and that they would not, ultimately, be happy?

That did not seem fair. Yet the church's teaching – camel, eye of needle, rich man, heaven – was very clear on this. Through its vast web of preachers, though, the church was the only organization with the power to shape, mould, and define what the masses believed. As a result, its version of the good life remained the dominant one – until the early 20th century.

Then, the shift in circumstances began to happen more rapidly, especially in the United States. That put the church's teaching even further out of step with day-to-day reality.

Worse, the church's advice, that people should be thrifty, moderate and not materialistic, was not delivering the levels of mass consumption that could keep up with mass production.

Fortunately, around this time, there was a new network, a direct competitor to the church's pulpits, if you like: the mass media of magazines, newspapers, cinema, and radio. The leaders of the secular world – the captains of consciousness – used that network to solve the problem of overproduction, and take advantage of the possibilities of mass production, by preaching a good life that was defined in material, consumer terms, like cars, toasters, radios, and dishwashers.

Happiness, according to this new gospel of consumption, could come in this life. To get it, you had to live a good life of profligate, conspicuous consumption – after all, the more you spent, the more work you would create for other people, and the more wealth you would create. To have more you had to spend more, you had to be materialistic: to covet the things thy neighbours, the Joneses, had – if not their donkeys, certainly their cars.

This innovative idea was not only counterintuitive, because it flipped the old truth on its head. It was also revolutionary: it sparked the consumer revolution. More importantly, it worked. It took us on an exciting journey to unprecedented material progress. It has also, unintentionally, led us into the perfect storm of *Stuffocation* today. Which means it is time, once again, to open our minds to another innovative, revolutionary idea.

Manifesto:
Why We Need Experience More than Ever

For a new value system to replace materialism, and be the answer to *Stuffocation*, it will have to solve all the problems that come with it – like pollution, overconsumption, and status anxiety. It should also take advantage of all the opportunities it contains – like the technologies that give us the benefits of access without the downsides of physical ownership.

It will have to appeal to everyone you would call a captain of consciousness in the 21st century – businesses, governments, you and me. It will have to provide profit for businesses, and jobs for people. It will need to produce taxable income, and a useful benchmark for governments. It should also satisfy our innate desires for happiness, meaning, and status.

Rather than defeatist and dull, it should be aspirational and inspiring. Instead of implying that we have reached the apex of human achievement and that from here on in we should just plateau, it should hold out the promise that life will be better in the future.

The way ahead, out of the storm of *Stuffocation*, is not minimalism, simple living, or the medium chill. Minimalism, I think, is too negative, too reductive. Simple living is too regressive. The medium chill lacks aspiration. The new value system that will solve *Stuffocation*, I think, is experientialism.

Experientialism will be good for all the stakeholders in our shared future. It will work, to begin with, for all of us. It will make us happier, healthier, richer, in every sense: less clutter, less regret, less anxiety, more meaning, more status, better conversations, more connections, a stronger sense of belonging.

To succeed in this new world, businesses, rather than trying to flog newly positioned but actually the same old stuff, will have to create genuinely new, engaging goods, services, and adventures that give us social and experiential currency – that is, a story to tell and an experience worth remembering.

And governments, instead of being fixated on increases in GDP and material progress, should shift their focus to improving wellbeing and experiential progress. A good start would be to raise psychologists to the same level as economists. We also need, alongside the new measures of society's wellbeing and progress, a new measure of personal progress that is as informative and simple as the figure that tells you your salary, but that expresses your success in experiential rather than material terms.

If we all – you, me, businesses, and governments – embrace experientialism, I think it can achieve in this century what materialism did in the last.

Just as materialism hauled billions out of poverty and delivered standards of living for the masses that would have sounded ludicrous in the first decades of the 20th century, so experientialism, I believe, will do something similar this century.

It will generate advances in wellbeing and quality of life that might sound, today at least, like they are the wishful thinking of an idealistic mind: shorter working hours, more time with family and friends, spending our time doing things we really enjoy.

As materialism delivered material progress that was almost impossible for most people to imagine before it happened, so experientialism will deliver experiential progress that is just as hard for most to imagine today.

Forecast:
the Rise of Experientialism

For all these reasons, then, we need to replace materialism with experientialism. And the good news is that we are. Because not only is experientialism exactly the sort of innovation that is likely to spread from the innovators to the mainstream, there are already signs that it is making that jump – even if they are, as you would expect at the beginning of experientialist era, still unevenly distributed.

There is Ron Inglehart's research, for instance, which shows that there is a long-term shift in our attitudes, away from materialism. There is Chris Goodall's analysis, which demonstrates that our behaviour is changing, and we are now consuming fewer materials.

There is the rising experience economy. There are the pioneer governments, measuring wellbeing and creating new benchmarks of progress. And then there are all the indications of the shift to experientialism in how people are choosing to spend their time and money: the young people living in smaller apartments in cities and not buying cars, the old people spending more on holidays and healthcare, the luxury consumers spending more on experiences rather than stuff, the collaborative consumers renting rather than buying, the millions reading e-books instead of physical books, and the billions sharing their experiences every day on Facebook, Instagram, and Twitter.

We are still, as I said, at the beginning. As the years pass, we will see more evidence of the rise of experientialism. There will be more people opting to work less and play more, and more brands delivering experience instead of physical clutter. In the next decades, the signs of experientialism will become more evenly distributed, just as the hallmarks of materialism – like luxury label goods, oversized watches and two-car garages – became more obvious as the 20th century progressed.

The last time Western society came to a crossroads, we solved the headache of overproduction, and the age-old issue of scarcity, by becoming materialistic. Then, as materialists, we became part of the problem of *Stuffocation*.

Now, as we arrive at our crossroads, we are becoming the answer to it. As we become experientialists, we are lessening our ecological footprints, clearing out the clutter, reducing our reliance on stuff. We are keeping up with the Joneses through experiences rather than objects. And we are starting to think of progress in experiential rather than material terms.

We have got enough and had enough of stuff.

We are realizing that, to show our status, to live a life that is meaningful, and to be happy in the 21st century – you and I and society in general – we all need experience more than ever.

Acknowledgements

"No author is an island", the poet John Donne almost wrote. That is especially true of non-fiction authors. A work of non-fiction may only have one name on the cover, but in truth it is the work of many people.

There are a huge number of people without whom the book you are holding in your hands would not exist. More than 100 people gave up their time to discuss the idea with me over tea, coffee, lunch, dinner, beer, wine, Skype, Skype video call, telephone, and email. There are the people, especially on America's West Coast and in Australia, who got up early or stayed up late so that the timings worked for them and me. There are the people whose work I have drawn on, both directly and indirectly. (I have tried to credit all those in the Endnotes. If any are missing, please let me know, and I will rectify the situation.)

So it may be my name on the front, but in many ways, *Stuffocation* stands on the hard work, good nature, and, yes, shoulders of many others. Given I wanted a clean cover, though, there was no way we'd have got all those names on the front.

I'm going to start by thanking my case studies, the people who shared the most, because they shared not only their ideas, but their lives. So, thank you: Ryan Nicodemus, Joshua Fields Millburn, Tammy Strobel, Graham Hill, Olga Sasplugas, Courtney Carver, Ben Howell, Sarah Howell, Marianne Cantwell, Jim Whyte, Sue Lenet, Bertrand Lenet, Dave Roberts, Jenn Roberts, Cliff Hodges, Deborah Richmond.

And then there's my case studies' friends and families, who helped bring their wives, husbands, daughters, sons, mothers, fathers, and friends' stories to life by adding the sort of details they had forgotten, didn't think were appropriate, or, let's be honest here, hoped weren't mentioned. So, thank you: Logan Smith, Tina Smith, Derek Hill, Hannah Wray, Mark Tuttle, Ren LeVally, Jenn Oslawski, Katherine Tickle, Dan Bosscher, Don Hodges, Hilda Hodges, Kai McDonald, Kathy Hettick, Hector Proud, Sarah Whyte, Emma Hutchinson, Andrew Bird, Andi Norris, and Coni Battle.

Then there are all the people who gave up so much of their time but whose stories ended up on the cutting-room floor. Editing is a nasty process that takes no prisoners. They don't say "kill your darlings" for nothing. Please know that your story did help me find the way forward, but there simply wasn't room to keep all the stories in – even if those stories include the sort of break-ups, breakdowns, breakthroughs, and gold bullion that make great stories. So, thank you: Rachel Jonat, Chris Wray, Colin Wright, Joshua

Becker, Simon Smith, Jeff Dobbs, Chris Concannon, Neal Gorenflo, Nicole Yau, Teresa Carey, Valeska von Mühldorfer, Ethan Segal, Fredrik Lofgren, Rakesh Banburi, Mike Benson, and Roberto Gonzalez.

Then there are all the experts, who have spent, in many cases, decades in their field. Your dedication to discovery, and to challenging the status quo and the conventional wisdom, is exactly the sort of thing that raises the fog a bit more, so that people like me can have a better view of the direction the world is turning. Thank you for that, and also, among other things: for your suggestions of more avenues to explore, for challenging and inspiring me over lunch and email and phone and Skype, for responding to far more fact-checking emails than strictly necessary, for patiently explaining how you do what you do, and for pushing me to re-examine whether I believed in what I believe – and whether I really was reading the data right.

So, thank you: Richard Thaler, Oliver James, Barry Schwartz, Stuart Ewen, Robert Fogel, Chris Goodall, Michael Schrage, Ron Inglehart, Ryan Howell, Jeanne Arnold, Darby Saxbe, Travis Carter, Leaf van Boven, Tom Gilovich, Brian Wansink, Geoffrey Miller, Danny Miller, Rupert Pennant-Rea, Garson O'Toole, Daniel Franklin, John Andrews, Rob Hyndman, Corinne Shefner-Rogers, Jim Dearing, Juliet Schor, Anna Coote, Benjamin Kline Hunnicutt, Pippa Norris, Trudi Toyne, Felipe Fernandez-Armesto, Avner Offer, Peter Stearns, Joe Pine, Jim Gilmore, Grant McCracken, Blake Mycoskie, Rob Symington, Alice Marwick,

Harry Parr, Sam Bompas, Jules Evans, Bob Cummins, Bernice Steinhardt, Chris Hoenig, Mark Tungate, Ann Mack, Albert Cañigueral, Anna-Maren Ashford, James O'Shaughnessy, Joe Goodman, Alastair Humphreys, Richard Layard, Tim Kasser, Vicki Robin, Gabriel Rossman, Janice Rutherford, and Eve Fisher.

Thank you to all the great people who put up with me being the worst of customers – stay for ages, spend very little – and brought me croissants, cake, one-and-a-half-shot cappuccinos, and smokey Russian caravan tea at the Hampshire Hog, the Thatched House, Brackenbury Deli, and Artisan.

Thank you also to the various libraries which have housed and helped: the LSE, the Imperial War Museum, the British Library, the Schlesinger Library (especially Ellen Shea), and the Hoover Presidential Library (in particular Spencer Howard).

Thank you to everyone who has believed in *Stuffocation* and worked – often tirelessly, at short notice, and late into the night – with me to make it happen: my agent Charlie Viney, my publisher Christopher Lascelles, copy editor Sue Browning, indexer Janice Rayment, web developer Tony Kurisankal, cover designer Ruby Epsilon, and publicist Patrick Mcaleenan.

Then there are all my friends, both old and new, who have inspired me, and who have helped with contacts, ideas, suggestions, data, Palaeolithic, psychological and economic knowledge, and the use of a Nespresso machine, a heater, and a home to write in: Ewen Brown, Adrian Sandiford, Catherine Mayer, Dan and Jacqueline Bosscher, Marilyn Wallman, Ian Sorrell, Julian Ellerby, James Kennedy, Daniel and Flip Antoine, Susan Herbert, Peter Markham, Gary Horne, Sophy Roberts, Nick Redman, Sean Thomas, Steve Tooze, Philipp Schwalber, George Collings, and, of course, Edwin Blanchard. The biggest thank yous here must go to Wendy Mandy, for helping me believe I had it in me, and Caroline van den Brul, for exceptionally insightful comments on an early draft.

A huge thank you to Jenny and Alan and Rob – for your love and support, my education, a love of stories, and myriad experiences.

A planet-sized thank you to my wife, partly for the discussions and the patience, but mostly for agreeing that instead of us having the extension you wanted, I could write the book I believed in.

Finally, thank *you* for reading my book. I think the ideas it contains are going to change the world. I hope you agree, and that you have already started to see the signs of experientialism rising, both in your own life, and in the lives of those around you.

Endnotes

INTRODUCTION

How We've Had Enough of Stuff

Page 1. Ryan Nicodemus and Joshua Fields Millburn

The best way to find out about Ryan Nicodemus and Joshua Fields Millburn, their books, their book tour (coming to your city soon), and how they help people get rid of what doesn't matter, is by visiting their fantastic website www.theminimalists.com.

Page 9. The Story of Stuff

Watch the Story of Stuff and read Story of Stuff, Referenced and Annotated Script, which contains evidence for the video's statements, at www.storyofstuff.org.

Page 9. "Four out of five were materialistic in 1970"

Ronald Inglehart, "The Silent Revolution in Europe: Intergenerational Change in Post-Industrial Societies", *American Political Science Review* Vol. 65, No. 4, December 1971. For updates since then, see Ronald Inglehart, "Changing Values among Western Publics from 1970 to 2006", *West European Politics* Vol.

31, Nos. 1–2, January–March 2008; also, the World Values Survey (www.worldvaluessurvey.org). Many make sense of the shift to less materialistic values by referring to Abraham Maslow, "A Theory of Human Motivation", *Psychological Review* Vol. 50, No. 4, 1943. Also, read about a generational shift to post-materialism in David Brooks, "The Experience Economy", *New York Times*, 14 February 2011.

Page 10. Advertising agency research

This research was conducted by an advertising agency called Euro RSCG Worldwide, which, in the time it's taken me to write the book, has become Havas Worldwide. The research paper is called The New Consumer (www.thenewconsumer.com). I calculated the number of people who might have had enough of stuff based on The New Consumer statistics that 67% believe most of us would be better off if we lived more simply, and that there are 63.23 million people in the UK, and 313.9 million in the US. Sources for those figures: World Bank and US Census Bureau.

Page 11. Affluenza and status anxiety

For the best introduction on how mass consumption is leading to mass depression, read Oliver James, *Affluenza* (London: Vermilion, 2007). For the primer on the concept of status anxiety, read Alain de Botton, *Status Anxiety* (London: Hamish Hamilton, 2004). They are quite different in style. James's is chatty, like having a conversation with an intelligent friend. De Botton's is written like a philosophical conversation starter. Each is well worth reading.

Page 11. "An environmentalist will tell you..."

For the environmentalist's view, read Greenpeace reports, most sensible newspapers, and the UN-commissioned IPCC report. For an alternative and fascinating view, read Peter H Diamandis and Steven Kottler's *Abundance: The Future Is Better Than You Think* (New York: Free Press, 2011).

Page 11. Ageing population

On the ageing population's heightened interest in experiences rather than material goods, consider 20th-century business success Malcolm Forbes, whose maxim was "he who dies with the most toys wins". When, as the owner of a lot of very big, expensive toys, like a 151-foot yacht with a helicopter pad, he died in 1990, not long after a $2 million 70th birthday party in Morocco, it didn't seem excessively unreasonable. It does now.

As people get older their priorities shift "from material things to ethereal things. Boomers are more interested in acquiring more experiences over more 'stuff'" – according to Matt Thornhill, an expert on older consumers who is co-author of *Boomer Consumer* (Carlsbad, California: Linx Corp, 2007) and founder of a consulting company targeting the elderly called Boomer Project. Source of this quote: Paul Hyman, "Baby Boomers: Every Silver Lining Has a Touch of Grey", *CRM Magazine*, February 2012.

People's consumption peaks around the age of 50, according to the way Kenneth Gronbach, author of *The Age Curve: How to Profit from the Coming Demographic Storm*, reads US Bureau of Labor Statistics. That is the time, he says, when people's earnings and consumption are at their highest and when they own their biggest homes. Source: as above.

Page 11. Growing population

There will be around 9 billion by 2050, according to John Andrews and Daniel Franklin (eds.), *Megachange: The World in 2050* (London: Economist, 2011). See also, the French Institute of Demographic Studies (Ined)'s forecast that there will be 9.7 billion by 2050, up from just over 7 billion today.

Page 11. The rise of the global middle class

Consider, for example, the opening statement in Dominic Wilson, Alex L. Kelston, Swarnali Ahmed, "Is this the BRICs Decade?", *Goldman Sachs' BRICs Monthly Issue*, 10/03, May 2010: "The last decade saw the BRICs make their mark on the global economic landscape. Over the past 10 years they have contributed over a third of world GDP growth and grown from one-sixth of the world economy to almost a quarter (in PPP terms). Looking forward to the coming decade, we expect this trend to continue and become even more pronounced."

Or consider the final sentence in Catherine Wolfram, "Rising Middle Class Fuels Global Energy Surge", Bloomberg.com, 17 January 2012: "There is no doubt that the rise of the global middle class is a positive development. Yet, if we don't forecast and plan accordingly, it could lead to dire unexpected environmental consequences and cause dramatic increases in energy prices that ultimately diminish the very livelihoods we are trying to improve."

Page 11. The move to cities and fewer cars

For more on the move to cities, consider the fact that humans officially became an urban species in 2007: since then, more than 50% of us have lived in cities. Source: Ricky Burdett and Deyan Sudjic, *The Endless City: The Urban Age Project* (London: Phaidon Press, 2007). Also: "One hundred years ago, 2 out of every 10 people lived in an urban area. By 1990, less than 40% of the global population lived in a city, but as of 2010, more than half of all people live in an urban area. By 2030, 6 out of every 10 people will live in a city, and by 2050, this proportion will increase to 7 out of 10 people." Source: World Health Organization

Also, Ariel Schwartz, "We Are Approaching Peak Car Use", *Fast Company*, 5 July 2011, and Richard Florida, *The Great Reset: How the Post-Crash Economy Will Change the Way We Live and Work* (New York: HarperBusiness, 2011). For a quick introduction, read Richard Florida, "The Fading Differentiation between City and Suburb", *Urban Land Magazine* (urbanland.uli.org), January 2013.

For Ruth Milkman's view on why people are disillusioned with capitalism, see Ruth Milkman, Stephanie Luce and Penny Lewis, *Changing the Subject: A Bottom-up Account of Occupy Wall Street in New York City* (City University of New York).

Page 12. "Researchers like Tom Gilovich have shown that this is not the case"

Tom Gilovich and Leaf van Boven, "To Do or to Have? That Is the Question", *Journal of Personality and Social Psychology* Vol. 85, No. 6, 2003. There is more on why experiences make us happier than material goods in Chapter Eight.

Page 12. Rising costs, stagnating incomes

See Richard Dobbs et al., *Resource Revolution: Meeting the World's Energy, Materials, Food, and Water Needs*, a report from McKinsey & Company (November, 2011). Also, "Hitting our Limits?", *The Economist*, 14 October 2011.

Page 13. "A technologist..."

For examples of technology facilitating the shift from owning material things to experience, consider the success of Spotify, Zipcar, and the Kindle. Various sources, including: "All Eyes on the Sharing Economy", *The Economist*, 9 Mar 2013.

The Perfect Storm

Page 14. "Applied more than 5,000 times"

Source: Everett M Rogers, *Diffusion of Innovations* (New York: Free Press, 1962, fifth edition, 2003)

Sherlock Holmes and the Mystery of the Krispy Kremes

Page 16.

This story draws on a number of reports, including: Peter Laing, "Cops Tackle Krispy Kreme Traffic Chaos – and Pick up a Box of Doughnuts", *Deadline News*, 15 February 2013; Shiv Malik, "Krispy Kremes Cause Chaos in Edinburgh Streets", *The Guardian*, 15 February 2013; and Harriet Arkell, "Jam Doughnuts: Hundreds of Motorists Bring Traffic Chaos to M8 as They Queue for Opening of New Krispy Kreme", *Mail Online*, 15 February 2013.

To make sense of evolutionary psychology and how it relates to consumerism, read the funny and engaging Geoffrey Miller, *Spent: Sex, Evolution and the Secrets of Consumerism* (New York: William Heinemann, 2009). In the UK, the paperback is Geoffrey Miller, *Must-Have: The Hidden Instincts Behind Everything We Buy* (London: Vintage, 2010). Not as funny, but as inspiring, and brilliant at helping us understand why we make (often bad) decisions on food, is Brian Wansink, *Mindless Eating: Why We Eat More Than We Think* (London: Bantam, 2006, reprint edition, 2010).

Page 17. "Krispy Kreme's Original Glazed contains two hundred and seventeen kilocalories, including three grams of protein, twenty-two grams of carbohydrates and thirteen grams of fat. The calorie counts go up from there."

Source: Krispy Kreme nutritional information.

Page 19. We are now living in an age of material abundance.

Various sources, including: Avner Offer, *The Challenge of Affluence* (Oxford: Oxford University Press, 2006), and John Kenneth Galbraith, *The Affluent Society* (New York: Houghton Mifflin Harcourt, 1958).

Page 19. "A shirt, before the Industrial Revolution, cost around £3,000 in today's money."

I asked an historian by the name of Eve Fisher to explain. Here's the reply she emailed me:

"Take a standard medieval man's shirt, a la Breughel's *Peasant Wedding*, etc., long sleeves, yoke, some smocking, band collar, hemmed, wrists, etc. Estimate it takes 7 hours to sew a shirt like that by hand - cutting the fabric, sewing, finishing inside and out, etc. Now, you have to have the cloth to sew. This would have been relatively fine, dense cloth. An historical reconstruction site (National Geographic) figured a good weaver could produce 2 inches an hour. It would have taken at least 4 yards of fabric, but you can't just have the 4 yards on a loom. It takes at least 1–2 feet at each end for a warp, and so 4 × 3 = 12 feet plus 3 feet at the end = 15 feet, 15 × 12 = 180 inches, divide by 2 = 90 hours. And you have to produce the thread/yarn to weave with. There would have been 15–20 threads per inch, we'll say he's poor and only gets coarse cloth, 15 threads. The fabric would have been a yard wide, so that would be 15 × 36 = 540 threads, each 15 feet long, just for the warp, a little less for the weft, but we'll just double it, so 1080 × 5 yards = 5,400 yards of thread. This would have taken about 400 hours to weave. (This is also the reason why women were defined by spinning – 'spinsters' - to make all that thread, fabric, etc., took a TREMENDOUS amount of time and energy.) So 7 + 90 + 400 = 497, or round to 500 hours of hand labor to make one shirt. Multiply by minimum wage of $7.00 = $3,500.00 for a shirt. No wonder fabric was never, ever thrown out, but worn to pieces, and then cut down for the kids, and then turned into diapers, rags, etc. Also why peasants had one set of work clothes, and a set of 'best' clothes (Sundays, holidays, etc.). Because that of course is just the shirt - you'd still need breeches/stockings, vest and jerkin for a man; skirt, bodice for a woman. And a cloak would be nice."

Page 20. Humans have many motivations – why focus on status, meaning, and happiness?

There are many things people want. I chose to stick with these three because I think they are a simple way to cover most of the basic human desires. For more, read Alain de Botton, *Status Anxiety* (London: Penguin, 2005); Roman Krznaric, *How to Find Fulfilling Work* (London: Macmillan, 2012); and Tim Kasser, *Values and Human Wellbeing*, a commissioned research paper for The Bellagio Initiative, November 2011; Geoffrey Miller, *Spent: Sex, Evolution and the Secrets of Consumerism* (New York: William Heinemann, 2009); S H Schwartz, "Universals in the Content and Structure of Values: Theory and Empirical Tests in 20 Countries", in M. Zanna (ed.), *Advances in Experimental Social Psychology* Vol. 25 (New York: Academic Press, 1992); and also Steven Reiss, *Who Am I?* (New York: Berkley Books, 2000).

CHAPTER ONE

The Farm Boy Who Discovered
the Secret to Forecasting

Page 27.

If *The Economist* will let you in, get hold of the 1984 Christmas edition – less for the veracity of this story and more for the adverts. They are mostly for cigars, whisky, and business travel, and all aimed squarely at middle-aged business men. With thanks to Daniel Franklin for letting me see look through the archives.

The dustmen story has become quite a meme at *The Economist*. It first appeared in *The Economist* Christmas Edition, 1984. It has also featured in "Garbage in, garbage out", *The Economist*, 3 June 1995, for example, and in *"The Future's Rubbish", The World in 2012* (London: The Economist, 2011).

Page 29. "How could the dustmen do so well compared with people who have been trained to know and who had far more information, the so-called experts? And, which is more worrying, what is the point in trying to forecast the future if an expert's forecasts are no more accurate than a prediction from the proverbial man on the street, no better, you might say, than rubbish?"

It has been pointed out to me that this could be offensive to dustmen. Can't see it myself, but just to be clear: it is not my intention to insult dustmen. Dustmen do possess expertise, but not, generally, in the field of forecasting. (If you are a dustman with forecasting skill, or know one who has an uncanny ability to know what's next, please let me know by emailing james@stuffocation.org.)

Forecasts Are Not Facts, They Are Maps

Page 29.

For Nassim Nicholas Taleb's dismal view of forecasting, read Nassim Nicholas Taleb, *The Black Swan* (New York: Penguin, 2007). The story of the turkey is borrowed, as Taleb notes, from the philosopher Bertrand Russell.

Using the Past to Tell the Future

Page 31.

I am indebted to three sources for this section: Peter N Stearns, "Why Study History?", American Historical Association, 1998; Nate Silver, *The Signal and the Noise* (New York: Allen Lane, 2012); and Rob Hyndman, "Why are some things easier to forecast than others?", 18 September 2012, on his blog, Hyndsight (www. robjhyndman.com/hyndsight).

Page 32. "In the 1970s, the high temperature forecasts were wrong, on average, by about six degrees. Today they are only wrong by half that amount, three degrees. When hurricane forecasters predicted where a hurricane would hit land in the 1980s they were usually out by 350 miles. Today, their predictions are only wrong by 100 miles."

If you're not ready – yet – to take on all of Nate Silver's *The Signal and the Noise*, read Nate Silver, "The Weatherman Is Not a Moron", *New York Times*, 7 September 2012.

The Farm Where the Corn Did Not Grow Tall

Page 34.

For Everett Rogers's version of his life, read Everett M Rogers, *The Fourteenth Paw* (Singapore: Asian Media Information and Communication Centre, 2008). My version also draws on conversations with people who knew him (especially his wife, Corinne Shefner-Rogers) and the following: Everett M Rogers, *Diffusion of Innovations* (New York: Free Press, 1962, fifth edition, 2003); Thomas E Backer, James Dearing, Arvind Singhal, Thomas Valente, "Writing with Ev—Words to Transform Science into Action", *Journal of Health Communication* Vol. 10, 2005; Arvind Singhal, "Everett M Rogers, an Intercultural Life: From Iowa Farm Boy to Global Intellectual", *International Journal of Intercultural Relations* Vol. 36, No. 6, 2012; Arvind Singhal and James Dearing, *Communication of Innovations: A Journey with Ev Rogers* (Thousand Oaks, California: Sage, 2006).

I have Corinne Shefner-Rogers to thank for sending me Bruce Ryan and Neal Gross's original paper: "The Diffusion of Hybrid Seed Corn in Two Iowa Communities", *Rural Sociology* Vol. 8, No. 1, 1943.

There is an excellent analysis of the paper in Malcolm Gladwell, The Tipping Point (New York: Little, Brown, 2000). (But why did Gladwell never mention Everett Rogers, who had made sense of it all? I'm going to ask him one day and find out.)

Page 34. The Corn Song

Many sources, including Arvid Huisman, "That's where the tall corn grows", *The Daily Freeman-Journal*, 19 November , 2012. Watch people singing the Corn Song at the Fifth Annual UI Libraries Staff Recognition Celebration, uploaded 4 June 2012 to YouTube.

Using the Present to Forecast the Future

Page 38.

For an excellent introduction to forecasting, read the first chapter of Martin Raymond, *The Trend Forecaster's Handbook* (London: Lawrence King, 2010). I have Martin Raymond to thank for introducing me to the field of forecasting, and teaching me a great deal of what I know about it.

For good examples of forecasting from the past, take a look at two prescient texts: Alvin Toffler, *Future Shock* (New York: Random House, 1970), and Daniel Bell, *The Coming of Post-Industrial Society* (New York: Basic Books, 1973).

CHAPTER TWO

The Original Mad Men
and the Job of Creating Desire

Page 43.

To understand where the ideas came from that influenced the original Mad Men – people like Edward Bernays and Earnest Elmo Calkins and Christine Frederick – read Wilfred Trotter, *Instincts of the Herd in Peace and War* (London: Macmillan, 1916); Gustave Le Bon, *The Crowd: A Study of the Popular Mind* (London: Unwin, 1903); Edward Bernays, *Propaganda* (New York: H Liveright, 1928, IG Publishing, 2005 edition); Edward Bernays, *Crystallizing Public Opinion* (New York: Liveright, 1923); Stuart Ewen, *Captains of Consciousness* (New York: McGraw-Hill, 1976); Stuart Ewen, *PR! A Social History of Spin* (New York: Basic Books, 1996); Matthew Hilton, *Consumerism in 20th-century Britain* (Cambridge: Cambridge University Press, 2003).

To understand the birth of consumerism, read Mark Tungate, *Adland: A Global History of Advertising* (London: Kogan Page, 2007, second edition 2013), Frank Trentmann (ed.), *The Oxford Handbook of the History of Consumption* (Oxford: Oxford University Press, 2012), Grant McCracken, *Culture and Consumption* (Bloomington: Indiana University Press, 1988), Jan de Vries, *The Industrious Revolution* (Cambridge: Cambridge University Press, 2008).

The scene from Hoover's life was inspired by "Happiness Machines" and "The Engineering of Consent", A Century of the Self, Adam Curtis, BBC, 2002, television. It was informed by "Hoover Sees Prosperous Era", *Houston Post Despatch*, 11 May 1925, and "Advertising Is a Vital Force, Says Hoover", *Boston Daily Globe*, 11 May 1925.

Thank you to the "Quote Investigator", Garson O'Toole, and to Spencer Howard, archives technician at the Hoover Presidential Library, for making sure the quotes in *Stuffocation* are correct.

Page 44. "In the sixty years since the Civil War's end, the population had increased by a factor of three, from 35 to 114 million. Over the same period, output had risen between twelve and fourteen times."

This, and much of this section, is sourced from a number of compelling accounts of this time: Jeffrey Kaplan, "The Gospel of Consumption", *Orion Magazine*, May/June 2008; Giles Slade, *Made to Break* (Cambridge: Harvard University Press, 2006); Vance Packard, *The Hidden Persuaders* (New York: Pelican, 1957), and Vance Packard, *The Waste Makers* (New York: Pelican, 1960). Simon N. Patten, *The New Basis of Civilization* (New York: Macmillan, 1907) and Victor Lebow's "Price Competition in 1955", *Journal of Retailing*, Spring 1955, were also useful.

Page 44. "The American people had reached, so the US secretary of labor James J Davis told The New York Times, the point of "need saturation".

Source: Jeffrey Kaplan, "The Gospel of Consumption", *Orion Magazine*, May/June 2008.

Page 45. "By 1927, the country's textile mills could produce enough cloth for the whole year by operating only six months of the year. Less than a fifth of America's shoe factories could produce a year's supply of footwear."

Source: again, Jeffrey Kaplan, "The Gospel of Consumption", *Orion Magazine*, May/June 2008.

Page 46. Bernard Mandeville

Read Bernard Mandeville, "The Fable of The Bees: or, Private Vices, Public Benefits" (1714) online.

Page 47. Captains of consciousness

The best place to find out about the role of the "captains of consciousness" in creating the "consumptionism" which has become the hallmark of 20th century society, is Stuart Ewen, *Captains of Consciousness* (New York: McGraw-Hill, 1976).

The New and Improved Throwaway Culture

Page 48.

For a man who made a living writing simple copy that really spoke to people, Earnest Elmo Calkins's autobiography is very hard to read. Still, if you want to find out more about him, it's the thing to read: Earnest Elmo Calkins, *Louder Please! The Diary of A Deaf Man* (New York: Scribners, 1937). On Calkins's tilt towards obsolescence, read Earnest Elmo Calkins, "Beauty the New Business Tool", *The Atlantic*, August 1927; also, Roy Sheldon and Egmont Arens, *Consumer Engineering: A New Technique for Prosperity* (New York: Harper Brothers, 1932).

Page 51. "The topic of how to create the new regular buying consumer... would be discussed at meetings of the New York Sales Managers' Club and the New York Advertising Club, and in the pages of leading trade publications like Printer's Ink and Advertising and Selling."

Sources: Giles Slade, Made to Break (Cambridge: Harvard University Press, 2006); and Janice Rutherford, Selling Mrs. Consumer: Christine Frederick and the Rise of Household Efficiency (Athens, Georgia: University of Georgia Press, 2003).

Page 51. "We must induce people," wrote another adman, J George Frederick, in a lead article in Advertising and Selling in 1928, "to buy a greater variety of goods on the same principle that they now buy automobiles, radios

and clothes, namely: buying goods not to wear out, but to trade in or discard after a short time."

Source: Giles Slade, *Made to Break* (Cambridge: Harvard University Press, 2006).

The Birth of Death Dating

Page 51. "American men bought 150 million throwaway collars and cuffs in 1872."

Source: Giles Slade, *Made to Break* (Cambridge: Harvard University Press, 2006).

Page 53. "The same process of industrial mutation – if I may use that biological term," Schumpeter wrote, "incessantly revolutionises the economic structure from within, incessantly destroys the old, incessantly creating a new one. This process of Creative Destruction is the essential fact about Capitalism."

From Joseph Schumpeter, *Capitalism, Socialism and Democracy* (New York: Harper, 1942).

Page 54. Christine Frederick

For more on Christine Frederick, read Christine McGaffey Frederick, *Selling Mrs. Consumer* (New York: Business Borse, 1929); also Janice Rutherford, *Selling Mrs. Consumer: Christine Frederick and the Rise of Household Efficiency* (Athens, Georgia: University of Georgia Press, 2003).

Page 54. Bernard London

Find Bernard London, *Ending the Depression Through Planned Obsolescence* (1932) on Wikimedia.org.

Page 54. Henry Ford's resistance to obsolescence. "We want the man who buys one of our cars never to have to buy another," he had stated in 1922. "We never make an improvement that renders any previous model obsolete."

Source: The Henry Ford (www.thehenryford.org).

Richard Nixon in the Kitchen and the Best Idea of the 20ᵗʰ Century

Page 57.

Sources for the story of Nixon, Khrushchev and the kitchen include William Safire, "The Cold War's Hot Kitchen", *New York Times*, 23 July 2009; also, various articles in BBC.co.uk, New York Times archives, History.com, and old newscasts on YouTube.com.

Read the transcript – to which I've made minor alterations for the sake of grammar and ease of reading – at the Freedom of Information Act Reading Room (www.foia.cia.gov).

Page 61. The best idea of the 20th century?

For an excellent reading of the benefits of capitalism, read Michael Schuman, "How To Save Capitalism", *Time Magazine*, 30 January 2012; Martin Wolf, "Is the Age of Unlimited Growth Over?", *Financial Times*, 3 October 2012; and Stephen Moore and Julian L. Simon, "The Greatest Century That Ever Was: 25 Miraculous Trends of the Past 100 Years", *Policy Analysis*, No. 364, December 15, 1999.

Page 61. "By 2030, so many believe, we may even have eradicated poverty."

Read more about ending poverty in "Poverty: Not Always with Us", *The Economist*, 1 June 2013, and Mark Tran, "New UN goals call for end to extreme poverty by 2030", *The Guardian*, 30 May 2013.

CHAPTER THREE

Barbra Streisand and the Law of Unintended Consequences

Page 63.

The best place to read about the story of Ken Adelman and Barbra Streisand is on Adelman's website, www.adelman.com. If you do, it's worth looking up some of the things Streisand's supporters said about Adelman.

Page 63. For the picture of Streisand's home...

Actually, maybe we should all just leave her alone. Don't you think enough people have looked by now?

The Prince and The Rabbit-Proof Fence

Page 66.

For a full version of the story of how rabbits came to Australia, read Mark Kellet, "Rabbits in Australia", *Australian Heritage*, Autumn 2006.

The story of Thomas Austin was greatly helped by reading British History Online (www.british-history.ac.uk); also, "The Acclimatisation Society", *The Melbourne Argus*, 21 April 1864, and "The Late Mr Thomas Austin", *The Melbourne Argus*, 18 December 1871.

The Law of Unintended Consequences

Page 69.

For more on Robert Merton's law of unintended consequences, read Robert K Merton, "The Unanticipated Consequences of

Purposive Social Action", *American Sociological Review* Vol. 1, No. 6, December 1936.

Page 69. "Change is caused by lazy, greedy, frightened people looking for easier, more profitable and safer ways of doing things. And they rarely know what they are doing."

From Ian Morris, *Why the West Rules—For Now: The Patterns of History and What They Reveal About the Future* (New York: Farrar, Straus and Giroux, 2010).

Mad Men, Silent Spring

Page 71.

This scene is in "The Gold Violin", Mad Men, New York, AMC, 2008, television.

Rachel Carson, *Silent Spring* (New York: Houghton Mifflin, 1962) is quite a read.

Page 73. "Environmental damage has really only got worse through the years"

Source: UN-commissioned IPCC report.

Page 73. "The greatest extinction of plant and animal species since the dinosaurs died out"

Source: The Center for Biological Diversity (www.biologicaldiversity.org).

The Dark Side of Materialism

Page 73.

For the three seminal texts on why materialism and meritocracy makes us feel joyless, anxious, and depressed, read three works by a philosopher, a psychologist, and an economist: Alain de Botton, *Status Anxiety* (London: Penguin, 2005), Oliver James, *Affluenza* (London: Vermilion, 2007), and Tibor Scitovsky, *The Joyless Economy: An Inquiry into Human Satisfaction and Consumer Dissatisfaction* (Oxford: Oxford University Press, 1976).

Page 74. Richard Easterlin's research

Richard Easterlin, "Does Economic Growth Improve the Human Lot? Some Empirical Evidence", in Paul A. David and Melvin W. Reder (eds.), *Nations and Households in Economic Growth: Essays in Honor of Moses Abramovitz* (New York: Academic Press, 1974).

Down the years, other scholars have challenged Easterlin's findings. For example, Betsey Stevenson and Justin Wolfers, "Economic Growth and Subjective Well-Being: Reassessing the Easterlin Paradox," *Brookings Papers on Economic Activity*, Economic Studies Program, The Brookings Institution, Vol. 39, No. 1, Spring 2008. The subject is now much debated. Who to believe and agree with? My view is that the objective data can be given the subjective spin that suits your beliefs. If you take other research into account, for example, Oliver James's *Affluenza*, it is clear which is correct.

Page 74. "But, as Bentham once observed, while he liked the first cup of coffee very much, the second was far less enjoyable."

Source: Tibor Scitovsky, *The Joyless Economy: An Inquiry into Human Satisfaction and Consumer Dissatisfaction* (Oxford: Oxford University Press, 1976).

Page 74. "Economists and sociologists have names for this: the law of diminishing marginal utility and hedonic contrast."

These are, of course, not quite the same, but they are related concepts.

Page 75. "Material goods... useful for self-expression"

For a very readable text on why material goods matter for self-expression and signifying status, read Daniel Miller, *Comfort of Things* (London: Polity, 2008). It is painstakingly researched, and brilliantly written.

Page 77. "From the 1970s to the turn of the century, mental illness in children and adults in developed countries doubled. A quarter of Britons now suffer emotional distress. Americans are three times more likely to be depressed today than in the 1950s. The level of emotional illness, it turns out, increases with income inequality, which also tends to be higher in English speaking nations. The more a society becomes like the United States of America – the most wasteful, most status-obsessed and most materialistic country on Earth – the higher the rate of emotional distress."

Source: Oliver James, *Affluenza* (London: Vermilion, 2007).

From the Pyramid to the Pancake

Page 78.

The idea of the pyramid to the pancake comes to me from two sources. The first was a lecture given by the political theorist Joseph Nye at the House of Commons. The second was something Dr James Bellini said to me back in 2009. I thank both of them.

Page 79. "Fifty Shades of Grey was rejected by professional agents. Its author published herself via an online e-book and print-on-demand publisher, and was then picked up by a mainstream publisher. It then became the fastest selling paperback ever."

Various sources, including: Ronald H Balson, "Bestseller Success Stories that Started Out as Self-Published Books", *Huffington Post*, 8 October 2013.

Page 79. Jenna Marbles

Watch the amazing Jenna Mourey get ready to go to work as a dancer in her "How to Trick People Into Thinking You're Good Looking" video at YouTube.

Page 79. Tavi Gevinson

Read about the time the twelve-year-old blogger sat front row in "Tavi Gevinson: 13-Year-Old Fashion Blogger Skips School, Attends Fashion Week", *Huffington Post*, 17 November 2009.

Page 79. Social media's effect on politics

For the impact of Facebook and Twitter on Egypt, Iran, and the Occupy Movement, consider Jose Antonio Vargas, "Spring Awakening: How an Egyptian Revolution Began on Facebook", *New York Times*, February 17, 2012, and Jared Keller, "Evaluating Iran's Twitter Revolution", *The Atlantic*, 18 June 2010.

CHAPTER FOUR

I Love to Count:
the 33, 47, 69 and 100
Things of Minimalism

Page 83.

Read more about Tammy Strobel at www.rowdykittens.com.

The 39 Socks

Page 89.

All the minimalists here have blogs. Some also write books about minimalism. Many also run courses to help people downsize their stuff and get more out of life.

Courtney Carver: www.bemorewithless.com

Nicodemus and Fields Millburn: www.theminimalists.com

Nicole Yau: www.castlesintheair.com

Colin Wright: www.exilelifestyle.com

Chris Wray: www.twolessthings.com

Rachel Jonat: www.theminimalistmom.com

Leo Babauta: www.zenhabits.com

CHAPTER FIVE

The Anthropologist
and the Clutter Crisis

Page 99.

Much of this chapter is drawn from the excellent, frightening, and very readable, Jeanne E Arnold, Anthony P Graesch, Enzo Ragazzini, Elinor Ochs, *Life at Home in the Twenty-first Century* (Los Angeles: Cotsen Institute of Archaeology Press, 2012).

For more on the Chumash, read Jeanne E. Arnold, *Foundations of Chumash Complexity* (Los Angeles: Cotsen Institute of Archaeology, 2004).

For complex societies in Peru, see Michael Moseley, *Pre-Agricultural Coastal Civilizations in Peru*, (Burlington, NC: Carolina Biological Supply Company, 1977).

Clutter Kills

Page 110.

The information in this section is based on Darby Saxbe and Rena Repetti, "No Place Like Home: Home Tours Correlate with Daily Patterns of Mood and Cortisol", *Personality and Social Psychology Bulletin* Vol. 36, No. 1, 2010.

Why hasn't something so important had more coverage before? I have some theories: does it not suit the media agenda, as Rachel Carson's discoveries did not in the 1960s? Or has it simply been overlooked? I don't know the answer.

Is Getting Rid of Stuff Enough?

Page 115.

For a smart, scholarly take on how many things we have – including toasters, towels, and clothes – and how we can change from a perspective of lack to one of plenty, read Juliet Schor, *Plenitude: The New Economics of True Wealth* (New York: Penguin, 2010). For a primer on the subject, read Stacy Mitchell, "Is Your Stuff Falling Apart? Thank Walmart", Grist.org, 9 November 2011. For the fashion angle, read Elizabeth L. Cline, *Overdressed: The Shockingly High Cost of Cheap Fashion* (New York: Penguin Portfolio, 2012).

Page 118. "The amount the average Briton spent on clothing almost doubled between 1990 and 2004."

Source: Julian M Allwood et al., "Well Dressed? The Present and Future Sustainability of Clothing and Textiles in the United Kingdom", University of Cambridge Institute for Manufacturing, 2006.

Page 118. "There are twice as many things in her wardrobe today than there were in 1980, and there are 22 things in there she has never worn."

Source: Sean Poulter, "In every woman's closet, 22 items she never wears - and the guilty complex that stops them clearing wardrobes out", *Daily Mail*, 26 January 2011.

CHAPTER SIX

The Good Life and the Cage-Free Family

Is the Good Life the Simple Answer?

Page 127.

The opening quote is sourced from Episode One, *The Good Life*, London, BBC, 1975, television.

Read more about Diogenes of Sinope in Diogenes Laertius, *Lives and Opinions of Eminent Philosophers*. Now out of copyright, it is available online and in various editions.

For a complete, and poetic, account of Thoreau's time in the woods, read Henry David Thoreau, *Walden; or, Life in the Woods* (Boston: Ticknor and Fields, 1854).

For more on Duane Elgin's discovery of, and research on, the voluntary simplicity movement, read Duane Elgin, *Voluntary Simplicity: Toward a Way of Life that is Outwardly Simple, Inwardly Rich* (New York: William Morrow, second edition, 1993). Another book I found very useful was Vicki Robin and Joe Dominguez, *Your Money or Your Life* (New York: Penguin, 1992, 2008).

The Complicated Side of Simple Living

Page 132. "Most years, there are 300 days of sunshine in Taos. In summer, the temperatures are balmy too. They are not in winter. On average, 305 inches of snow falls."

Source: Taos Ski Valley Chamber of Commerce.

Page 136. "The way to make sense of this is, as behavioural psychologists have showed time and again, that people do not necessarily behave in a rational, logical way."

To understand this, read Daniel Kahneman, *Thinking, Fast and Slow* (New York: Penguin, 2011), and Richard Thaler and Cass Sunstein, *Nudge* (New York: Penguin, 2008). For the best visualization of how the two parts of the brain work together, read about the elephant and its rider in Jonathan Haidt, *The Happiness Hypothesis: Putting Ancient Wisdom to the Test of Modern Science* (London: Arrow, 2007).

Not Simple, but Simpler Living

Page 138.

To read a more complete account of how LeVally and Harris came down from the mountain, and struggled with that decision, read www.cagefreefamily.com.

CHAPTER SEVEN

A Man Named Dave
and the Medium Chill

Page 141.

Read about the medium chill from the man who created it in his two seminal posts: David Roberts, "The Medium Chill", Grist.org, 28 June 2011; David Roberts, "The medium chill, revisited", Grist. org, 1 May 2013.

For more on the working week, read Benjamin Kline Hunnicutt, *Work Without End and Free Time: The Forgotten American Dream* (Philadelphia, Pennsylvania: Temple University Press, 2013); also Benjamin Kline Hunnicutt, *Kellogg's Six-Hour Day* (Philadelphia, Pennsylvania: Temple University Press, 1996); and Benjamin Kline Hunnicutt, *Work without End: Abandoning Shorter Hours for the Right to Work* (Philadelphia, Pennsylvania: Temple University Press, 1988). Also, see Anna Coote, Andrew Simms, Jane Franklin, *21 Hours* (London: New Economics Foundation, 2010); John Quiggin's "The Golden Age", *Aeon Magazine*, September 2012; and Sharon Beder, *Selling the Work Ethic: From Puritan Pulpit to Corporate PR* (Melbourne: Scribe, 2000).

Why the Medium Chill Matters

Page 145.

The "6.23 express to Paddington" is a generic idea. The 7.44am from Henley-on-Thames to London's Paddington is the most overcrowded train in the UK. Source: British government. But, interestingly, there is a 6.23 *from* Manchester's Paddington station to Middlesbrough that packs so many commuters on it has been dubbed the "Sardine Express".

Can Dave Save Us from Stuffocation?

Page 149.

The tale of the average Palaeolithic woman comes from Geoffrey Miller, *Spent: Sex, Evolution and the Secrets of Consumerism* (New York: William Heinemann, 2009).

For the rise of "clock-time" and what the Industrial Revolution did to our working week, read Benjamin Kline Hunnicutt's works mentioned above.

For more on threshold earners, see Tyler Cowen, "The Inequality That Matters", *The American Interest*, January/February 2011. For an excellent deconstruction of that article, read political columnist Reihan Salam, "Threshold Earners and Gentleman Hackers", *National Review*, 28 December 2010.

Page 153. "There is no sign of the 'social snowball' or 'tipping point' that would suggest that the medium chill is set to make the leap along the adoption curve."

I spent a lot of time thinking about this. I know a number of people who deliberately do not seek to maximise income, and prefer time and life instead. Then there are the numbers of part-time workers rising dramatically in recent years. But I think much of that has been forced on people. So although I think we will see a rise in people choosing the medium chill, and it could become much more important as a value system and lifestyle choice, I do not think the evidence is convincing enough yet to make me try to convince you. As it stands, the medium chill is a subset of this wider idea of experientialism.

CHAPTER EIGHT

The Experientialists (part one): Escaping the Cubicle

Page 161. "By the 1950s, when you could see the Jet Age and the Space Race reflected in so many cars' chrome tail-fins"

For example, the 1955 Chrysler 300F, the 1957 Chevrolet Bel Air Convertible, and the 1958 Aston Martin DB4.

Page 161. Dirk Jan De Pree

For an introduction to the story of Dirk Jan De Pree and the cubicles, read Julie Schlosser, "Cubicles: The Great Mistake", *Fortune Magazine*, 22 March 2006, and Marc Kristal, "An Idea Whose Time Has Come", *Metropolis Magazine*, June 2013.

Marianne and the Free-Range Lifestyle

Page 169.

For more on the Free-Range movement, see www.free-range-humans.com, and Marianne Cantwell, *Be A Free Range Human* (London: Kogan Page, 2013).

To Do or to Have? That Is No Longer in Question

Page 175.

The most important paper for this chapter is Tom Gilovich and Leaf van Boven, "To Do or to Have? That is the Question", *Journal of Personality and Social Psychology* Vol. 85, No. 6, 2003.

It is informed by many others, including:

Leonardo Nicolao, Julie R. Irwin, and Joseph K. Goodman, "Happiness for Sale: Do Experiential Purchases Make Consumers Happier than Material Purchases?", *Journal of Consumer Research* Vol. 36, No. 2, 2009.

Elizabeth W. Dunn, Daniel T. Gilbert, Timothy D. Wilson, "If Money Doesn't Make You Happy, Then You Probably Aren't Spending It Right", *Journal of Consumer Psychology* Vol. 21, No. 2, April 2011.

Tim Kasser, *The High Price of Materialism*, (Cambridge, Massachusetts: MIT Press, 2002).

Tim Kasser et al., "Materialistic Values: Their Causes and Consequences", in *Psychology and Consumer Culture: The Struggle for a Good Life in a Materialistic World*, eds. Tim Kasser and Allen D Kramer (Washington: American Psychological Association, 2004).

Leaf van Boven, "Experientialism, Materialism, and the Pursuit of Happiness", *Review of General Psychology* Vol. 9, No. 2, June 2005.

Elizabeth Dunn and Michael Norton, "Don't Indulge. Be Happy", *New York Times*, 7 July 2012.

Elizabeth Dunn and Michael Norton, *Happy Money: The Science of Spending* (New York: Simon & Schuster, 2013).

Travis Carter and Thomas Gilovich, "I Am What I Do, not What I Have: The Centrality of Experiential Purchases to the Self-Concept", *Journal of Personality and Social Psychology* Vol. 102, No. 6, 2012.

Travis Carter and Thomas Gilovich, "The Relative Relativity of Material and Experiential Purchases", *Journal of Personality and Social Psychology* Vol. 98, No. 1, 2010.

Ryan T Howell, Paulina Pchelin, Ravi Iyer, "The Preference for Experiences Over Possessions: Measurement and Construct Validation of the Experiential Buying Tendency Scale", *The Journal of Positive Psychology* Vol. 7, No. 1, January 2012.

Emily Rosenzweig and Thomas Gilovich, "Buyer's Remorse or Missed Opportunity? Differential Regrets for Material and Experiential Purchases", *Journal of Personality and Social Psychology* Vol. 102, No. 2, 2012.

Tori DeAngelis, "Consumerism and Its Discontents", *American Psychological Association* Vol. 35, No. 6, June 2004.

Tim Kasser and Allen D Kanner (eds.), *Psychology and Consumer Culture: The Struggle for a Good Life in a Materialistic World* (Washington, DC: American Psychological Association, 2003)

Peter A Caprariello, Harry T Reis, "To do with others to have (or to do alone?): The value of experiences over material possessions depends on the involvement of others", University of Rochester, 2012.

CHAPTER NINE

The Experientialists (part two): Hippies with Calculators

When you are in London, visit Bertrand Lenet's restaurant. It may be a cliché to say it, but it is like a little bit of France in London. It scored 4.1 out of five stars on Google when I last looked. (I recommend the steak frites). It is called Gastro, 67 Venn St London SW4 0BD. Telephone: +44 (0) 20 7627 0222.

Part-time Hippy, Full-time Professional

If you want to drive from London to Ulan Bator, you can do it with the Mongol Rally.

The Rise of the Hippies with Calculators

Page 197.

Deborah Richmond's BrandYoga is at www.brandyoga.com.

The business that Olga Sasplugas runs, still, with Graham Hill is selling a ceramic version of the iconic New York City coffee cup. Visit www.wearehappytoserveyou.com to see, and perhaps buy, the cups.

Join Escape the City today at www.escapethecity.com.

Alice Marwick has now turned her PhD into a book: Alice Marwick, *Status Update: Celebrity, Publicity, and Branding in the Social Media Age* (Yale: Yale University Press, 2013).

CHAPTER TEN

Facebook Changed How We Keep up with the Joneses

Page 201.

For the seminal work on consumption and status, read Thorstein Veblen, *Theory of the Leisure Class* (New York: Macmillan, 1899).
    If you haven't already, watch a TED lecture at www.ted.com.

Page 206. "If you have high status, people laugh at your jokes more, you earn more, you get invited out to more parties. You are also more likely to live longer, feel more important and loved, and have a more attractive partner."

Various sources, including: Alain de Botton, *Status Anxiety* (London: Hamish Hamilton, 2004).

Page 207. FOMO

See the FOMO reports by advertising agency JWT: Fear of Missing Out, May 2011, and Fear of Missing Out (FOMO), March 2012 Update. Take particular note of figures 2F and 2G in the Appendix. If you compare them you can see how social media is speeding the shift from materialism to experientialism – as people are more able than ever to get status from experiential rather than material goods. My reading, of course, is that conspicuous living is replacing conspicuous consumption in its importance for our status and our lives.

Is Experientialism the Answer to Stuffocation?

Page 211. Ron Inglehart

Again, Ron Inglehart, "The Silent Revolution in Europe: Intergenerational Change in Post-Industrial Societies", *American Political Science Review* Vol. 65, No. 4, December 1971. To see the shift away from materialistic values, see the World Values Survey (www.worldvaluessurvey.org).

Page 211. The changing make-up of our economy

Compare the type of items in Simon Kuznets, *National Income, 1929-32* (Cambridge, MA: NBER, June 1934) with those in today's economies. Consider also, Francisco J Buera and Joseph P Kaboski. "The Rise of the Service Economy", *American Economic Review* Vol. 102, No. 6, 2012. For an easy introduction, see the video infographic "The iPhone Economy" at www.nytimes.com.

For the definitive text on consuming fewer materials, read Chris Goodall, "Peak Stuff", *Carbon Commentary*, 2011. And read Chris Goodall, *Sustainability* (London: Hodder & Stoughton, 2012). Keep up with the latest news via Goodall's excellent blog www.carboncommentary.com.

This chapter was also informed by Tyler Cowen, *The Great Stagnation* (New York: Dutton, 2011), and Robert J Gordon, "Is US Economic Growth Over? Faltering Innovation Confronts the Six Headwinds", Centre for Economic Policy Research, September 2012.

Page 212. "In 2007, the average American bought almost twice as many items of clothing each year compared to 1991. But by 2012, the number they were buying had stopped rising, and even fallen slightly, from 67 to 64 items."

Source: See notes for the section in Chapter Five called *Is Getting Rid of Stuff Enough?*

Page 212. "People in the UK and Ireland prefer experiences to material goods."

This statement is based on survey data from nationally representative surveys conducted in December 2012 (with thanks to James Kennedy). We asked: "Please think of the last time you spent money on something that made you really happy. Was this an 'object' or an 'experience'?"

In the UK, 30% said object, 12% said they could not remember making a purchase that made them happy, 7% said not sure, and 51% said experience.

In the Republic of Ireland, 40% said object, 5% said they could not remember making a purchase that made them happy, 4% said not sure, and 51% said experience.

Page 212. "The demise of the hardback and the rise of e-books"

For example, Alison Flood, "Hardback sales plummeting in age of the ebook", The Guardian.co.uk, 12 August 2011.

Page 212. "Plummeting sales of recorded music and the boom in live music and festivals"

Source: Thomas K Grose, "Live, at a Field Near You", *Time*, 14 November 2011.

Page 212. "People in their sixties spend more on holidays than any other age group"

Source: a report, published January 2013, from a website called TravelSupermarket, which questioned 5,000 holidaymakers. The report found that the over-60s are most likely to spend the most money on holidays, and that they spend an average of £794 on travel and accommodation each year. See "The silver pound: Holidaymakers in their sixties spend more than other age groups", *Daily Mail*, 28 January 2013. Also, research from the International Council of Shopping Centers, a trade body, states that over-55s spend more than 50% of the money spent on holidays in the US.

Page 212. "The emergence of extreme sports and challenges like Tough Mudder"

See Richard Askwith, "Tough Mudder: The obstacle courses for adults that are now worth $250m", *The Independent*, 3 May 2013.

Page 212. "The doubling in the number of people working part-time in recent years"

For example, Matt Chorley, "Part-time Britain: Record numbers now have jobs but most finding employment work for less than 25 hours", *Mail Online*, 11 September 2013. Also, Mehroz Baig, "The Rise in Part-time Employment", *Huffington Post*, 16 October 2013.

For more on the Boston Consulting Group's luxury reports, visit www.bcg.com.

Page 213. "In an era of over-consumption, people are realizing that there is more than just buying products," said Jean-Marc Bellaiche, a senior partner at the Boston Consulting Group. "Buying experiences provides more pleasure and satisfaction."

Source: Andrew Roberts, "Building Luxury Brand Loyalty via Exclusive Experiences", *Bloomberg Businessweek*, 31 January 2013.

Page 213. Millennials living in cities and not buying cars.

Consider Robert Wright, "Transport: Freed from the Wheel", *Financial Times*, 6 October 2013. This states that "Young city dwellers are driving less, forcing the motor industry to rethink the role of the car". Also, read Jordan Weissman, "Why Don't Young Americans Buy Cars?", *The Atlantic*, 25 March 2012; and John Arlidge, "Baby, you can share my car", *Sunday Times*, 10 March 2013, which states that: in 2008, only 30% of 16-year-old Americans held driving licences, down from 50% a generation ago, that 80% of under-25s in Tokyo do not have a car, and that in Germany, the share of young households without cars rose from 20% to 28% from 1998 to 2008.

Page 213. Millennials choosing to live in small, city-centre apartments

See Richard Florida, *The Great Reset: How the Post-Crash Economy Will Change the Way We Live and Work* (New York: HarperBusiness, 2011). For a rigorous analysis of the millennials' housing aspirations, read Nathan Morris, "Why Generation Y is Causing the Great Migration of the 21st Century", on the website of a design firm called Placemakers (www.placemakers.com), 9 April 2012.

Page 213. "Rather than owning a thing": millennials not so interested in material objects

Various sources, including Tammy Erickson, "Meaning Is the New Money", HBR Blog Network, 23 March 2011; and David Brooks, "The Experience Economy", *New York Times*, 14 February 2011.

Page 213. The rise of services like Zipcar, Spotify, and Netflix

For excellent introductions to how these companies operate, read Rachel Botsman and Roo Rogers, "Beyond Zipcar: Collaborative Consumption", *Harvard Business Review*, October 2010; and, for the rise of these services, read "All Eyes on the Sharing Economy", *The Economist*, 9 Mar 2013.

CHAPTER ELEVEN

Are You Experienced?
Your Government Wants to Know

Page 215.

This chapter is informed by many sources, including Roger Cohen, "The Happynomics of Life", *New York Times*, 12 March 2011; Richard Layard, *Happiness: Lessons from a New Science* (London: Penguin, 2011).

Page 215. "This great nation will never be intimidated," George W Bush declared. "People are going about their daily lives, working and shopping and playing, worshipping at churches and synagogues and mosques, going to movies and to baseball games." And Tony Blair told the British people "they should go about their daily lives: to work, to live, to travel and to shop".

Note that the view that Tony Blair and George Bush simply encouraged their people to shop after the attacks of 9/11, 2001 has been challenged – for example, by political consultant Karl Rove – but I believe the point holds good: that politicians, and many of us too, had come to largely measure our progress, and certainly our national status, in terms of GDP.

Counting, the Economists' Way

Page 216.

There are many accounts of the effects of the Depression: John Steinbeck, *The Grapes of Wrath* (New York: Viking Press, 1939) is arguably the most visceral and best.

Page 216. "By 1932, 25% of the working population was unemployed."

Source: various histories of the Great Depression, including The Econ Review (www.econreview.com).

Page 217. "Unemployment soared to 25% in the UK"

Source: Stephen Constantine, *Unemployment in Britain Between the Wars* (London: Longman, 1980).

Page 217. "30% unemployed in Australia"

Source: Australian government figures.

Page 218. Simon Kuznets

Read more about the rise of economics and the life of Simon Kuznets in Robert Fogel, *Simon S Kuznets April 30, 1901–July 9, 1985* (Cambridge, MA: NBER, 2000); and Simon Kuznets et al., *National Income, 1929-32* (NBER, June 1934).

Page 218. "As recently as the late 19th century, economics was considered of such little importance that at Oxford University, for example, there was only one part-time lecturer, and at American universities it was merely one section of one segment of an entire course"

Sources: Robert Fogel, *Simon S Kuznets April 30, 1901–July 9,*

1985 (Cambridge, MA: NBER, 2000); and Gerard M Koot, *English Historical Economics, 1870-1926 : The Rise of Economic History and Neomercantilism* (Cambridge: Cambridge University Press, 1987). Particular thanks for help with finding this detail about the rise of economics in the UK go to Avner Offer.

Page 221. "And by the late 1950s, with backing from the International Monetary Fund, Kuznets's method was adopted by all countries."

By "all countries", I am referring here to the major Western countries. Of course, Simon Kuznets's work was supplemented by many other economists, including, for example, Richard Stone and Alexander Eckstein. With thanks to three economists at the London School of Economics for their assistance with this: Olivier Accominotti, Steve Broadberry, and Tamas Vonyo.

What Have The Economists Ever Done for Us?

Page 221.

This scene, of course, is a from *Monty Python's Life of Brian*, with kind permission. For the sake of brevity, it has been edited slightly. With thanks to Jill Foster and Holly Gilliam for their assistance.

The Limits to GDP

Page 225. "Increases in GDP per capita do improve wellbeing, up to around $75,000 or £50,000 per capita"

Source: Daniel Kahneman, Angus Deaton, "High Income Improves Evaluation of Life But Not Emotional Well-Being", *Proceedings of the National Academy of Sciences* Vol. 107, No. 38, 7 September 2010.

For the drunkard's search, read Abraham Kaplan, *The Conduct of Inquiry: Methodology for Behavioral Science* (San Francisco: Chandler Publishing, 1964).

For more on substitution, read Daniel Kahneman, *Thinking, Fast and Slow* (New York: Penguin, 2011).

For a moving version of what GDP does not measure, look up Robert Kennedy's 1969 speech set to (almost) stirring music on YouTube.

To find out more about alternatives to GDP, read Tim Jackson, *Prosperity Without Growth* (London: Earthscan, 2009) and Joseph E Stiglitz, Amartya Sen and Jean-Paul Fitoussi, *Mismeasuring Our Lives* (New York: New Press, 2010).

Also, Jules Evans, "Beyond GDP: Towards a Better Measurement of National Wellbeing in France and the UK", Franco-British Council report, 2 February 2011.

Jon Gertner, "The Rise and Fall of the GDP", *New York Times*, 13 May 2010.

Nicolas Sarkozy Has a Problem

Page 229. Sarkozy's popularity nose-diving

Source: Crispian Balmer, "French fall out of love with smitten Sarkozy", *Reuters*, 4 February 2008.

Page 229. Sarkozy "stalked the vast halls of the Élysée Palace"

Source: Cécile Alduy, "Life as Sarkozy's Secret Speechwriter", *The Atlantic*, 26 March 2013.

Sarkozy's thoughts here are taken from his foreword in Joseph E Stiglitz, Amartya Sen and Jean-Paul Fitoussi, *Mismeasuring Our Lives* (New York: New Press, 2010).

Page 230. Substitution

For more on substitution, and especially the difference between the "remembering self", and the "experiencing self", see Daniel Kahneman, *Thinking, Fast and Slow* (New York: Penguin, 2011).

Page 231. "As many methods as there are countries"

The Wikiprogress.org pages on Subjective Well-being have been invaluable here, as has Bernice Steinhardt et al., "Key Indicator Systems: Experiences of Other National and Subnational Systems Offer Insights for the United States", United States Government Accountability Office, Report to Congressional Addressees, 2011. Useful websites for progressive measures of social progress include: www4.hrsdc.gc.ca for Canada's Indicators of Well-being in Canada (IWC); uwaterloo.ca/canadian-index-wellbeing for The Canadian Index of Wellbeing (CIW); Australian Bureau of Statistics's www.abs.gov.au for Measuring Australia's Progress (MAP); www.oecdbetterlifeindex.org for the Organisation for Economic Co-operation and Development (OECD)'s Better Life Index; hdr.undp.org for the UN's Human Development Index (HDI); www.grossnationalhappiness.com for Bhutan's Gross National Happiness (GNH); and www.stateoftheusa.org for The State of the United States of America (SUSA).

Page 233. "Barry Schwartz recently proposed a psychological parallel to the Council of Economic Advisers that was created in 1946, a 'Council of Psychological Advisers for the US President'."

Source: Barry Schwartz, "Move Over Economists: We Need a Council of Psychological Advisers", *The Atlantic*, 12 November 2012.

Page 235. "Joseph Stiglitz says, 'what we measure affects what we do'"

Source: Joseph Stiglitz, "The great GDP swindle", Theguardian. com, 13 September 2009.

CHAPTER TWELVE

Scenes from the Experience Economy

Page 239.

For more on Punchdrunk, see www.punchdrunk.com.

The Pilot and the Pig's Ear

Page 241.

For more on Bompas and Parr, visit www.jellymongers.co.uk

"Everyone is an autobiographer nowadays"

Page 248. "We live in a cluttered time of too much information"

We consume the equivalent of 174 newspapers' worth of information every day, according to a researcher at the University of Southern California called Dr Martin Hilbert, as reported in Richard Alleyn, "Welcome to the information age – 174 newspapers a day", *Daily Telegraph*, 11 February 2011.

CHAPTER THIRTEEN

The Experientialists Who Love Stuff

Page 251. "Consumer spending makes up around 65% of the British, and just above 70% of the US economy"

Various sources, including: Martin Wolf, "Britain must fix its banks – not its monetary policy", *Financial Times*, 6 June 2013; Hale Stewart, "Consumer Spending and the Economy", FiveThirtyEight, *New York Times*, 19 September 2010.

The Secret Loot in the Experience Economy

Page 253.

For more on Secret Cinema, visit www.secretcinema.org.

Page 257. Fabien Riggall once boasted about getting people to pay £50 each to see a film

Read Nick Curtis, "Secret Cinema: how to get 25,000 people to pay £50 for a film ticket, without knowing what the film is", *Evening Standard*, 7 December 2012.

Graham: the Minimalist Who Loves Stuff

Page 261.

See Graham Hill's work at www.treehugger.com, his new company LifeEdited at www.lifeedited.com, and see www.ted.com for his talks.

Follow Colin Wright at www.exilelifestyle.com.

For an example of how people are still shopping in a time of too much stuff, consider Emily Sheffield, "How We Shop Now", *British Vogue*, February 2013. Sheffield writes that "a fashion consultant called Anita Borzyszkowska says: 'So I am actually spending more per item, but there are fewer buys.'" And Sheffield quotes a report from high-net worth consumer specialist Ledbury Research, which points to "consumers adopting a 'less is more' mentality. So they are focusing more on quality and good experiences than 'look at me' purchases."

The New 'n' Improved Features and Benefits of the Experience Economy

Page 267.

This section – and much of the chapters about the experience economy – is inspired and informed by B Joseph Pine II and James H Gilmore, *The Experience Economy* (Boston: Harvard Business School Press, 1999) and B Joseph Pine II and James H Gilmore, *The Experience Economy Updated Edition* (Boston: Harvard Business School Press, 2011). For a quick introduction to the subject, read B Joseph Pine II and James H Gilmore, "Welcome to the Experience Economy", *Harvard Business Review*, July 1998.

More on TOMS shoes: www.toms.com.

More on the Common Threads Initiative between eBay and Patagonia: www.patagonia.com/us/common-threads.

Watch Puma's Clever Little Shopper disappear on YouTube.

Stay with Airbnb: www.airbnb.com.

Rent a car from Zipcar: www.zipcar.com .

Get your music from Spotify: www.spotify.com.

Page 271. "London, one of the world's most visited cities"

Source: Deborah L. Jacobs, "The 20 Most Popular Cities In The World To Visit In 2012", *Forbes*, 20 June 2012. In the 2013 rankings, Bangkok pipped London to the number one spot.

CHAPTER FOURTEEN

What about the Chinese?

Page 277.

The description of Liu Dandan, Zhou Zhou, and Richard Lu is taken from the photoshoot for Bill Saporito, "A Great Leap Forward: Can China's famously thrifty workers become the world's big spenders?", *Time*, 31 October 2011. Thanks here to Bill Saporito, Zohair Abdoolcarim, Adrian Sandiford, Austin Ramzy, and Chen Jiaojiao for their help with Liu Dandan, Zhou Zhou, and Richard Lu.

Page 278. "More than a billion people in countries like India, Indonesia, Vietnam, Nigeria, and Brazil, will be joining them as middle-class, conspicuous consumers."

Various sources, including: Linda Yueh, "The rise of the global middle class", BBC.co.uk, 19 June 2013.

The Next Great Leap Forward

Page 281. "In the West, it took 150 odd years from the start of the Industrial Revolution to lead to overproduction. After that, it took just under 80 years or so in the West for the consumer revolution to lead to overconsumption and Stuffocation."

I'm taking the start of the Industrial Revolution as around 1780, and the "moment" of overproduction as 1929, and pegging Stuffocation to 2013. Cultural sweeps are rarely neat, so these are slightly arbitrary estimates.

Page 282. "In 2012, for instance, there were overproduction problems in [Chinese] industries ranging from coal, cotton and ship-building to clothing, solar cell and construction."

Various sources, including Colyapi, "The danger of Chinese overproduction", *China Daily Mail*, 8 January 2013; Walden Bello, "China and the Crisis of Overproduction", GlobalPolitician.com; and Dexter Roberts, "To Fix Overproduction, China Wants to Supersize Industries", Bloomberg BusinessWeek, 25 January 2013.

Page 283. "For stability and growth – in China as well the rest of the world – The World Bank and the International Monetary Fund both want the Chinese to become high-spending consumers."

Source: Louis Kuijs, "How to further boost consumption?", World Bank, 2012 (http://go.worldbank.org/OGWG0M41K0); and IMF Press Release No. 13/260, July 17, 2013, in which the IMF's directors "underscored the importance of [China] transitioning to a new growth path that is more consumption-based".

Page 283. "Advertising, the industry most likely to engineer consumers rather than products, is exploding. In 1976, there weren't even ten advertising agencies in the whole country. By 2001, there were 70,000. By 2010, 234,000. And by the end of 2012, that had shot up to 377,000."

Sources: Kong Liang and Laurence Jacobs, "China's Advertising Agencies: Problems and Relations", *International Journal of Advertising*, 22 June 1994; Ying Fan, "Advertising and Public Relations in China", in *Communicating with 1.3 billion people in China*, Handbook of Corporate Communication and Public Relations, ed. by Sarah Oliver (London: Routledge 2004); "China's Advertising & Marketing Industry Research Report", My Decker Capital, January 2012; "China's ad industry rises to world's second: SAIC", *China Daily*, 27 April 2013, which cites Zhang Mao, the head of China's State Administration for Industry and Commerce (SAIC).

Page 283. "The Chinese government is explicitly intent on creating consumers as well, and borrowing ideas from the American experiment of the 20th century."

Source: Louis Kuijs, "How to further boost consumption?", World Bank, 2012 (http://go.worldbank.org/OGWG0M41K0).

Page 284. "The value of e-commerce in China in 2012, from a standing start a few years ago, was almost the same as the entire economy of the Republic of Ireland."

This comparison is based on the value of e-commerce in China in 2012 at $210 billion, and the Republic of Ireland economy for that year, $220 billion. Sources: Eurostat; Kenneth Rapooza, "China E-Commerce Rises 64.7% In 2012", *Forbes*, 29 March 2013.

Page 284. "Frequent demonstrations and riots as people put their environment and quality of life before growth"

Various sources, including: J T Quigley, "Chinese Government Will Spend $277 Billion to Combat Air Pollution", *The Diplomat*, 27 July 2013; and Sui-Lee Wee, "China offers rewards to six regions to fight air pollution", *Reuters*, 14 October 2013, which notes that "Protests over pollution in China are becoming common, to the government's alarm. Authorities have invested in various projects to fight pollution and even empowered courts to mete out the death penalty in serious pollution cases."

Page 284. "Stalling levels of happiness: since 1990, the average Chinese person's material living standard has increased by four times, for instance, yet happiness has not increased at all."

Source: Richard Easterlin et al., "China's Life Satisfaction, 1990–

2010", University of Southern California, Los Angeles, Proceedings of the National Academy of the Sciences, May 2012; or Richard Easterlin, "When Growth Outpaces Happiness", *New York Times*, 27 September 2012.

Page 285. "In China, the experiential luxury sector – which includes days out at spas, playing golf and going on holiday – is growing around 25% faster than the personal luxury goods sector."

This is calculated from the following statistics: that, while sales of personal luxury goods in China are rising 22% per year, sales of luxury experiences are growing at 28% each year. Source: Boston Consulting Group.

Page 285. "It took China around a third of the time to go from the start of its industrialization to overproduction – around 60 years."

I'm taking industrialization to have begun in the late 1950s in the Great Leap Forward. The historian Niall Ferguson believes that China is "cramming a century's worth of industrialisation and urbanisation into about 30 years". A report by the McKinsey Global Institute is even more bullish, claiming that China's industrialization has proceeded at ten times the speed of Britain's. Source: Tong Wu, "China's industrial revolution is happening on a new planet", Phys.org, 19 September 2013.

Page 285. "If [China] continues to follow a similar, accelerated path, it will reach overconsumption by 2037."

By 2037, really? The various factors that are causing *Stuffocation* over here now are likely to be more, and less, relevant, in China in the future. The environment, for example, is likely to be a far more pressing problem. In terms of the personal, at-home, clutter crisis aspect of *Stuffocation*, though, it is unlikely that the average Chinese will reach the same material standard of living as we have in the West for far more years.

CONCLUSION

Why You Need Experience More Than Ever

The source for this story is, of course, years of conversations with my grandfather and grandmother, Jack and Pam Wallman – as well as the note Granddad gave me on the day he died.

The thinking about the good life was inspired by, among other texts, Aristotle, *Nicomachean Ethics* (Cambridge: Hackett, trans. by Terence Irwin, 1985).

Index

Also by Crux Publishing

OPEN by David Price

'From every perspective OPEN will open your mind to some of the real implications of digital technologies for how we live and learn in the 21st century.'

SIR KEN ROBINSON,
world-leading expert on education and creativity

What makes a global corporation give away its prized intellectual property? Why are Ivy League universities allowing anyone to take their courses for free? What drives a farmer in rural Africa to share his secrets with his competitors?

A collection of hactivists, hobbyists, forum-users and maverick leaders are leading a quiet but unstoppable revolution. They are sharing everything they know, and turning knowledge into action in ways that were unimaginable even a decade ago. Driven by technology, and shaped by common values, going 'open' has transformed the way we live. It's not so much a question of if our workplaces, schools and colleges go open, but when.

Packed with illustration and advice, this entertaining read by learning futurist, David Price, argues that 'open' is not only affecting how we are choosing to live, but that it's going to be the difference between success and failure in the future.

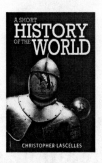

A Short History of the World
by Christopher Lascelles

'A clearly written, remarkably comprehensive guide
to the greatest story on Earth - man's journey from the
earliest times to the modern day. Highly recommended.'
DAN JONES, author of *The Plantagenets:
The Kings Who Made England*

A Short History of the World is a short and easy-to-read history book that relates the history of our world from the Big Bang to the present day. It assumes no prior knowledge of past events and 32 maps have been especially drawn to give the reader a better understanding of where events occurred.

The book's purpose is not to come up with any ground-breaking new historical theories. Instead it aims to give a broad overview of the key events so that non-historians will feel less embarrassed about their lack of historical knowledge when discussing the past. The result is a history book that is reassuringly epic in scope but refreshingly short in length – an excellent place to start to bring your knowledge of world history up to scratch!

For the latest news on Stuffocation, visit

www.stuffocation.org

CPSIA information can be obtained at www.ICGtesting.com
Printed in the USA
LVOW08s1804270214

375431LV00008B/1172/P

Water is Rising in the Classroom

TRUE TERROR DREAMS OF TEACHERS

Water is Rising in the Classroom

TRUE TERROR DREAMS OF TEACHERS

Collected by **ELLIOT LILIEN** ~ Illustrated by **LARAINE ARMENTI**

Martin and Lawrence Press ~ Groton, Massachusetts

Martin and Lawrence Press
P.O. Box 682
Groton, Massachusetts 01450

Cover and book design: Laraine Armenti

Printed in the United States of America

Elliot Lilien, 1939–, Laraine Armenti 1958–
Water is Rising in the Classroom, True Terror Dreams of Teachers

ISBN 0972168745
1. Humor — Non-Fiction 2. Education 3. Psychology

*Some readers were aghast at the personal nature
of the material, yet the dreamers overwhelmingly
did not object to the inclusion of their dreams.
I am grateful that they shared them with us. —E.L.*

*For Elliot Lilien, who made his students believe
we were much smarter than we were. —L.A.*

Laraine Armenti does not know and has never met any of the dreamers quoted in this book, except Elliot Lilien, whose picture does not look like him either.

Preface

When the idea of a contest comparing terror dreams of teachers was first discussed at Concord-Carlisle High School in Massachusetts, it was thought that the exercise would be good entertainment for the staff. When the dreams were revealed to the faculty, however, most everyone found them remarkable; something no one had expected.

About thirty percent of the teachers admitted to having the dreams and I wondered if CCHS was unique, or if teachers at other schools had had similar experiences. After researching about twenty schools it became clear that nightmares exist in all types of schools. No matter what kind of school is considered, approximately the same percentages will apply as at Concord-Carlisle. Teachers of longer tenure are more likely to have dreams, but young teachers also have them, and many of their dreams are the most vivid.

My friends in the independent schools surmised that private school teachers would have fewer dreams because their experience was generally less threatening. That contention is not borne out by the material I gathered. There seems to be no difference in the dreams of teachers in schools where the parents' income is high compared to less wealthy schools. I could find no difference in the dreams of female and male teachers.

It is interesting that the dreams do not go away, even if the dreamer gets out of education. I interviewed an eighty-three year old woman who had quit teaching in her forties. She still had nightmares. I still have terror dreams despite retiring in 2000.

Students have similar dreams to teachers, although they do not have ones in which they have responsibility for others. Students dream about being unprepared. I still have law school dreams although I graduated in 1964. I cannot find the building in which my moot court trial is to be heard and wander around downtown Manhattan, knowing nothing about the case. I am curious about the dreams of air traffic controllers or policemen. The dreams of soldiers seem good candidates for the same category.

Teachers' nightmares occur most often in late August and on Sunday nights — that makes sense. And dreams are recurrent. The dreamers have the same dream, over and over. It does not require a highly analytical ability to discover what motivates the dreamers. They fear they will lose control, be humiliated, entirely forget their expertise, or be harassed into hysteria by the demands of the job. They fear that an unmanageable child will be introduced into their room. However, these anxieties are expressed in original ways, frequently very amusing.

Most teachers, when shown the dreams, find them revealing, and worthy of discussion. Readers may recognize their own terror dreams within these pages and recall others they had forgotten.

As a teacher I sometimes ran into people who thought teaching was easy. These were never teachers or former teachers — always those who had never attempted the task. This book shows some of the stress and anxiety associated with the profession. It illustrates "teacher fears." As such it may be useful in showing teachers they are not alone. Then again it's just interesting. You might, if you read the book, learn something.

Contents

~

Overwhelmed

~

WATER IS RISING IN THE CLASSROOM

Overwhelmed

In my dream there is one week left in the school year. Water is rising in the classroom. It rises until the top of my head is on the ceiling. None the less I continue to teach, aware that there is only one week to go and I'll probably make it.

Kathryn Codd
Newton North High School
Newton, Massachusetts

Overwhelmed

I'm asleep in my dream. I wake up and go to class totally unprepared, when a huge metal bookcase falls on me and kills me.

Jim Newton
Lincoln-Sudbury High School
Sudbury, Massachusetts

TRUE TERROR DREAMS OF TEACHERS

6

Overwhelmed

I'm stuck on the slide on the playground —
in the middle of the slide. The kids are
playing all around me. I try to get their
attention but they ignore me.

Beth Gainer
Blanchard School
Boxborough, Massachusetts

I'm the art teacher and I'm late. I'm running,
feeling dreadful anxiety. In the distance I can
see the class but I can't get to them. I scream.
They can't or won't hear. There are chandeliers
in the room. The principal is watching.

Diane Hosmer
Blanchard School
Boxborough, Massachusetts

Overwhelmed

I am teaching forty students in a covered bridge in Maine. Railroad tracks run down the middle of the bridge, the train is choo-chooing in the distance, and no one will listen to me.

Wilson Flight
Concord-Carlisle High School
Concord, Massachusetts

In my dream there is an earthquake. I shout and no one listens.

Sue McAlister
Whitin Middle School
Uxbridge, Massachusetts

WATER IS RISING IN THE CLASSROOM

Overwhelmed

The principal keeps a puppy in his bathroom. Whenever the teachers feel anxiety they are allowed to go in there and pet the puppy. The puppy is a yellow lab.

Cindy Plunkett
Blanchard School
Boxborough, Massachusetts

I have a severe case of diarrhea in a compulsory teachers meeting.

Barbara Boudrot
Concord Middle School
Concord, Massachusetts

Overwhelmed

As I'm teaching the walls and ceiling are falling
down on me. I begin to hold them up, first with
one hand, then with the other. I continue
teaching, holding up the walls and the ceiling.

Bill Miller
Concord Middle School
Concord, Massachusetts

WATER IS RISING IN THE CLASSROOM

Overwhelmed

On the first day of class I start to walk from the back of the room to the front. Making my way down the aisle, I realize I am getting shorter and shorter. By the time I reach the front of the class I'm so small I can't see over the top of the desks.

Barbara Boudrot
Concord Middle School
Concord, Massachusetts

Overwhelmed

I dream that a crowd of vicious, angry,
screaming parents has surrounded my house
at night. They continually chant "More! More!
Do more! Do more!"

Philip Benincasa
Principal, Alcott School
Concord, Massachusetts

~

Discipline

~

WATER IS RISING IN THE CLASSROOM

Discipline

I take one student outside into the hall to talk
to him for disciplinary reasons, and when I
return, rows two through five are missing.
Not just the students, the desks, everything.

Elliot Lilien
Concord-Carlisle High School
Concord, Massachusetts

I have the "honors" kindergarten class and
I'm trying to get them to line up on the
playground. I can't get them to do it. I turn
to my assistant and observe, "If this is the
"honors" kindergarten class, what must the
others be like?"

Katie Balducci
Willard School
Concord, Massachusetts

WATER IS RISING IN THE CLASSROOM

Discipline

I am the school librarian. I dream that the students are playing hockey in the library. They are also writing foul graffiti on the walls while the game is going on, while others are decorating for Christmas.

Jeff Smith
Middlesex School
Concord, Massachusetts

In my dream my students totally refuse to do anything.

Jon Bassett
Weston High School
Weston, Massachusetts

In my dream, all the students in my class are cheating during a test.

Paul Quain
Buckingham, Browne & Nichols
Cambridge, Massachusetts

Discipline

A student steals my T-Bird. He's tattooed. My dream recurs over and over.

Mal Grant
Sanborn School
Concord, Massachusetts

I go outside of my classroom to find the most disruptive kids in school having drag races in the halls, which are somehow wide enough to accommodate two cars side by side. I am infuriated, not only because of the reckless abandon with which they are running over fellow students and faculty, but also because they have very nice cars: Aston Martins and Lamborghinis. It is frustrating that they are from such unpunishable wealth and that they can show off their money with impunity.

Then the door to the classroom I just left turns into one of those futuristic blast doors from Star Wars and slides closed with a hiss. No matter how much I press the button it won't open, because my students keep pressing the button to close it on the other side, keeping me outside and in danger of being flattened by the racing cars.

David Nurenberg
Concord-Carlisle High School
Concord, Massachusetts

WATER IS RISING IN THE CLASSROOM

Discipline

I was playing a giant board game with my friends and several of my most disruptive students. One of the students got up from the table, sprouted claws from her hands and chased me around the room, trying to skewer me. I backed into an alcove in the wall, just out of reach of her slashing claws. One of my friends tossed me a phone and I kept trying to dial the police and cry for help — a scene similar to the ones from Jurassic Park, where the tyrannosaurus's mouth can't get through the cave, but it keeps trying nevertheless.

David Nurenberg
Concord-Carlisle High School
Concord, Massachusetts

Discipline

A student has run away from me and hidden in
a woodchuck hole. We pursue him and, when
we find him he peeps out and says "I like it
better here."

Sam Slarsky
Blanchard School
Boxborough, Massachusetts

I'm appalled to discover a discipline problem
from years ago reappears in my class.

Dan Farber
Buckingham, Browne & Nichols
Cambridge, Massachusetts

Discipline

I am trying to get back for the first day from
Lake Mooselookmiguntic. A dozen kids are
jumping on my desks when I arrive.

Linda Bradley
New Suncook School
Lovell, Maine

I dream I'm on a nature field trip for five days.
There are no study plans. We're in unheated
cabins. It rains the whole time and I'm stuck
with 68 kids.

Sam Slarsky
Blanchard School
Boxborough, Massachusetts

~

Keeping Up

~

WATER IS RISING IN THE CLASSROOM

Keeping Up

I have died and gone to heaven. Saint Peter gives me permission to go back to Earth for one day so that I can grade tests and return homework.

Yvonne Farino
Concord-Carlisle High School
Concord, Massachusetts

In my dream I am endlessly highlighting student reports on states.

Lauren Grady
Blanchard School
Boxborough, Massachusetts

Keeping Up

I'm sitting on a beach with the principal. A student comes by in the water riding on a bomb. "Karen, you're the Guidance Chair," the principal says, "go defuse that bomb." So I swim out and defuse it. Then I am appointed to give a special seminar to the whole staff on defusing bombs. While I'm giving the training session, my assistant leans over and says to me, "No one is listening." "Keep going," I reply. "We need the professional development points."

Karen Bushey
Concord-Carlisle High School
Concord, Massachusetts

Keeping Up

I'm teaching my class when I notice outside the window that the students have my cats and are playing volleyball with them. The cats run by and are trampled. Chaos breaks out when an ex-date rolls a bomb into the room. I have a secret code for bombs and I'm trying to get the students to pay attention so I can warn them.

Rachel Childs
Lincoln-Sudbury High School
Sudbury, Massachusetts

In my dream there is a nuclear attack and I have to shepherd the Alcott students into a "safe" place. I'm thinking of my own family as we await our fate.

Chris Gill
Alcott School
Concord, Massachusetts

Keeping Up

I'm sitting in the back row of the all-district training session prior to the first day of classes. A speaker is presenting to the group when I decide I could get something done while listening. I decide to shave my legs. As I slowly drag the razor over one leg the principal and superintendent approach me and say, "You are doing an inappropriate thing." I pop out of my seat and say, "You don't give me enough time to get anything done — just let me shave my legs."

Barbara Anderson
Suncook School
Lovell, Maine

I'm given a cart to teach art and must wheel it from class to class.

George Wood
Concord Middle School
Concord, Massachusetts

Keeping Up

As I'm going over my grades in preparation for the end of the semester I begin to think that I've had a somewhat light load. Then I discover that there is a section I've never met. So I go down to the room and there they are — they have been waiting in the room for eleven weeks and they are in a very resentful mood. So I put a pile of novels three feet tall on the front desk and say, "Well, this stuff is pretty straightforward. I think we can do it in a week."

Steven Teichgraeber
Concord Academy
Concord, Massachusetts

A whole semester has gone by and I never attended a class I was assigned, either because I missed it on my schedule, or it wasn't there. I find out the final exam is today.

Amy Salvatore
Fenn School
Concord, Massachusetts

WATER IS RISING IN THE CLASSROOM

Keeping Up

It's the first day of school. I must tell the
principal that I'm pregnant and won't be able
to fulfill my contract. But I can't find the school
because someone has moved the trees and
the building.

Rosie White
Suncook School
Lovell, Maine

I pass out materials. As I'm giving directions,
another teacher comes in, collects my materials
and leaves.

Carol Boudreau
Blanchard School
Boxborough, Massachusetts

Keeping Up

I'm sitting on the beach in my bikini when I remember that the sixth graders have started a day early and my class is meeting. I rush up to the classroom in my bathing suit. All the students are there and the principal is waiting in the doorway.

Sarah Oelkers
Concord Middle School
Concord, Massachusetts

I'm home vacuuming. The phone rings. I answer it and I'm told my class is waiting.

Cynthia Katz
Concord Academy
Concord, Massachusetts

I'm in the wrong place and the class is waiting. An authority figure discovers me.

Cindy Broyer
Suncook School
Lovell, Maine

~

Harassed

~

WATER IS RISING IN THE CLASSROOM

Harassed

Ten nine year olds are taking a violin lesson
from me. They are sitting in a semi-circle,
while I am writing on the board. As I look
around I see them all holding their violins in
the correct positions — only they are all giving
me the finger.

Christopher Borg
Groton School
Groton, Massachusetts

A student with a boom box on his desk turns
it up. "You know that isn't allowed! Now put
that away," I shout. When I next turn around,
every student in the class has a boom box
playing loudly.

Andrei Joseph
Concord-Carlisle High School
Concord, Massachusetts

WATER IS RISING IN THE CLASSROOM

Harassed

I'm a drama coach. In one dream, during a
major performance, the students make up an
entirely new play. As I yell at them, they laugh.

Bill Plott
Lincoln-Sudbury High School
Sudbury, Massachusetts

Harassed

On the first day of school there is a professional
workshop. It is to be interspersed with student
performances. Along with three of my
colleagues, I choose to be shot and buried
in cement instead.

Joanna Glazer
Concord-Carlisle High School
Concord, Massachusetts

Previous to my dream, a kindergarten student
said in class, "You don't have the same nipples
as the music teacher." "WHAT?" I asked.
"Oh, no — dimples," he corrected himself. Then
I dreamed I was topless in class, reading a book.

Robin Cicchetti
Willard School
Concord, Massachusetts

WATER IS RISING IN THE CLASSROOM

Harassed

A long-snouted happy brown bear is chasing me around the schoolyard.

Mary Sperazzo
Blanchard School
Boxborough, Massachusetts

I am teaching when I notice that there are bears just outside my classroom, on the other side of a screen door. The students want to feed the bears with peanut butter and jelly sandwiches, but I have read that if you feed bears they never go away. I am desperately trying to stop them from slipping the sandwiches to the bears.

Lara Antkowiak
Concord-Carlisle High School
Concord, Massachusetts

Harassed

I was teaching my health class and they were
completely out of control. At the same time
they were enjoying my efforts to control them.
Then a group of electricians came into the room
and began stringing wire for an intercom
system. I got my foot caught in the wire as they
began pulling it through a hole in the wall.
I did a one-legged dance as my foot was
dragged closer and closer to the wall. I spotted
a student who I'd coached to the State
Championship in javelin but my plea for help
was futile as he laughed loudest of all.

Glenn Moore
Boonton, New Jersey

TRUE TERROR DREAMS OF TEACHERS

59

~

Chaos

~

WATER IS RISING IN THE CLASSROOM

Chaos

I taught horseback riding. My dream begins
with the fat girls in the class unable to get on
the horses. Then the horses all try to roll in the
mud. I jumped out of my bed and announced
to the room, "Everybody must make a circle to
the right." My roommate woke up and replied,
"Okay."

Nancy McPherson
Boxborough, Massachusetts

Chaos

My aide, dressed in a colonial outfit, is trying to jump out of my car while I'm driving. I grab her dress and try to pull her back in.

Beth Gainer
Blanchard School
Boxborough, Massachusetts

TRUE TERROR DREAMS OF TEACHERS

WATER IS RISING IN THE CLASSROOM

Chaos

I am taking kids on a field trip in a fancy bus when we are suddenly zooming down a dirt path in the woods, barely staying on the road. At one point we do a 180 degree turn when we decide we are heading the wrong way. Then I realize one of my students is driving. That's when the police come. I quickly jump into the driver's seat and tell all the kids to pretend I've been driving the whole time.

Alison Sanders-Fleming
Lincoln-Sudbury High School
Sudbury, Massachusetts

It is the first day of school (kindergarten) and the end of the day busses leave. But I teach through the departure of the busses and when I line up my kids, all the busses are gone. "Stop the busses," I yell, and I chase them in my slippers in a cold sweat.

Beverly Gauthier
Alcott School
Concord, Massachusetts

Chaos

I'm teaching when the door opens and the
Special Ed teacher comes in with a new student
— a girl who's one foot tall. She has to be given
a special seat up front so she can see. When the
class continues I forget about her, and, in my
enthusiasm, I place-kick her and she goes down
like a bowling pin. As I, full of remorse for not
following the Ed Plan, bend over to help her up,
the door opens and the Special Ed teacher
appears again — this time with a student who
is half boy, half dog. He has to be given a seat
at the side of the room so the other students
don't step on his tail.

Andrei Joseph
Concord-Carlisle High School
Concord, Massachusetts

WATER IS RISING IN THE CLASSROOM

Chaos

In my dream a Down Syndrome student who is
very heavy has caught his finger in a car door
and so is brought to the nurse where he goes
out of control and begins to destroy the nurse's
office. Things get worse as a detective arrives
and is pulled around by his necktie.

Joe Pacenka
Lincoln-Sudbury High School
Sudbury, Massachusetts

I'm in charge of a girl in a wheelchair. I realize
that the wheelchair girl has deflated the tires
of my car.

Lois McWalter
Concord Middle School
Concord, Massachusetts

~

Expertise

~

74

Expertise

I'm coaching basketball and have lost my
glasses. I'm so blind I can't see the court
or the players.

Kristen Stiefel
Middlesex School
Concord, Massachusetts

In my dream my students are in the halls
discussing what I taught them. They understand
nothing that I've said and I'm too embarrassed
to interrupt them.

Anne Colman
Concord Academy
Concord, Massachusetts

Expertise

As I, naked, attempt to write my name on the board on the first day of class, the chalk keeps disintegrating.

Janet Kresl Moffet
Weston High School
Weston, Massachusetts

I'm teaching in a strange school rather than my usual school. The chalk refuses to write. I'm trying to talk myself out of the dream unsuccessfully, knowing that it is only a dream.

Jim Williams
Lincoln-Sudbury High School
Sudbury, Massachusetts

I'm naked and roller skating down the hall, pretending everything is okay.

Allison Sanders-Fleming
Lincoln-Sudbury High School
Sudbury, Massachusetts

TRUE TERROR DREAMS OF TEACHERS

Expertise

In my dream I was assigned to teach math, although I'm a social studies teacher. I stood up before the class and said, "That's all I know. Have a nice year." When I went to the main office afterwards, my mail box was missing.

Lee Marsh
Weston High School
Weston, Massachusetts

I teach ceramics. I dream the pieces inside the kiln blow up.

Nancy Arkuss
Fenn School
Concord, Massachusetts

WATER IS RISING IN THE CLASSROOM

Expertise

The class is people in their thirties. I am teaching with no trousers and notice that fact along about the same time as the class. I think to myself, "They're adults. They'll understand."

Dan Sanford
Concord Academy
Concord, Massachusetts

I am unprepared, I don't know what block it is, what books I'm using, or what class is coming. I ask everyone to help me and I suddenly realize I'm not wearing any pants.

Mark Fidler
Buckingham, Browne & Nichols
Cambridge, Massachusetts

Expertise

One of the 5th graders I worked with is teaching me snowboarding. We are at the top of a very high mountain and he says, with flashing colored hair, "Are you sure you want to go through with this?"

Marge Maurukas
Blanchard School
Boxborough, Massachusetts

My room is empty. I have no ideas. I notice that all the other teachers on the hall are doing quite well. I am the only one who is not functioning.

Liz Merrill
Willard School
Concord, Massachusetts

84 WATER IS RISING IN THE CLASSROOM

Expertise

I have invited the School Committee, the
Superintendent and the Principal to see my
class. They are seated in the back. The students
start coming into the room and I realize
I don't know any of them. Not only that,
but I've forgotten which subject I'm teaching
and there are no plans.

Robin Neumann
Concord Middle School
Concord, Massachusetts

The department head comes into my class
and embarrasses me in front of the students.
He says, "I wouldn't have to be here if you
were doing your job."

Annaliese Navaro
Middlesex School
Concord, Massachusetts

I am a music teacher. Before the concert
I peek at the audience and see the President
of the United States, all my college professors
and the Supreme Court are in the house. Then
only four members of my chorus show up and
none of them know the music.

Julie Clinch
Blanchard School
Boxborough, Massachusetts

WATER IS RISING IN THE CLASSROOM

A Final Note

I would like to hear from you. I continue to collect
teachers' nightmares. Please write to me about your
terror dreams, your thoughts about this book, and
to receive information about my current projects.

Elliot Lilien
62 Chester Road
Boxborough, MA 01719

Bookstores please contact Elliot Lilien or:

Martin and Lawrence Press
P.O. Box 682
Groton, Massachusetts 01450
978-448-6651
rmpm@charter.net